TENNESSEE LEGAL RESEARCH HANDBOOK

by

Lewis L. Laska

University of Tennessee at Nashville

Member of the Tennessee Bar

Introduction by
Justice Joseph W. Henry
Tennessee Supreme Court

WILLIAM S. HEIN & CO., INC.
LAW BOOK PUBLISHERS

1977

First Printing

Cite as in this example:

Laska, *Tennessee Legal Research Handbook* §115

or

L. LASKA, TENN. LEGAL RES. HANDBOOK § 115

ISBN 0-930342-04-6

Library of Congress No. LC 77-071305

Printed in the United States of America

INTRODUCTION

All Tennessee judges and lawyers can attest to the urgent need for a comprehensive legal research handbook for use in preparing briefs and opinions. *Tennessee Legal Research Handbook* will meet that need.

Lewis Laska's book is a guide to the quick and effective use of legal materials by all concerned with research in any area of Tennessee's government or laws. It encompasses Tennessee law from the Watauga Association Compact, generally recognized as the first written constitution adopted by Americans, to current legal publications. It is filled with citations to source materials relating to our statutory laws, court rules, practice aids, administrative and governmental procedures, and a wide assortment of other reference material, much of which is hard-to-find.

This handbook is a "must" for legal scholars and writers of the bench and bar because it will aid in finding peripheral and background materials that are essential to quality research, but are all too often elusive. Likewise, this book will serve those who are in the legislative and executive branches of our state's government because it is a road map to effective research and documentation.

A copy of Mr. Laska's book should be on the desk of every lawyer, judge and public official in Tennessee. In a time when we are being smothered by an avalanche of legal treatises, it is refreshing to find one that is of practical use to the practicing lawyer, irrespective of the size of his law firm, the situs of his office, or the nature of his practice.

I commend this book to my brother lawyers, my fellow judges, and my fellow Tennesseans as a vast storehouse of vital information.

Joseph W. Henry
Associate Justice
Tennessee Supreme Court

CONTENTS

Introduction iii

This Book and Its Use ix

Chapter I: Organic Law

Section 100   Organic Acts to 1772 2

§ 110   Early Self-Government, 1772-1789 3

§ 110(a)   Watauga Association Compact, 1772 3

§ 110(b)   Cumberland Compact, 1780 4

§ 110(c)   Franklinite Movement, 1784-1789 5

§ 115   Common Law Acceptance 6

§ 120   Territorial Government, 1790-1796 8

§ 130   The 1796 Constitution 9

§ 140   The 1834 Constitution 11

§ 150   Amendment and Secession, 1853-1862 13

§ 160   Military Government and Reconstruction, 1862-1869. 14

§ 170   The 1870 Constitution 15

§ 180   Constitutional Amendments, 1953-1972 16

Chapter II: Statutes

Section 200   Collections of Statutes Prior to 1955 19

§ 210   *Tennessee Code Annotated* 28

§ 220   The Format of T.C.A. 29

§ 230   Indexes and Non-statutory Material in T.C.A. 34

§ 240   Using T.C.A. 36

§ 250   Uniform Acts 37

§ 260   Special Compilations 42

Chapter III: Session Laws and Materials of Legislative Intent

Section 300   Session Laws 43

§ 310   Public Acts, Private Acts and Resolutions 43

§ 315   Bill Drafting Aids 46

§ 320   North Carolina and Territorial Session Laws 47

§ 325   State Session Laws: 1796 to Present 48

§ 330   Materials of Legislative Intent—Primary 49

§ 335   Journals of General Assembly: 1796 to present 49

§ 338   Legislative Debates: Recordings 50

§ 340   Materials of Legislative Intent and Services—Current . 50

§ 342   *Legislative Record* 50

§ 344   Unbound House and Senate Journals and
Chief Clerk's Index 51
§ 346   Unofficial Index to Legislation Introduced
in the General Assembly 51
§ 348   The Constituents "Hot Line" 52
§ 349   Proprietary Reporting Services 52
§ 350   Materials of Legislative Intent—Secondary 52
§ 352   Legislative Services (Council) Committee 53
§ 352(a)   Final Reports, 1954-1966 54
§ 352(b)   Topical Reports, 1966- 55
§ 354   Law Revision Commission 59
§ 354(a)   General Reports 59
§ 354(b)   Topical Reports 60
§ 360   General Assembly Reports 62

Chapter IV: Tennessee Courts and Court Reports

Section 400   Introduction 66
§ 401   Supreme Court: 1790-1870 67
§ 402   Supreme Court: 1870- 70
§ 404   Intermediate Appellate Courts: 1873-1925 71
§ 404(a)   Court of Chancery Appeals, 1895-1907 71
§ 404(b)   Court of Civil Appeals, 1907-1925 72
§ 406   Court of Appeals, 1925- 72
§ 408   Court of Criminal Appeals, 1967- 73
§ 410   Trial Courts 74
§ 412   Circuit Courts 75
§ 414   Criminal Courts 75
§ 416   Chancery Courts 76
§ 416(a)   The Growth of Equity 76
§ 416(b)   Cooper's Tennessee Chancery Reports 78
§ 418   Law and Equity Courts 78
§ 420   Courts of Special or Limited Jurisdiction 79
§ 422   General Sessions Courts 79
§ 424   County Judges, Probate Courts, and Juvenile Courts. 80
§ 426   Municipal Courts 81
§ 430   Official Court Reports 81
§ 432   Supreme Court Reports:
Tennessee Reports; Tennessee Decisions 82
§ 432(a)   Slip Opinions and Unofficial Reporting Services .. 83
§ 432(b)   Supreme Court Reports—Annotations 84
§ 433   Parallel Citation Tables 84
§ 434   Revisions of Tennessee Reports 85
§ 434(a)   Tennessee Reports, Cooper's Edition 87
§ 434(b)   Tennessee Reports, Shannon's Edition 89
§ 436   Features of the Supreme Court Reports 90
§ 438   Thompson's and Shannon's Unreported Cases 91
§ 438(a)   Miscellaneous Supreme Court Reports 91

§ 440   Intermediate Appellate Court Reports 93
§ 444(a) *Chancery Appeals Reports;*
Chancery Appeals Decisions 94
§ 444(b) *Tennessee Court of Civil Appeals Reports* 94
§ 446   *Tennessee Appeals Reports* 95
§ 448   *Tennessee Criminal Appeals Reports* 95
§ 450   Briefs and Appellate Records 96
§ 460   Court Calendars 96
§ 470   Executive Secretary to the Supreme Court 97
§ 480   Appellate Court Nominating Commission 97
§ 490   Judicial Standards Commission 98

Chapter V: Court Rules and Court Practice Aids

Section 500   Court Rules 99
§ 510   Court Rules and Procedure: pre-1970 100
§ 520   Court Rules and Procedure: 1970- 102
§ 530   Appellate and Bar Admission Rules 103
§ 540   Rules of Civil Procedure 104
§ 550   Rules of Criminal Procedure 106
§ 560   Local Rules 108
§ 570   Rules and Practice before Courts of
Limited Jurisdiction 108
§ 572   Domestic Relations Courts/Family Law 109
§ 574   Probate Courts, County Judges/Probate Law 109
§ 576   Juvenile Courts/Juvenile Law 110
§ 578   General Sessions Courts 111
§ 580   Federal Court Rules and Practice 111
§ 590   Judicial Conference and Judges Conference 113
§ 592   District Attorney General's Conference 114
§ 594   Judicial Council 114
§ 596   Advisory Commission on Rules 115

Chapter VI: Annotations, Digests, Indexes, and Citators

Section 600   Annotations 116
§ 610   Digests 117
§ 610(a) West's *Tennessee Digest* 118
§ 610(b) *Michie's Digest of Tennessee Reports* 118
§ 620   American Digest System 118
§ 630   Early Digests—Tennessee 119
§ 640   Indexes to Statutes, Session Laws, Reports 120
§ 640(a) Statutes 120
§ 640(b) Session Laws 120
§ 640(c) Index to Private Acts 121

§ 640(d) Index to Reports 121
§ 650   Citators—Shepard's *Tennessee Citations* 121
§ 660   Citators—early 123
§ 670   Shepard's *Southwestern Reporter Citations* 123

Chapter VII: Administrative Law and State Agency Publications

Section 700 Administrative Law 126
§ 710   Administrative Structure—Departments 126
§ 712   Administrative Structure—Commissions,
             Boards, Councils, and Committees 127
§ 720   Finding Current Administrative Law 129
§ 722   Administrative Law Sources: 1974-   130
§ 724   *Tennessee Administrative Register* 130
§ 726   *Official Compilation, Rules and Regulations of the
             State of Tennessee* 131
§ 728   Executive Orders 132
§ 730   *Opinions of the Attorney General* 132
§ 740   Public Documents, 1836-1954 135
§ 742   Public Documents, 1954- 136
§ 744   *List of Tennessee State Publications* 136
§ 750   Services and Holdings of the State Library
             and Archives 137
§ 752   Services and Publications of the State
             Planning Office 138
§ 754   Publications of the Comptroller 139
§ 756   Reports of the Public Service Commission 140

Chapter VIII: Local Government Law

Section 800 Municipal Corporations 141
§ 810   Home Rule and City-County Consolidation 142
§ 820   Ordinances—Larger Cities 142
§ 825   Ordinances—Smaller Cities 143
§ 830   Municipal Technical Advisory Service 144
§ 835   MTAS Publications 145
§ 840   Judicial Interpretation of Ordinances 145
§ 845   City Attorney Opinions 145
§ 850   County Government 146
§ 860   County Legislative-Administrative Activities 146
§ 870   County Technical Assistance Service 147

Chapter IX: Loose-leaf Services, Treatises,
Periodicals and Miscellaneous Publications

Section 900   Loose-Leaf Services 149
    § 910   Form Books 150
    § 920   Treatises and Practice Aids 151
    § 930   Reference Books, Bibliographies and
             Legal Writing Books 160
    § 940   Restatements 162
    § 950   Periodicals 163
    § 960   Directories 165
    § 970   Special Libraries 166

Appendix A   Session Laws 170
Appendix B   Journals 179
Appendix C   Tennessee Reports/Decisions 194

Index   199

This book describes the legal publications, the structure of the Tennessee judicial and governmental system, and the important resources necessary for effective research in Tennessee law.

It is primarily designed to aid law-related professionals *e.g.*, lawyers, law students, paralegals, but should also be helpful to laypersons, especially government employees and historians approaching the many sources of Tennessee law in a systematic manner. A reference book, this is not a treatise on legal research methodology, legal analysis, or legal writing. Little good is served by attempting to duplicate the many valuable books currently available on those subjects. A list of such books may be found here in section 930.

To the outsider, the Tennessee legal system appears immovable and unchanging. In truth, this is not so. Although deeply rooted in the past, the system is undergoing important changes today. Hence, this caveat: generalizations made here about the system and/or its literature should be carefully scrutinized to determine whether important modifications have been made. The researcher should be watchful for changes in these areas:

The Court Structure. On August 1, 1977 a Limited Constitutional Convention will meet in Nashville to make recommendations on thirteen subjects affecting Tennessee law and government. One of the more important of these is the Judiciary Article. The convention will consider the entire article and is expected to make important changes in the judicial structure. Accordingly, the careful researcher should read chapter 4 in concert with these developments.

Legislative Staff Support. In recent years General Assembly standing committees, *e.g.*, Senate Judiciary Committee, have taken on some of the legislative support functions heretofore performed by other entities, notably the Legislative Council Committee. It may be expected that the nature of legislature-related publications will be changing and chapter 3 should be consulted with this in mind.

Court Rules. Improvement of procedural law is the handmaiden of judicial reform. Hence it is not surprising that today attempts are being made to improve the law in this area, notably appellate and criminal rules. The researcher should monitor these developments carefully and utilize chapter 5 accordingly.

Administrative Law. A new Tennessee Administrative Procedures Act, passed in 1974, has opened new vistas for advocacy and research and the future of this act will greatly affect the usefulness of the sources described in chapter 7.

This book is the state's first work of this sort. Effort has been made to insure that it is as comprehensive as possible—and the author wishes to express sincere appreciation to Edward Martin of the Coffee County bar and Mary Schaffner, a student at Vanderbilt Law School, for their valuable insights and editorial assistance. Any shortcomings of this book are the author's sole responsibility and he would appreciate any errors or omissions being called to his attention.

Chapter I

ORGANIC LAW

Organic law is the fundamental law or constitution of a state by which the people establish a system of government. The organic law of Tennessee can be traced back several hundred years, at least to English colonial charters affecting Tennessee while it was still a part of North Carolina. But Tennesseans themselves early displayed a zeal for self-government. Their philosophy and experience, commonly called Jacksonian Democracy, has had profound effect on the nation and has left an indelible mark on the state's governmental and judicial system today.

The purpose of this section is to outline briefly the development of Tennessee's organic law and to list the better sources a legal researcher should consult to explore the law's evolution. Sources for research into *contemporary* organic (constitutional) law are described here in sections 170 and 180.

All of the organic law developments described in this section (and many more, such as slavery) are treated in detail in the most recent work on the state's constitutional history. It is:

> Laska, Lewis L. "A Legal and Constitutional History of Tennessee, 1772-1972." *Memphis State University Law Review* 6 (1976): 563-672.

Two necessary books for research on Tennessee constitutional history are:

> Caldwell, Joshua W. *Studies in the Constitutional History of Tennessee.* 2d rev. ed. Cincinnati: Clarke, 1907.

> McClure, Wallace M. *State Constitution-Making, with Especial Reference to Tennessee.* Nashville: Marshall and Bruce, 1916.

Because the legal researcher should be familiar with the state's historical and political development, the following four important research tools are quite helpful:

> Folmsbee, Stanley J., Robert E. Corlew, and Enoch L. Mitchell. *History of Tennessee.* New York: Lewis Historical Publishing Co., 1960. 2 vols. A one-volume

edition has been published as *Tennessee: A Short History.* Knoxville: Univ. of Tenn. Press, 1969. This is the latest and best of the state's scholarly histories.

Greene, Lee S., David Grubbs, Victor Hobday. *Government in Tennessee.* 2nd ed. Knoxville: Univ. of Tenn. Press, 1975.

Smith, Sam B., ed. *Tennessee History: A Bibliography.* Knoxville: Univ. of Tenn. Press, 1974. This massive 498 page bibliography compiled by one of the state's leading historians is a necessary first step in any historical research involving Tennessee.

White, Robert H. *Messages of the Governors of Tennessee, 1796-1907.* Nashville: Tennessee Historical Commission, 1952-1972. 8 vols. Probably the most important work of Tennessee historical writing by a single author, White's collection of documents and his analysis make this a necessary resource for Tennessee legal research.

§100   ORGANIC ACTS TO 1772

English title to what is now Tennessee must be traced back through the colonial charters of Virginia and North Carolina, notably the latter. These sometimes overlapping charters, granted in 1578, 1584, 1606, 1609, 1612, 1629, 1663, 1665, and with one exception, (that of Sir George Carteret, Lord Granville) surrendered in 1729, can be found in:

Thorpe, F. N., ed. *Federal and State Constitutions, Colonial Charters, and Organic Laws.* Vols. 5 and 7. Washington: Government Printing Office, 1909.

A descriptive analysis of the more important of these charters, as they relate to North Carolina and the present State of Tennessee, is provided by:

Bassett, John Spencer. *The Constitutional Beginnings of North Carolina, 1663-1729.* Johns Hopkins University Studies in Historical and Political Science, edited by Herbert B. Adams, series 12, no. 3. Baltimore: John Hopkins University Press, 1894.

Black, Roy W. "The Genesis of the County Organization in the Western District of North Carolina and the State of Tennessee." West Tennessee Historical Society *Proceedings* 2 (1948): 95-118.

Kavass, Igor I. and Bruce A. Christensen. *Guide to North Carolina Legal Research*. Buffalo: Hein & Co., 1973.

Parker, Mattie E. E., ed. *North Carolina Charters and Constitutions, 1578-1698*. Raleigh: Carolina Charter Tercentenary Commission, 1963.

The Peace of Paris (1763) extinguished French claims to the eastern Mississippi Valley and granted Great Britain title to the region, ending more than a hundred years of intrigue and conflict over the area. For discussion and documents regarding pre-Revolution exploration and settlement of Tennessee, a researcher should consult the works of the dean of Tennessee legal historians, Samuel Cole Williams. These include:

Williams, Samuel Cole. *Early Travels in the Tennessee Country, 1540-1800*. 1928. Reprint. Johnson City: The Watauga Press, 1972.

_____. *Dawn of Tennessee Valley and Tennessee History*. 1937. Reprint. Nashville: Blue and Grey Press, 1972.

§110   EARLY SELF-GOVERNMENT, 1772-1790

Tennessee had valuable experience with self-government over two decades prior to statehood. The most notable of these efforts were the Watauga Association Compact, the Cumberland Compact, and the Franklinite Movement.

§110 (a) WATAUGA ASSOCIATION COMPACT, 1772

The Tennessee experience with self-government began in 1772 when settlers along the Watauga River signed the Watauga Association Compact establishing a temporary unit of government, a magistrate's court of five members. Recognized by historians as the first written constitution adopted by American-born freemen, this document is described in:

Allen, Ben and Dennis T. Lawson. "The Wataugans and the 'Dangerous Example'," *Tennessee Historical Quarterly* 26 (1967): 173-147.

Caldwell, Joshua W. "The Watauga Association." *American Historical Magazine* 3 (1898): 312-15.

Goodpasture, Albert V. "The Watauga Association." *American Historical Magazine* 3 (1898): 103-20.

Williams, Samuel Cole. "The First Territorial Division Named for Washington," *Tennessee Historical Magazine*. (ser. 2) 2 (1932): 153-59, reprinted in White, Robert, ed. *Tennessee Old and New*. 2 vols. Nashville: The Tennessee Historical Commission and the Tennessee Historical Society, 1946. 1: 201-12.

§110(b) CUMBERLAND COMPACT, 1780

The first settlers on the Cumberland River at what is now Nashville followed the Wataugan example and drafted their own instrument of government in May 1780, now referred to as the Cumberland Compact. Legislative and judicial authority was vested in an elected twelve-man committee whose members were subject to recall. This provision for recall of elected officials is assumed by legal historians to be the first in the history of the United States.

Documents and discussion of the composition and activities of the Cumberland Association are found in:

Goodstein, Anita S. "Leadership on the Nashville Frontier, 1780 - 1800." *Tennessee Historical Quarterly* 35 (1976): 175-198.

Henderson, Archibald. "Richard Henderson: The Authorship of the Cumberland Compact and the Founding of Nashville." *Tennessee Historical Magazine* (ser. 3) 2 (1916): 155-74.

Horn, Stanley F. "The Cumberland Compact." *Tennessee Historical Quarterly* 3 (1944): 65-66.

Quarles, Robert T. and White, Robert H., eds. *Three Pioneer Tennessee Documents—Donelson's Journal, Cumberland Compact, Minutes of Cumberland Court.* Nashville: Tennessee Historical Commission, 1964.

Settlers in what is now the Clarksville area drafted a similar document. See:

Williams, Samuel C. "The Clarksville Compact of 1785." *Tennessee Historical Quarterly* 3 (1944): 237-247.

§110(c) FRANKLINITE MOVEMENT, 1784-1789

In 1784 a convention of east Tennesseeans drafted a provisional constitution for a new state they were attempting to establish. Called the State of Franklin, this sovereignty suffered a tumultuous existence until its collapse five years later.

For discussion of the Lost State of Franklin, as it is called, including a description of its constitution see:

Burch, Charles N. "Important Events in the Judicial History of Tennessee." *Tennessee Law Review* 15 (1938): 220-29.

Cannon, Walter F. "Four Interpretations of the History of the State of Franklin." East Tennessee Historical Society *Publications* 22 (1950): 3-18.

Fink, Miriam L. "Judicial Activities in Early East Tennessee." East Tennessee Historical Society *Proceedings* 7 (1935): 38-49.

Fink, Paul M. "Some Phases of the History of the State of Franklin." *Tennessee Historical Quarterly* 16 (1957): 195-213.

Garrett, William R., ed. "The Provisional Constitution of Frankland." *American Historical Magazine* 1 (1896): 48-63.

Goodpasture, Albert V., ed. "Constitution of the State of Franklin." *American Historical Magazine* 9 (1904): 399-408.

Lacy, Eric R. "The Persistent State of Franklin." *Tennessee Historical Quarterly* 23 (1964): 248-257.

Siousatt, St. George L. "The North Carolina Cession of 1784 in its Federal Aspects." Mississippi Valley Historical Association *Proceedings* 2 (1908): 35-62.

Williams, Samuel Cole. *History of the Lost State of Franklin.* 1933. Reprint. Nashville: Blue and Grey Press, 1972.

§115   COMMON LAW ACCEPTANCE

On December 22, 1789, North Carolina passed a second Cession Act offering the Tennessee area to the federal government. Chap. 3 [1789] N.C. Pub. Acts 31. Ten conditions were placed on the offer, one of them (number eight) provided that "the laws in force and use in the state of North Carolina at the time of passing this act, shall be and continue in full force within the territory hereby ceded until the same shall be repealed, or otherwise altered by the Legislative authority of the said territory." (The laws referred to here were both the statutory and common law). Tennessee became a federal territory (The Southwest Territory) when Congress passed the Cession Acceptance Act; (Act of April 2, 1790, ch. 6, 1 Stat. 106.) Thus Tennessee officially adopted North Carolina laws as her own at that time, even though such laws had been followed (and asserted) for about a quarter century.

What were the "laws in force and use in North Carolina" at that time? Certainly, these were the North Carolina statutes (see section 320) including the early statutes of limitations which led to so much land litigation in the early days of Tennessee.[1] Also included were English statutes "in force and use" in North Carolina so long as they were not inconsistent with the freedom and independence of that state, especially those statutes which were passed prior to 1607 when the Virginia charter was granted, which included what afterward became North Carolina and Tennessee. Green v. Allen, 24 Tenn. 169, 233 (1844). For a partial list of English statutes which became a part of North Carolina (hence Tennessee) common law, see Glasgow's Lessee v. Smith and Blackwell, 1 Tenn. 169 (1813). Equally important was North Carolina's acceptance of the common law of England. This had been accomplished by a statute which declared that "all such parts of the common law as were not destructive of, repugnant to, or inconsistent with the freedom or independence of North Carolina, were to be in full force within [North Carolina] except as this common law has

1. See Ch. 27 [1715] N.C. Pub. Acts in 1 E. SCOTT, LAWS OF TENNESSEE 14 (1821). See also, Cox, History of Adverse Possession Statutes of Tennessee, 6 MEM. ST. U. L. REV. 673 (1976). The best compilation of the North Carolina laws of this era is J. IREDELL, LAWS OF THE STATE OF NORTH CAROLINA, 1715-1790 (1791).

not (sic) been otherwise provided for, abrogated or repealed." Ch. 5, §2 [1778] N.C. Pub. Acts 22. An earlier North Carolina act had adopted both the English common law and statutes as the law in that colony, but the 1778 act spoke only of the common law.[2] Thus it could be said that the common law in its entirety and as a distinctive system of laws has never been in force in Tennessee, but only such part thereof has been in force in the state as had been adopted and was in force in North Carolina when ceded by North Carolina to the federal government. Howard v. State, 143 Tenn. 539, 546 227 S.W.36 (1921).

Territorial ordinances and acts sometimes modified North Carolina statutes or common law as Tennessee created her own jurisprudence. (See section 320). Later, the Tennessee Constitution of 1796 provided: "All laws and ordinances now in force and use in this territory, not inconsistent with this Constitution, shall continue to be in force and use in this state, until they shall expire, be altered or repealed by the legislature." Tenn. Const., art X, § 2 (1796). This language was repeated in the 1834 Constitution and likewise appears in our present document. Tenn. Const., art. XI, § 1. Accordingly, common law as it existed when the Tennessee constitution went into effect was made the law of Tennessee by that instrument, but those laws could be altered, amended, repealed or added to by subsequent legislatures. Henley v. State, 98 Tenn. 665, 41 S.W. 352, 39 L.R.A. 126 (1897). Rush v. Great Am. Ins. Co., 213 Tenn. 506, 376 S.W.2d 454 (1964).

Next, it should be noted that all pbulic and general statutes of the state, including the English statutes, and the statutes of North Carolina brought into this state, previously and then existing and in force, were, in effect, repealed by the Code of 1858 (Code sections 41, 42), except as therein compiled and re-enacted. State v. Miller, 79 Tenn. 620 (1883). (See section 200.) The same rule was applied respecting the Code of 1932 in State ex. rel. Moore v. Tutt, 175 Tenn. 412, 135 S.W.2d 449 (1940) and repeated in Tennessee Code Annotated. T.C.A.

2. See Ch. 31, §§6, 7 [1715] N.C. Pub. Acts in 1 E. SCOTT, LAWS OF TENNESSEE 22 (1821). The 1715 act was a gesture of law reform designed to mollify the already belligerent colonists. See Bassett, *The Constitutional Beginnings of North Carolina, 1663-1729.* Johns Hopkins University Studies in Historical and Political Science, series 12, no. 3 (1894) at 156.

§§1-204, 1-205. (See section 210.) Court decisions announced previous to the enactment of the Code of 1858, construing and applying the ancient English statutes, were *not* annulled by such Code. State v. Miller, 79 Tenn. 620 (1883); Moss v. State, 131 Tenn. 94, 173 S.W. 859 (1914).

In recent years the Tennessee Supreme Court has taken an expansive view of the scope of acceptance of North Carolina common law. In *Dunn v. Palermo*, 522 S.W.2d 679, 682 (Tenn., 1975) the Court said: "Thus it is that Tennessee (in 1796), through North Carolina, adopted the common law of England as it existed in 1776." The court was following language taken from Quarles v. Sutherland, 215 Tenn. 651, 389 S.W. 2d 249 (1965) and Smith v. State, 215 Tenn. 314, 385 S.W.2d 748 (1965), saying in *Dunn v. Palermo*, at 682:

"We adopted the common law: 'As it stood at (1776) and before the separation of the colonies . . . (it) being derived from the state of North Carolina, out of which Tennessee was carved. The Acts of North Carolina, 1715, C.31, and Acts of North Carolina 1778, C.5, preserved the common law, while Session (sic) Act 1789, c.3 provided for its continuance in the State of Tennessee."

Thus, while the holding in *Palermo* is sound (right of married woman to choose surname) some of the language used to describe acceptance of the common law is simplistic and perhaps rigid. A better description might be: "In 1790, Tennessee adopted as its law those elements of English and North Carolina statutory and common law as were in force in North Carolina at that time or in 1778, to the extent such laws were consistent with the freedom and independence of Tennessee and the customs and expectations of her people."

§120 TERRITORIAL GOVERNMENT, 1790-1796

What is now the State of Tennessee became a federal territory in 1790 and achieved a representative form of government four years later.[3]

3. An extended discussion of territorial government including the drive for admission to the union is included in Laska, *A Legal and Constitutional History of Tennessee, 1772-1972* 6 MEM. ST. U. L. REV. 579-582, 596-598 (1976) [hereinafter cited as Laska, *Legal and Constitutional History*].

The following organic acts and sources provide a description of the government and its activities during this period.

Cession Acceptance. Act of April 2, 1790; 1 Stat. 106. An Act to accept a cession of the State of North Carolina to a certain district of Western Territory.

Southwest Territory. Act of May 26, 1790; 1 Stat. 123. An Act **for** the Government of the Territory of the United States, South of the River Ohio.

Blount, William. *The Blount Journal, 1790-1796.* Edited by William R. Garrett. Nashville: The Tennessee Historical Commission, 1955.

Carter, Clarence E., ed. *The Territorial Papers of the United States,* IV *The Territory South of the River Ohio: 1790-1796.* Washington: Government Printing Office, 1936.

The Acts and Ordinances of the Governor and Judges of the Territory of the United States of America South of the River Ohio. Knoxville: Roulstone, 1793.

Acts Passed at the First Session of the General Assembly of the Territory of the United States South of the River Ohio. Knoxville: Roulstone.

Acts Passed at the Second Session of the First General Assembly of the Territory of the United States South of the River Ohio. Knoxville: Roulstone, 1795.

A compilation of early journals, including the constitutional convention journal, are found in *Journal of the Territorial Councils of the Senate and House of Tennessee.* Knoxville, Roulstone, 1794-1796. Reprint. Nashville: McKenzie and Brown, 1852. Until 1974, the original imprints were presumed lost. See Dobson, John. *The Lost Roulstone Imprints.* Knoxville: Univ. of Tennessee Library, 1975.

§130   THE 1796 CONSTITUTION

A full understanding of Tennessee's present constitution is greatly aided by exploring its antecedents, the constitutions of 1796 and 1834, because the state's present instrument (drafted in 1870) drew heavily from them.

Initially, two invaluable books must be consulted for thorough discussion of almost any issue of the state's three constitutions. These are:

Caldwell, Joshua W. *Studies in the Constitutional History of Tennessee*. 2d rev. ed. Cincinnati: Clarke, 1907.

McClure, Wallace M. *State Constitution-Making, with Especial Reference to Tennessee*. Nashville: Marshall and Bruce, 1916. This contains parallel presentations of the 1796 Constitution, the 1834 Constitution and amendments, and the 1870 Constitution.

The 1796 Constitution was described by Jefferson as "the least imperfect and most republican of the state constitutions" and was patterned after the North Carolina Constitution of 1776.[4] Documents and discussion of this constitution are:

Constitution of the State of Tennessee. Unanimously Established in Convention at Knoxville, on the Sixth Day of February, One Thousand Seven Hundred and Ninety-Six. Knoxville: Roulstone, 1796, Philadelphia, 1796.

Journal of the Proceedings of the Tennessee Constitutional Convention, Begun and Held in Knoxville, Jan. 11, 1796. Knoxville: Roulstone, 1796. Reprint. Nashville: McKenzie and Brown, 1852. This 1852 reprint, that included legislative journals for the years 1794-96, and is usually given the collective title *Journal of the Territorial Councils of the Senate and House of Tennessee*, was long considered the "official" journal because no copies of Roulstone's imprints had been found. However, one came to light in 1974 and is described in Dobson, John. *The Lost Roulstone Imprints*. Knoxville: Univ. of Tennessee Library 1975.

Barnhart, John D. "The Tennessee Constitution of 1796: A Product of the Old West." *Journal of Southern History* 9 (1943): 532-48. The author emphasizes

---

4. Commentators uniformly cite historian Ramsey as the authority for Jefferson's statement, but Ramsey does not document the quotation—and this writer has been unable to locate it. *See* G. RAMSEY, ANNALS OF TENNESSEE TO THE END OF THE EIGHTEENTH CENTURY 657 (1853) (1967 reprint). The 1796 Constitution is described in Laska, *Legal and Constitutional History*, at 582-596.

Pennsylvania, not North Carolina influence on the 1796 Constitution.

Haynes, Robert R. "The Origins and Development of the Constitution of Tennessee." M.A. thesis, George Peabody College, 1927.

Higginbothom, Sanford W. "Frontier Democracy in the Early Constitutions of Tennessee and Kentucky, 1772-1779." M.A. thesis, Louisiana State University, 1941.

Loveless, Walter A. "A History of the Constitutional Conventions of Tennessee." M.A. thesis, George Peabody College, 1930.

Rippa, Sol A. "The Development of Constitutional Democracy in Tennessee 1790-1835." M.A. thesis, Vanderbilt University, 1949.

Sanford, Edward T. "The Tennessee Constitutional Convention of 1796." Tennessee Bar Association *Proceedings* (1896): 92-135. This is the first scholarly description of the convention. Sanford, a Knoxville native, served as a United States District Judge for the eastern and middle districts of Tennessee from 1908 until 1923 when he was elevated to the United States Supreme Court.[5]

Williams, Charlotte. "Congressional Action on the Admission of Tennessee into the Union." *Tennessee Historical Quarterly* 2 (1943): 291-315.

Williams, Samuel C. "The Admission of Tennessee into the Union." *Tennessee Historical Quarterly* 4 (1945): 291-319.

§140   THE 1834 CONSTITUTION

Tennessee's increasing population and prosperity began to highlight weaknesses in the 1796 Constitution. Unhappy with legislative selection of judges and county officials, the misuse of private legislation, a land taxation system that ignored property values, and desiring express authorization for state

5. Laska, *Mr. Justice Sanford and the Fourteenth Amendment*, 33 TENN. HIST. Q. 210 (1974).

aid for internal improvements, the people sent representatives to a Nashville convention in May, 1834, which drafted a constitution that was approved by referendum that same year.[6]

Drafted in a fever of Jacksonian Democracy, this document's bold imprint clearly shines through in the Constitution of 1870, Tennessee's present organic law. This was the first Tennessee constitution to recognize three separate departments of government, providing for a Supreme Court to exercise appellate jurisdiction only. Local officers were to be popularly elected. A permanent capitol was to be selected by the legislature. The legislature was further required to pass laws fixing the rate of interest and was prohibited from suspending the general law for any individual or from passing special legislation. The cumbersome procedure for amending the constitution, still an integral part of present organic law, had its origins in the 1834 Constitution.

Again, the works of Caldwell, McClure and White ably describe this document as do the aforementioned theses. Other sources include:

> *Journal of the Convention of the State of Tennessee, Convened for the Purpose of Revising and Amending the Constitution Thereof.* Nashville: Banner and Whig Office, 1834.

> Cassell, Robert. "Newton Cannon and the Constitutional Convention of 1834." *Tennessee Historical Quarterly* 25 (1956): 224-242.

> Golden, Gabriel H. "William Carroll and His Administration: Tennessee's Business Governor." *Tennessee Historical Magazine* 9 (1925): 9-30.

> Kegley, Isabelle G. "The Work of William Carroll as Governor of Tennessee." M.A. thesis, Vanderbilt University, 1935.

> Mooney, Chase C. "The Question of Slavery and the Free Negro in the Tennessee Constitutional Convention of

---

6. The new constitution became effective January 1, 1835; some writers such as Robert T. Shannon and Robert H. White correctly refer to it as the 1835 Constitution. However, the common practice, as seen in *Tennessee Code Annotated,* is to use the year 1834. The document is described in Laska, *Legal and Constitutional History* at 599-615.

1834." *Journal of Southern History* 12 (1946). 487-509.

§150   AMENDMENT AND SECESSION, 1853-1862

The 1834 Constitution was regularly amended only once, in 1853, by a provision requiring the popular election of the judiciary and state's attorneys. The aforementioned works of Caldwell and McClure describe this amendment.

In 1861 the Tennessee legislature, expressly waiving "any opinion as to the abstract doctrine of secession," declared its independence from the federal government, entered into a military league with the Confederacy, and joined the Confederate States of America.[7] The better among numerous sources discussing this event are:

Fertig, James L. "The Secession and Reconstruction of Tennessee." Ph.D. dissertation. University of Chicago, 1898. Reprint. New York: AMS, 1968.

Henry, J. Milton. "The Revolution in Tennessee, February, 1861, to June, 1861." *Tennessee Historical Quarterly* 18 (1959): 99-119.

Neal, John Randolph. "Disunion and Restoration in Tennessee." Ph.D. dissertation, Columbia University, New York: Knickerbocker Press, 1899.

White, Robert H., ed. *House Journal*, General Assembly, Thirty-fourth session, 1861-62. Nashville: Tennessee Historical Commission, 1957.

————, *Messages of the Governors of Tennessee, 1857-1869*. Nashville: Tennessee Historical Commission, 1959.

Wooster, Ralph A. *The Secession Conventions of the South*. Princeton, N.J., Princeton University Press, 1962.

7. This episode and related issues such as slavery are described in Laska, *Legal and Constitutional History* at 617-621.

§160 MILITARY GOVERNMENT AND RECONSTRUCTION, 1862-1869

In 1862 Andrew Johnson was appontied Military Governor of Tennessee. During his tenure civil government was slowly re-established and a self-proclaimed constitutional convention in 1865 rescinded the Tennessee Declaration of Independence and amended the constitution by outlawing slavery. Reconstruction Governors Brownlow and Senter saw the state achieve political reconstruction including congressional representation in 1866.[8] The numerous sources discussing this era include:

> *Admission of Tennessee.* House of Representatives Miscellaneous Document No. 55, 39th Congress, 1st Session (1866).

> Alexander, Thomas B. *Political Reconstruction in Tennessee.* Nashville: Vanderbilt Univ. Press, 1950. Reprint. New York: Russell, 1968.

> Feistman, Eugene G. "Radical Disenfranchisement and the Restoration of Tennessee, 1865-1866." *Tennessee Historical Quarterly* 12 (1953): 135-151.

> Hall, Clifton R. "Andrew Johnson: Military Governor of Tennessee." Ph.D. dissertation, Princeton University, 1914. Reprint. Princeton: Princeton University Press, 1916.

> Neal, John Randolph. "Disunion and Restoration in Tennessee," Ph.D. dissertation, Columbia University, New York: Knickerbocker Press, 1899.

> Patton, James W. *Unionism and Reconstruction in Tennessee, 1860-1869.* 1934. Reprint. Gloucester, Massachusetts: P. Smith, 1966.

> *Report of the Joint Committee on Reconstruction.* House of Representatives Document No. 30, 39th Congress, 1st Session (1866).

> White, Robert H. *Messages of the Governors of Tennessee, 1857-1869.* Nashville: Tennessee Historical Commission, 1959.

---

8. This and other issues such as the franchise are described in Laska, *A Legal and Constitutional History* at 625-631.

§170   THE 1870 CONSTITUTION

Tennessee's present constitution was framed in 1870 and became effective that year. Its chief purpose was to seek rapid enfranchisement of Confederate sympathizers and to safeguard the state against gubernatorial overreaching as experienced during Reconstruction.[9]

The annotated text of the constitution is found in volume 1 of Bobbs-Merrill's Tennessee Code Annotated (1955). (See sections 210 and 220) Recent amendments and annotations are listed in the pocket supplements of that volume.

Earlier annotations include:

Anderson, Douglas, *Tennessee Constitutional Law.* Nashville: Brandon, 1896. This is a treatise *cum* annotation.

Grayson, D.L. *The Annotated Constitution and Code of Tennessee.* 2 vols. Chattanooga: Chattanooga *Times,* 1895. This is an annotation *cum* code.

Shannon, Robert T. *The Constitution of Tennessee, Annotated.* Nashville: Tennessee Law Book Co., 1916.

Sources for description and analysis in addition to the aforementioned theses are:

Caldwell, Joshua W. *Studies in the Constitutional History of Tennessee.* 2d rev. ed. Cincinnati: Clarke, 1907.

Combs, William H. "An Unamended State Constitution: The Tennessee Constitution of 1870." *American Political Science Review* 32 (1938): 514-24.

Combs, William H. and William E. Cole. *Tennessee, A Political Study.* Knoxville: University of Tennessee Press, 1940.

Journal of the Proceedings of the Convention of Delegates Elected by the People of Tennessee, to Amend, Revise or Form and Make a New Constitution for the State. Assembled in the City of Nashville, January 10, 1870. Nashville: Jones and Purvis, 1870.

McClure, Wallace M. *State Constitution-Making, with Especial Reference to Tennessee.* Nashville: Marshall and Bruce, 1916.

---

9. Laska, *Legal and Constitutional History* at 631-653.

Stanberry, George, W., II. "The Tennessee Constitutional Convention of 1870." M.A. thesis, University of Tennessee, 1940.

White, C.P., et al. Constitutional Problems of Tennessee in The University of Tennessee Record, Extension Series. Vol. 13, No. 2 (Knoxville, 1937).

Naturally, the state's law reviews should be consulted for articles dealing with specific issues of constitutional law, e.g., taxation, apportionment. Examples of such articles include:

Armstrong, Walter P., Jr. "Constitutional Limitations on Income Taxes in Tennessee." Vanderbilt Law Review 27 (1974): 475-489.

Cox, Archibald. "Current Constitutional Issues—Reapportionment." Tennessee Law Review 30 (1962): 28-35.

Note, "Constitutional Provisions Regulating the Mechanics of Enactment in Tennessee." Vanderbilt Law Review 5 (1952): 614-621.

§180   CONSTITUTIONAL AMENDMENTS, 1953-1972

The 1870 Constitution became, in time, the nation's oldest unamended state constitution and was not modified until 1953. That year a limited constitutional convention was called. It suggested eight changes, the more important affecting the governor's power and term, legislative pay, and state-municipality relations.[10] This was by far the state's most successful convention, but this procedure has been utilized with reasonable success three times since, in 1959, 1965, and 1971.[11]

Documents and discussions relevant to these amendments

10. Laska, Legal and Constitutional History at 653-663.
11. Laska, Legal and Constitutional History at 663-671. The 1976 General Assembly passed a public act, Chapter 848, providing for a referendum on the holding of another limited constitutional convention. The convention call was limited to thirteen items, the most important ones being the uniform interest rate and judicial reform. The referendum, held August 5, 1976, approved the convention which is scheduled to convene August 1, 1977. See, A. HOPKINS et al., ISSUES IN THE TENNESSEE CONSTITUTION (1976).

are:

Allen, Tip H. and Coleman B. Ransome, Jr. *Constitutional Revision in Theory and Practice, Part 2, Tennessee: A Case Study of the Limited Convention.* University, Alabama: Bureau of Public Administration, University of Alabama, 1962. This is the leading study of the 1953 convention.

Beeler, Roy H. *Right of the Legislature to Call a Limited Constitutional Convention.* Nashville: State of Tennessee, 1946.

Bureau of Public Administration. *Papers on Constitutional Revision* 2 vols. *The University of Tennessee Record, Extension Series.* Vol. 23, April and July 1947.

Cortner, Richard C. *The Apportionment Cases.* Knoxville: University of Tennessee Press, 1970.

Denny, Raymond. "The Tennessee Constitutional Convention." *Tennessee Law Review* 23 (1953): 15-23.

Frierson, W.F. and Cecil Sims. *Report of the Constitution Revision Commission.* Nashville: State of Tennessee, 1946.

Hopkins, Anne, et al. *Issues in the Tennessee Constitution.* Nashville: Tennessee League of Women Voters, 1976. This is a leading discussion of topics facing the 1977 convention.

Journal and Proceedings of the Constitutional Convention of the State of Tennessee, 1959. Nashville: Limited Constitutional Convention, State of Tennessee, 1959.

Journal and Proceedings of the Limited Constitutional Convention of the State of Tennessee, 1965. Nashville: Limited Constitutional Convention of 1965, 1965. Note that the prime impetus for this convention was the need to reapportion the legislature following the decision in *Baker v. Carr.*

Journal and Proceedings of the Limited Constitutional Convention of 1971. Nashville: Limited Constitutional Convention, State of Tennessee, 1971.

Nelson, William R. "The Limited Constitutional Convention: The Tennessee Experience." *Public Administration Survey* 19 (1972): 1-7.

Overman, Edward S. *Taxation of Public Utilities in Tennessee.* Knoxville: Bureau of Public Administration, 1962. Improper taxation led to the 1971 convention.

Perry, Jennings. *Democracy Begins at Home: The Tennessee Fight on the Poll Tax.* New York: Lippincott, 1944. The poll tax, as a requirement for voting, was removed altogether by the 1971 amendment.

For a list of studies prepared for use by the delegates to these conventions see the notes in:

Laska, Lewis L. "A Legal and Constitutional History of Tennessee." *Memphis State University Law Review* 6 (1976): 563-672.

Here again, the state's law reviews should be consulted for research in specific issues of constitutional law. Examples of articles include:

Grant, Daniel R. "Metropolitan Problems and Local Government Structure: An Examination of Old and New Issues." *Vanderbilt Law Review* 22 (1969) 757-773.

Mendelson, Wallace. "Paths to Constitutional Home Rule for Municipalities." *Vanderbilt Law Review* 6 (1952): 66-78.

Chapter II

STATUTES

§200   COLLECTIONS OF STATUTES PRIOR TO 1955

A reliable and logical collection of legislative enactments is among the foremost needs of anyone who deals with the law. It is not surprising, therefore, that among the earliest books printed in Tennessee one finds attempts to compile, revise, and codify the state's statutes.

The contemporary legal researcher may feel that the present code, Tennessee Code Annotated, is the only relevant one for his purposes but will quickly change his mind when the object of his research requires deeper probing into the legislative and codification history of the act in question. Puzzling references to the 1858 Code, Shannon's Code, Williams' Code, the 1932 Code, and its 1950 Supplement, are made comprehensible when seen in context of the panoply of Tennessee codes.[1] The following is a bibliographical, chronological narrative of Tennessee codification designed to guide a serious researcher through the labyrinth of Tennessee statutes.

The state was only seven years old when George Roulstone, the state printer, undertook as a private enterprise the first publication of the state's statutes in 1803. Untrained in the law, Roulstone merely reprinted the session laws to date and

---

1. The best history of the state's codification was **prepared**, quite appropriately, by one of the state's leading codifiers and legal writers, Samuel C. Williams. *See,* Williams, *A History of Codification in Tennessee,* 10 TENN. L. REV. 61, 165 (1932). Legal writers tend to draw heavily on each other's work and Williams was no exception. *See also,* Goodpasture, *An Account of the Compilations of the Tennessee Statutory Laws,* 7 AM. HIST. MAG. 69 (1902). Checklists of Tennessee compilations and codes are included in three sources. These are: CHECK LIST OF ACTS AND CODES OF THE STATE OF TENNESSEE, 1792-1939. Special Publications Series No. 5, Nashville: Tennessee Historical Records Survey Project, 1940; CHECK-LIST OF TENNESSEE STATUTES (Part IV) in PRELIMINARY CHECK-LIST OF TENNESSEE LEGISLATIVE DOCU-MENTS. Nashville: State Library and Archives, 1954; Pimsleur, CHECK-LISTS OF BASIC AMERICAN LEGAL PUBLICATIONS. AALL Publications Series No. 4, Section 1, South Hackensack, N.J. Fred B. Rothman, 1962.

included an index. In short, his work was simply a compilation[2] of Tennessee laws. This, one of the state's rarest books, is:

>Laws of the State of Tennessee, 1794-1801. Knoxville: Roulstone, 1803.

Roulstone's work set the Tennessee pattern of codification as a private, proprietary venture, and although the legislature authorized several revisions[3] during the next fifty years, Tennessee had no official codification[4] of its statutes until 1858.

The first in an impressive line of statutory offerings authored by revisers trained in the law was published in 1809. Also the first book printed in Nashville, it is:

>Haywood, John. *A Revisal of all the Public Acts of the State of North Carolina and the State of Tennessee.* Nashville: Bradford, 1809. A second revised edition of this compilation appeared in 1812, a third in 1815.

Haywood's work was later superseded by a similar compilation that included some marginal notes, this one also written by a judge. Commonly called Scott's Revisal, it is:

>Scott, Edward. *Laws of the State of Tennessee, including those of North Carolina Now in force in this State. From the year 1715 to the year 1820, inclusive.* 2 vols. Knoxville: Heiskell and Brown, 1821.

Scott's work met with legislative approval after the fact, but in 1825 the legislature established the state's first successful codification commission, appointing two commissioners "to digest and revise the statute laws." The term "digest" is unfortunate in that it implies some sort of annotation. Rather, what the legislature intended was inclusion of "lead-lines," or short statements of the substance of sections, appended by references to acts summarized. After some delay because of the death of one of the authors, the work finally appeared in 1831 and is

---

2. A *compilation* is a mere collection and arrangement of the laws in force. It usually excludes only those laws expressly repealed and does not make changes in substance or form.

3. A *revision* includes compilation but contemplates the omission of expressly or impliedly unconstitutional acts. Likewise, it means changes in form but not in substance in order to achieve clarity and brevity, to fill in omissions, and to remove typographical errors, redundancies, and inconsistencies.

4. A *codification* means both compilation and revision, but includes changes in substance.

generally known as Haywood and Cobbs' Revisal. It is:

> Haywood, John and Cobbs, Robert L. *The Statute Laws of
> the State of Tennessee of a Public and General Nature.*
> Knoxville: F. S. Heiskell, 1831.

A new constitution in 1834 prompted a new compilation
of statutes. This one, a novel arrangement of acts by both
chronological and alphabetical order, contained some modest
annotations. Having been written by two men who later became
the state's leading jurists, it was very popular with the bar. It is:

> Caruthers, R. L. and Nicholson, A. O. P. *A Compilation
> of the Statutes of Tennessee, of a General and Per-
> manent Nature, from the Commencement of the
> Government to the Present Time. With Judicial
> Decisions and forms.* Nashville: James Smith, 1836.
> Note that this compilation was supplemented twice
> by Judge Nicholson in 1846 and 1848.

The great codification movement of the 1840's and 1850's
made an appearance in Tennessee in 1858 with the enactment
of what is generally referred to as the Code of 1858. After a
false start in 1844, the legislature appointed two commissioners
in 1852 giving them power "to revise and digest the general
statutes and to suggest amendments or alterations." Although
the two codifiers ultimately found they could not work together,
the Code was a success because it was the first such revision—
codification to be arranged analytically by part, title, chapter,
and article. This revision, together with the suggested amendments, was enacted in its entirety and is therefore the state's
first official code.[5] It is:

> Meigs, Return J. and Cooper, William F., eds. *The Code of
> Tennessee.* Nashville: Eastman and Co., 1858.

Note that this code was supplemented beginning in 1871
and that later editions included acts of the two successive
years. As before, however, this was a private venture. These two
policies, unsystematic supplementation and proprietary codifica-

5. State v. Runnels, 92 Tenn. 320, 332, 21 S.W. 665, 666 (1892). Note
that legislative attempts to *amend* unofficial codes (Milliken & Vertrees',
Shannon's) were appropriately rebuffed by the Tennessee Supreme Court.
Burnett v. Turner, 87 Tenn. 123, 127 10 S.W. 194, 196 (1888); Memphis
Street Railway Co. v. State, 110 Tenn. 598, 604, 75 S.W. 730, 734 (1903).

tion, were to be the hallmarks of Tennessee codification for the next sixty years. The supplement is:

Shankland, James H. *Public Statutes of the State of Tennessee Since the Year 1858. Being in the Nature of Supplement for the Code.* Nashville: Paul and Tavel, 1878.

Despite a new constitution in 1870 (the appearance of which usually mandates a new code) the state could not afford another code revision, so two lawyers took it upon themselves in 1871 to issue a compilation that drew as its model the existing code. This unofficial code gained a measure of respectability when the legislature purchased a large quantity for public purposes upon the author's agreement to supplement their work, making it current through 1873. The compilation (together with the tipped-in supplement) is generally referred to as Thompson and Steger's Code. One of the chief merits of this work lay in its annotations, the first serious attempt at such in Tennessee jurisprudence. This compilation is:

Thompson, Seymour D. and Steger, Thomas M. *A Compilation of the Statute Laws of the State of Tennessee, Of a General and Permanent Nature, Compiled on the Basis of the Code of Tennessee, with Notes and References, Including Acts of Session of 1870-71.* 3 vols. St. Louis: W. J. Gilbert, 1872. Volume 3 appeared late in 1872.

This compilation went through three editions, the latest appearing in 1873, and was supplemented earlier that year. The cumulative supplement is:

Thompson, Seymour D. and Steger, Thomas M. *Supplement for the Statute Laws of Tennessee, Embracing the Acts of 1871, 1872, and 1873, with an Index.* St. Louis: W. J. Gilbert, 1873.

The next attempt at recodification came in 1883 when the legislature appointed two commissioners "to revise, digest and codify" the law. Following the general format of the Code of 1858, the revisers made only modest substantive changes yet added some annotations and devised new section numbers. This massive tome was much relied upon by the bar despite the fact that it failed to gain official legislative approval. Called the

"M & V Code" or Milliken and Vertrees' Code it is:

> Milliken, W. A. and Vertrees, John J. *The Code of Tennessee, Being a Compilation of the Statute Laws of the State of Tennessee, of a General Nature, in force June 1, 1884.* Nashville: Marshall and Bruce, 1884.

Following a now familiar pattern in Tennessee codification, this work was supplemented twice in 1893 and 1895 by Robert Shannon, a man who was to figure prominently in Tennessee codification and law reporting for the next forty years. The supplements, sometimes referred to as Shannon's (first) Supplement, are:

> Shannon, Robert T. comp. and ed. *Code Supplement, Embracing the Public and Permanent Statutes of the State of Tennessee, from 1885 to 1893, Inclusive, Properly and Consecutively Arranged with Reference to the Sections of the Code of 1884, (Milliken and Vertrees) whether Amending, Repealing, or Enacting Wholly New Law.* Nashville: Marshall and Bruce, 1893. A second edition by the same title was issued in 1895 and included acts passed to that year.

The next twenty years can be viewed as the bizarre era of Tennessee codification as the bar was met by a proliferation of proprietary, unofficial "codes" and supplements.

In 1895 a Chattanooga lawyer published a code which was so quickly superseded it is seldom ever mentioned by legal historians. It is:

> Grayson, D. L. *The Annotated Constitution and Code of Tennessee.* 2 vols. Chattanooga: Chattanooga *Times,* 1895.

Capitalizing on the reputation he earned supplementing the Milliken and Vertrees' Code, Shannon published in 1896 a massive new compilation complete with new section numbers and extensive annotations. It very quickly superseded the Milliken and Vertrees' Code. Unfortunately, the success of this code stifled the movement for a new official code. This work is referred to as Shannon's Code of 1896 and is:

> Shannon, R. T. comp., annot. and ed. *Public Permanent Statutes of a General Nature, Being an Annotated*

*Code of Tennessee, the Annotations Showing the
Construction of the Statutes and Constitution of the
State by the Supreme Court, and Also Its Decisions
upon kindred subjects, Together with the Declaration
of Independence, Articles of Confederations, Consti-
tution of the United States, Constitution of Tennessee,
Laws for Naturalization, Laws for Authentication of
Laws and Records, and the Chancery Rules.* Nashville:
Marshall and Bruce, 1896.

Naturally, this work was supplemented in the usual fashion.
Generally referred to as Shannon's (second) Supplement, it is:

Shannon, Robert T., comp. *Supplement to Shannon's Code,
Embracing the Existing Permanent and Public Stat-
utes of the State of Tennessee Enacted Since Shannon's
Code of 1896, Properly and Consecutively Arranged
with References to the Sections Thereof, whether
Amending, Repealing, or Enacting Wholly New Law.
With Annotations.* Nashville: Marshall and Bruce,
1904.

In 1912 two Nashville lawyers published a quasi-supple-
ment to Shannon's Code which was simply an index to statutes
passed since 1897. This work is:

Farrell, Jr., Norman and J. S. Laurent. *An Annotated Index
to the Public and General Statutes of Tennessee, From
1897 to 1911 Inclusive.* Nashville: Marshall and
Bruce, 1912.

The next offering by way of codification and annotation
(the latter by now seen as an important adjunct to such codes)
was a backward step for Tennessee jurisprudence. An out-of-
state publisher had purchased Shannon's annotations to his
code and sought to revise and update them by way of a new
code. Published in 1915 to 1917, and generally referred to as
the Thompson-Shannon Code, it was an awkward and incomplete offering causing its original draftsman untold frustration
and lost revenue. It is:

Thompson, Frank M., et al. annot. and rev. *Thompson's
Shannon's Code of Tennessee, 1917. Containing the
Public and Permanent Statutes of a General Nature*

with Annotations Showing the Construction of the
Statutes and Constitution of the State by the Courts,
and Also the Decisions upon kindred Subjects. Being
a Revision of Shannon's Code of 1896. Louisville:
Baldwin Law Book Company, 1917. A second edition
appeared in 1918.

Although the publisher sent purchasers certain revised
parts, this work was supplemented only once, in 1920. It is
sometimes referred to as Baldwin's Code although, correctly, it
was only a supplement. It is:

Spahr, Neal B., comp. and ed., with Seymour, Charles B.,
annot. *Baldwin's Cumulative Code Supplement of*
Tennessee, 1920. Supplementing and Continuing
Thompson's Shannon Code, 1917 and Shannon's
Code, Louisville: Baldwin Law Book Company, 1920.

The "Code War of 1917" was touched off when the
prodigious Shannon produced that year a new code, complete
with rewritten, exhaustive annotations that outshone its step-
brother. This five volume effort called Shannon's Code of 1917
was the author's masterpeice, and its appearance prevented the
Thompson-Shannon Code from being enacted as the official
code. The resulting imbroglio actually prevented *either* from
receiving legislative favor, yet in time the 1917 code gained
greater bar acceptance because it was better indexed and supplemented. The work is:

Shannon, Robert T., comp., ed., annot. *A Compilation of*
the Tennessee Statutes of a General Public Nature, In
force on the first Day of January, 1917, Together
with which are noted the Existing Local Statutes.
5 vols. Nashville: Tennessee Law Book Company,
1917-18.

Note that another edition in two large volumes called the
"County Edition" was quite popular.

Although numbered sequentially, the massive indexes to
this work were issued subsequent to the code's appearance. They
are:

Shannon, R. T. *Index to Shannon's Code of the Statutes*
of Tennessee, Issued in 1917 and 1918. Nashville:
Tennessee Law Book Publishing Company, 1919.

Shannon, R. T. *Index-Digest to Notes and Annotations in Shannon's Code of Tennessee. Issued in 1917 and 1918.* Nashville: Tennessee Law Book Company, 1922.

Finally, a supplement to the code, covering the years 1917-1925, was issued. It is:

Shannon, Robert T. *Supplement to Shannon's Annotated Code of 1917, With Annotations.* Indianapolis: Bobbs-Merrill, 1926.

The above supplement was so large that it required a separate index which was published late the same year. It is:

Shannon, Robert T. *Index to Notes and Annotations in Shannon's Code. Supplement Issued in 1926.* Nashville: Tennessee Law Book Publishing Company, 1926.

A decade of intense lobbying by the bar led to legislative creation of a new code commission in 1929—only the second such commission in the state's history—with the power to codify, revise and amend the statutes. The work of the commission, however, was subject to legislative amendment and enactment. The three commissioners were Shannon, Samuel C. Williams, and George Harsh. Despite the withdrawal of Shannon, the work was completed within two years and was enacted substantially as drafted.[6] This, of course, was an official code, taking effect January 1, 1932. It is:

Williams, Samuel C., Shannon, Robert T., Harsh, George. *The Code of Tennessee 1932.* 3 vols. Kingsport: Southern Publishers, Inc., 1931.

Note that enactment of the Code was prospective, and that prior to its effective date the legislature passed "amending" laws which were published as a "supplement" in 1932. This is:

Baldwin, William E. *Baldwin's Tennessee Code Supplement, 1932, Annotated Supplementing 1932 Official Code of Tennessee.* Cleveland: Baldwin Law Publishing Company, 1932.

The Baldwin Company issued one more supplement until, like so many others before, it abandoned the practice of Tennessee codification. The supplement is:

6. Trabue, *The New Tennessee Code*, 10 TENN. L. REV. 155 (1932).

Baldwin, William E. *Baldwin's Tennessee Code Service, 1933, Annotated.* Cleveland: Banks-Baldwin Law Publishing Company, 1933.

The 1932 Code, with inclusion of the 1931 acts, was published in a one-volume edition by the Michie Company in 1932. It is:

Michie, A. Hewson and Charles W. Sublett. *Michie's Tennessee Code of 1932.* Charlottesville: Michie Company, 1932.

Note that this code was supplemented in the following years: 1933, 1934, 1935 (twice), 1936, 1933-37 (a cumulative supplement), and 1937 (a second supplement).

In 1938 the Michie Code of 1932 was revised to include the acts to 1938 and added expanded annotations. It was supplemented in 1939, 1941, and 1943. It is:

Michie, A. Hewson, Chas. W. Sublett, Beirve Stedman. *Michie's Tennessee Code of 1938, with Complete Annotations.* Charlottesville: Michie Company, 1938.

Only two years after the original Michie's Tennessee Code of 1932 appeared, yet another unofficial code was published. Compiled by judge-historian, Samuel C. Williams, this code was much more fully annotated than previous codes, and soon became the most accepted codification for Tennessee. Generally referred to as the Williams' Code, it is:

Williams, Samuel C., comp. and annot. *Annotated Code of Tennessee.* 8 vols. Indianapolis: Bobbs-Merrill, 1934.

Until 1939 the Williams' Code was published by Bobbs-Merrill. Cumulative pocket supplements were printed in 1935, 1936, 1937, and 1938.

In 1939, the Michie Company gained control of its erstwhile competitor's product, and for the next four years it issued cumulative pocket supplements to the newly renamed Michie's Williams' Code.

The first volume of the first edition of this "revised" code (one that already had been supplemented four times!) appeared in 1941. Volume four was replaced that year. Volume three was replaced in 1942 and volumes one and two in 1943. This curious set bearing the hybrid title of two well known codes and the imprint of two publishers was the last unofficial codification. It was supplemented cumulatively from 1943-1949, 1951 (including the 1950 Official Code Supplement), and in 1952. The final supplements, for the years 1953 and 1954, were non-cumulative. Also, in 1952 Michie published as a part of the index supplement a table of comparative code sections. This was necessary because the 1950 Official Code Supplement assigned to certain acts section numbers that were different than those in Williams' codification. The 1950 Supplement also renumbered certain sections of the Code of 1932.

In 1945 the legislature authorized a temporary code commission to revise, compile and codify all Tennessee statutes passed subsequent to those included in the Code of 1932. Following a couple of false starts, the commission's Code Supplement was approved by the legislature in early 1951. It followed the general scheme of the Code of 1932 and is generally referred to as *1950 Code Supplement.* It is:

Code Commission (Tomlinson, Sr., Pride, Hugh Stanton, Frank Fowler, and Robert L. Harris). *Supplement to the Code of Tennessee.* 2 vols. Nashville: Rich Printing Company, 1952.

Note that the provisions of the Code Supplement were subordinated to any other statutes enacted by the legislature of 1951. These acts, plus those enacted by the 1953 legislature were, of course, later codified in Tennessee Code Annotated.

§210   TENNESSEE CODE ANNOTATED

A temporary code commission composed of Chief Justice A. B. Neil, Attorney-General Roy H. Beeler, and Harry Phillips (now Chief Judge, Sixth Circuit Court of Appeals) was established by the legislature in 1951. Because of the report of this Commission, in 1953 the legislature created a permanent code commission and authorized the publication of an official annotated code to be supplemented systematically. T.C.A. §§1-101 to -114. Drafted under the direction of Judge Sam B. Gilreath, the code, including annotations, is owned by the state although publication is the financial responsibility of the publisher. The present code commission is charged with codification of new acts, accomplished in cooperation with the publisher, Bobbs-Merrill. Supplements appear in the late fall of each year, and enactment of this codification is the first task of the next legislative session. Enacted in 1955 and generally referred to as "T.C.A." or Tennessee Code Annotated, Tennessee's present official annotated code became effective January 1, 1956.[7] It is:

> Gilreath, Sam B., consult. ed. Tennessee Code Annotated. Indianapolis: Bobbs-Merrill, 1955. 25 vols., with supplements.

§220   THE FORMAT OF T.C.A.

Tennessee's early codes (both official and unofficial) were usually divided into the four Blackstonian divisions: "Public Rights," "Private Rights," "Redress of Civil Injuries," and "Crimes." Within these parts topics were usually arranged alphabetically or, less often, by subject. A further sub-classification was by sections, which were, however, numbered consecutively. Indexing and supplementation was often inadequate and never timely. The problems with such codes are manifest. For example, is the topic "negotiable instruments" a public or a private right? Consecutive section numbering left no room for inserting numbers of code sections assigned to new statutes enacted by succeeding legislatures. A system of subnumbering that incorporated decimals and alpha-numerics sprang up in the prior codes and proved bewildering to bench and bar alike.

To remedy these defects the commission decided to utilize seventy-one titles which together with constitutional materials and the index, were to be placed in thirteen volumes. The titles have not changed since 1955 although their placement has been slightly altered due to an increase from thirteen to twenty-five volumes.[8]

7. Phillips, Tennessee Code Annotated, 23 TENN. L. REV. 268 (1954).

8. Volume 8 (titles 42-47) was replaced in 1964 with two volumes, 8 and 8A, the former incorporating titles 42-46, the latter 47 and title 48 from volume 9. Volume 9 in turn was replaced in 1966 with a new volume 9 (incorporating titles 49 and 50) and 9A, including titles 51, 52, and 53, the latter title taken from volume 10. Volume 10 in turn was replaced in 1968 with a new volume 10 (incorporating titles 54-56) and a new volume

Shown below are the titles appearing in the 1977 code. Through title forty-one the various titles are arranged by general topics similar to specialized codes, to wit:

Vol. 1.   Constitutions
Vol. 2.   Political Code - State Governmental Organization
Vol. 2A. Political Code - Local Governmental Organization
Vol. 3.   Political Code - Military and Public Officers
Vol. 3A. Political Code - Administrative Provisions
Vol. 4.   Courts and Procedures
Vol. 5.   Courts and Procedures
Vol. 5A. Court Rules
Vol. 6.   Probate Matters
Vol. 6A. Mental Health - Domestic Relations
Vol. 7.   Criminal Code
Vol. 7A. Criminal Procedure

Titles 42 to 71, (that is, Volumes 8 through 12) are

10A, incorporating titles 57-59. Also in 1968 the publisher issued a special supplement containing the General Corporation Act which is now included in the cumulative supplement to volume 8A. Volume 2 was replaced in 1971 with a new volume 2 (incorporating titles 1-4) and with a new volume 2A (incorporating titles 5, 6). Volume 3 was replaced in 1973 with a new volume 3 (incorporating titles 7, 8) and with a new volume 3A incorporating titles 9-15. The index volume, number 13, became so unwieldy that in 1974 it was replaced with a new volume 13 (index letters A to D), 14 (E to O), and 15 (P to Z). Volume 7 was replaced in 1976 with a new volume 7 (incorporating titles 38, 39) and a new volume 11 (incorporating titles 60-63) and a new volume 11A (incorporating titles, 64-66). Volume 12 was replaced in 1976 with a new volume 12 (incorporating title 67 code sections up to §67 - 3905) and a new volume 12A (incorporating title 67 code sections to §67 - 6045 and titles 68-71). Volume 16 was added in 1977. It incorporates the parallel reference tables formerly in Volume 1. See section 230. Volume 9 was replaced in 1977 with a new volume 9 (incorporating only title 49) as was volume 9A replaced with a new 9A (incorporating only titles 50-51) and a new volume 9B was added (incorporating titles 52-53). Volume 6 was replaced in 1977 with a new volume 6 (incorporating only titles 30-32) and a new volume 6A was added (incorporating titles 33-37). Volume 5A (Court Rules) was added in 1977.

arranged alphabetically, not by general topics, beginning with "Aeronautics" and ending with "Weights and Measures." Following are all of the code titles by volume as of 1977.

VOLUME 1

Constitutions

Title

VOLUME 2

1. Code and Statutes
2. Elections
3. Legislature
4. State Government

VOLUME 2A

5. Counties
6. Municipal Corporations

VOLUME 3

7. Military Affairs—Civil Defense
8. Public Officers and Employees

VOLUME 3A

9. Public Finances
10. Public Libraries and Archives
11. Public Parks, Forests and
    Recreational Systems
12. Public Property, Printing and Contracts
13. Public Planning and Housing
14. Public Welfare
15. Public Records

VOLUME 4

16. Courts
17. Judges and Chancellors
18. Clerks of Courts
19. Justices of the Peace
20. Civil Procedure
21. Proceedings in Chancery
22. Juries and Jurors

32

V O L U M E 5

23. Remedies and Special Proceedings
24. Evidence and Witnesses
25. Judgments
26. Execution
27. Appeal and Review
28. Limitation of Actions
29. Attorneys at Law

V O L U M E 5A

Court Rules

V O L U M E 6

30. Administration of Estates
31. Descent and Distribution
32. Wills

V O L U M E 6A

33. Mentally Ill and Mentally Retarded Persons
34. Guardianship—Estates of Incompetents
35. Fiduciaries and Trust Estates
36. Domestic Relations
37. Juveniles

V O L U M E 7

38. Prevention and Detection of Crime
39. Criminal Offenses

V O L U M E 7A

40. Criminal Procedure
41. Prisoners—Penal and Reformatory Institutions

V O L U M E 8

42. Aeronautics
43. Agriculture and Horticulture
44. Animals and Animal Husbandry
45. Banks—Financial Institutions
46. Cemeteries

V O L U M E 8A

47. Commercial Instruments and Transactions
48. Corporations and Associations

V O L U M E 9

49.   Education

V O L U M E 9 A

50.   Employer and Employee
51.   Fish, Game and Wildlife Resources

V O L U M E 9 B

52.   Food, Drugs and Cosmetics
53.   Health and Safety

V O L U M E 10

54.   Highways, Bridges and Ferries
55.   Holidays
56.   Insurance

V O L U M E 10A

57.   Intoxicating Liquors
58.   Mines and Mining
59.   Motor and other Vehicles

V O L U M E 11

60.   Oil and Gas
61.   Partnerships
62.   Professions, Businesses and Trades
63.   Professions of the Healing Arts

V O L U M E 11A

64.   Property
65.   Public Utilities and Carriers
66.   Sports and Athletic Events

V O L U M E 12

67.   Taxes and Licenses, §67-101 to §67-3905

V O L U M E 12A

67.   Taxes and Licenses, §67-4001 to §67-6045
68.   Timber

34

69.   Trade Practices—Trade-Marks and Labels
70.   Waters, Waterways, Drains and Levees
71.   Weights and Measures

Combined General Index
Volume 13 A—D
Volume 14 E—O
Volume 15 P—Z

V O L U M E   16
Tables

This codification is further systemized by section number-ing that attempts to follow a logical pattern based on title, chapter, and section. That is, the title number comes first, followed by a hyphen, then the chapter number (usually one digit but sometimes two when a title has numerous chapters), with the last two digits showing the section number within the chapter. For example, the statute abolishing survivorship in joint tenancy is T.C.A. §64-107. That is, it is title sixty-four (Property), chapter one, section seven. The codification of the Uniform Commercial Code prompted a minor change in the numbering system relating to the U.C.C. The various articles of the U.C.C. have been codified as chapters and an extra hyphen placed between the chapter number (*nee* article) and the section number itself. For example, the statute abolishing seals on sales contracts is T.C.A. §47-2-203. That is, it is title forty-seven (Commercial Instruments and Transactions), chapter two (Sales) section 203.

A very important feature of Tennessee Code Annotated is the legislative history of each code section which appears in parenthesis below each section. This history simply provides the session law origin of the present code section, together with its previous code section number and amendments, if any. See section 600.

§230   INDEXES AND NON-STATUTORY MATERIAL IN T.C.A.

Each volume of the code is indexed and a general index of three volumes (Vol. 13, A-D; Vol. 14, E-O; Vol. 15, P-Z) is provided. Also each volume except the first contains a ready-reference index in the last pages of the supplement. Arranged alphabetically, it is a convenient shortcut into the volume in hand.

The index references for a particular subject are to code sections including the title. For example:

Consortium
damages for wife's loss of   25-109

A surprising amount of non-statutory material is included in the code. The following are in Volume 5A (1977):

1.   Rules of the Tennessee Supreme Court. (indexed) See Sections 500 and 530. Note that besides establishing rules for appellate practice and procedure these rules encompass:
    A.   Licensing of Attorneys
    B.   Canons of Judicial Ethics
    C.   Rules for Disbarment of Attorneys
2.   Rules of the Court of Appeals (indexed). This includes the Court of Criminal Appeals.
3.   Rules of Civil Procedure (indexed). See section 540.
4.   Code of Professional Responsibility.
5.   Index to Articles and Memorials of Tennessee Judges and Lawyers.

Other important materials are in Volume 16, notably the parallel reference tables. These tables show where code sections from earlier codes and session laws by number are codified in T.C.A. Such tables are invaluable to a researcher wishing to trace the language of an early act or statute. These tables are:

1.   1932 Code and 1950 Code Supplement
2.   Williams' Code
3.   Shannon's Code and Supplement (This is Shannon's Code of 1917.
4.   Code of 1858
5.   Acts from 1715 to present

This volume also includes mortality and annuity valuation tables based on the 1970 census, interest tables and a perpetual calendar.

§240   USING T.C.A.

Proper use of Tennessee Code Annotated requires skillful manipulation of its Combined General Index, Vols. 13-15. This is true even though a researcher may have confidence that the statute sought will be found in a particular title or volume because no system of codification can draw precise lines between areas of the law, or expect to draw within its nomenclature scheme all laws in some way relevant. For example, willful polluting of water is a felony in Tennessee. T.C.A. §70-337. Should this appear in the criminal code or be shown under the title Waters, Waterways, Drains and Levees?

Unfortunately, inadequate indexes have been the bane of the Tennessee bar, and criticism has been frequently leveled at the current index. Accordingly, the researcher is well advised to familiarize himself first with the terminology of T.C.A., then to peruse the index for the most pertinent subject, and to opt for several alternate subjects should the first one(s) prove unfruitful. For example, should "peace bonds" not be readily discovered, one might look under "bonds and undertakings" before finding the appropriate entry, namely, "bond to keep the peace."

Other suggestions for using T.C.A. include:

1.   Each volume has its own complete index so reference to the Combined General Index is not always necessary.

2.   A general table of contents for the entire T.C.A. indicating the location of titles is included on the inside cover and flyleaf of the Combined General Index volumes.

3.   Each volume contains its own detailed table of contents and its spine summarizes its contents. For example, the spine of Volume 4 reads "Courts and Procedure."

4.   The index does not distinguish between statutes in the volume and those in the cumulative pocket supplements. *Therefore, it is imperative that the supplement to a volume be consulted to locate all current law relevant to the subject being researched.*

All public and general acts passed prior to the enactment of Tennessee Code Annotated in 1955 were expressly repealed or repealed by failure of incorporation with certain exceptions. T.C.A. §1-204 (1955). The exceptions dealt with certain state bond provisions (T.C.A. §1-206 (1955)) and those of a private or local nature, although a variety of other statutes were likewise untouched, such as those dealing with county boundaries, regulation of local courts, and occupant, entry and similar land laws. For a complete list see T.C.A. §1-205 (1955). In any event, local laws, that is, Private Acts, are not published in Tennessee Code Annotated. See sections 310 and 640(c).

§250   UNIFORM ACTS

A variety of uniform or suggested model state acts have been enacted in Tennessee.[9] Also, the effects of such acts are apparent in a variety of statutes that draw heavily on these models but are not complete adoptions. For example, the real estate broker licensing act is patterned after a real estate industry supported law. It is not indexed in Tennessee Code Annotated under uniform acts however. Precisely, the term uniform and/or model act refers to those drafted by the National Conference of Commissions on Uniform State Laws or a similar organization such as the appropriate committee (or section) of the American Bar Association. In T.C.A. the term "uniform" has also been applied to acts that attempt to insure uniform activities across the state, for example, the uniform county road law.

Shown below are the "uniform acts" in force in Tennessee together with some information as to their origin. The year of its adoption is shown in parenthesis.

Absence as Evidence of Death and Absentees' Property Law (1941); T.C.A. 30-1801 - 30-1815 (1977).

Administrative Procedures Act (1974); See section 722.

Aeronautics Law (1923); T.C.A. 42-101 - 42-111 (1964). Support for this act was withdrawn by the Conference in 1943 because of obsolescence.

---

9. An excellent discussion of these acts enacted in Tennessee up to 1952 may be found in *Comment, Tennessee and the Uniform Acts*, 22 TENN. L. REV. 407 (1952).

Anatomical Gift Act (1969); T.C.A. 53-4201 - 53-4290 (1977).

Anti-Gambling Act (1955); T.C.A. 39-2031 - 39-2037 (1975). This was a model act drafted by the Conference in collaboration with the American Bar Association.

Business Corporation Act. Enacted as "Tennessee General Corporation Act," (1968); T.C.A. 48-101 - 48-2007 (Supp. 1976). This act replaced the Business Corporation Act of 1929. T.C.A. 48-101 - 48-931 (repealed). In 1957 the Conference withdrew support for its own Business Corporation Act and endorsed the Model Business Corporation Act drafted by the American Bar Association. For discussion of the Tennessee act see "The New Tennessee General Corporation Act: A Symposium," *Tennessee Law Review* 36 (1969): 324-361. See also, Paul J. Hartman, *Business Corporation Study* 4 vols. Nashville: Tennessee Law Revision Commission, 1964-65. See also, "The General Corporation Act." *Tennessee Bar Journal* 5 (November, 1968): 5-73.

Business Records as Evidence Act (1957); T.C.A. 24-712 - 24-715 (Supp. 1976). Support for this uniform act was withdrawn by the Conference in 1966 because it was superseded by the Uniform Rules of Evidence and the Uniform Interstate and International Procedure Act.

Commerical Code (1963); T.C.A. 47-1-101 - 47-9-507 (1964). Tennessee adopted the 1962 Revision. It superseded the Bill of Landing Act, Negotiable Instrument Law, the Sales Act as amended, the Stock Transfer Act, Trust Receipts Act, Warehouse Receipts Act as amended, Conditional Sales Act, and Chattel Mortgage Act, many of which had been enacted in the state. See section 920, specifically, "Uniform Commercial Code."

Common Trust Funds Act (1953); T.C.A. 35-401 - 35-405 (1977). Amended version, 1952.

Contribution Among Tortfeasors (1968); T.C.A. 23-3101 - 23-3106 (Supp. 1976). Revised Act, 1955.

Controlled Substances Act. Enacted as "Tennessee Drug Control Act of 1971" (1971); T.C.A. 52-1408 - 52-1448 (1977). Superseding the Narcotic Drug Law (1937);

T.C.A. 52-1301 - 52-1304, 52-1309, 52-1311, 52-1313, 52-1319 - 52-1323 (repealed).

County Uniform Road Law (1974); T.C.A. 54-1001 - 54-1017 (Supp. 1976). This is an act of local origin.

Criminal Extradition Act (1951); T.C.A. 40-1001 - 40-1034 (1975). Revised Act, 1936.

Declaratory Judgments Act (1923); T.C.A. 23-1101 - 23-1113 (1955). Armstrong, "Uniform Declaratory Judgments Act Adopted in Tennessee," *Tennessee Law Review* 1 (1923): 38-47.

Execution of Wills Act (1941); T.C.A. 32-101 - 32-111 (1975). This is a model act.

Extradition of Persons of Unsound Mind Act (1917); T.C.A. 33-1001 - 33-1011 (1977). Conference support of this act was withdrawn in 1954 because of obsolescence.

Federal Tax Liens Act (1927); T.C.A. 64-2110 - 64-2115 (1976). The Conference suggested revisions in 1962 and 1966.

Fiduciaries Act (1953); T.C.A. 35-201 - 35-214 (1977).

Flag Act (1923); T.C.A. 39-1601 - 39-1606 (1975). Support for this act was withdrawn by the Conference in 1966.

Foreign Depositions Act (1923); T.C.A. 24-906 (1955). This uniform act was withdrawn by the conference in 1966 and in favor of the Uniform Interstate and International Procedure Act.

Foreign Probated Wills Act (1919); T.C.A. 32-501 - 32-505 (1977). Conference support for this act was withdrawn in 1943 because of obsolescence. See Execution of Wills Act.

Fraudulent Conveyances Act (1919); T.C.A. 64-308 - 64-321 (1976).

Fresh Pursuit Law (1939); T.C.A. 40-809 - 40-815 (1975). Neither a uniform nor model act as described above.

Gifts to Minors Act (1957); T.C.A. 35-801 - 35-810 (1977). The conference revised this act in 1965 and 1966.

Insurers Liquidation Act (1939); T.C.A. 56-1301, 15-1303, 56-1304, 56-1314, 56-1331. (1968) This was a model act.

Interstate Arbitration and Compromise of Death Taxes Act (1951); T.C.A. 30-1638 - 30-1643 (1977).

Judicial Notice of Foreign Laws Act (1943); T.C.A. 24-607 - 24-612. (1955) This uniform act was withdrawn by the conference in 1966, being superseded by Uniform Rules of Evidence and Uniform Interstate and International Procedure Act.

Limited Partnership Act (1919); T.C.A. 61-201 - 61-230 (1976).

Management· of Institutional Funds Act (1973); T.C.A. 35-1101 - 35-1109 (1977).

Motor Vehicle Operator's and Chauffeur's License Law (1957); T.C.A. 59-701 - 59-718. (1968). This was neither a uniform nor model act as described above. See Vehicle Code.

Out of State Parolee Supervision Act (1939); T.C.A. 40-3626 (1975). Neither a uniform nor model act as described above.

Partnership Act (1917); T.C.A. 61-101 - 61-142 (1976).

Photographic Copies of Business and Public Records as Evidence Act (1971); T.C.A. 24-711 (Supp. 1976).

Principal and Income Act (1955); T.C.A. 35-701 - 35-715 (1977). This act has been amended and revised by the conference in 1958 and 1962.

Probate Code, Intestate Succession—Ch. 529 and 538 [1976] Tenn. Pub. Acts 355, 424.

Proof of Foreign Statutes Act (1923); T.C.A. 24-616 (1955). Superseded by Uniform Rules of Evidence and Uniform Interstate and International Procedure Act.

Reciprocal Enforcement of Support Act (1953); T.C.A. 36-901 - 36-929 (1977). The 1958 amendments were enacted in Tennessee. The Conference revised the act in 1968.

Relocation Assistance Act (1972); T.C.A. 13-1901 - 13-1917 (1973).

Residential Landlord and Tenant Act (1975); T.C.A.
64-2801 - 64-2864 (1976). Note, "An Overview of the
Tennessee Residential Landlord and Tenant Act." *Memphis State University Law Review* 7 (1976); 109-128.
See also, T.C.A. 53-5501 - 53-5507 (1977); the latter is
not a uniform act as described above.

Securing Attendance of Witnesses from Within or Without
a State in Criminal Proceedings Act (1939); T.C.A.
40-2429 - 40-2438 (1975). Revision, 1936.

Simplification of Fiduciary Security Transfers Act (1959);
T.C.A. 35-901 - 35-911 (1977).

Simultaneous Death Act (1941); T.C.A. 31-501 - 31-508
(1977). The Conference amended this act in 1953.

Standards Code for Factory-Manufactured Mobile Homes
(1972); T.C.A. 53-4801 - 53-4814 (1977). This is not
a uniform or model act as described above.

Testamentary Additions to Trusts Act (1961); T.C.A.
32-307 (1977).

Vehicle Code (1951); T.C.A. 59-201 - 59-211, 59-301 -
59-330, 59-801 - 59-881, 59-1001 - 59-1015, 59-1016 -
59-1017, 59-1018 - 59-1030, 59-1201 - 59-1240. (1968)
This was neither a uniform nor model act as described
above but the code, its amendments, and revisions have
been endorsed by the conference in 1946, 1948, and
1970.

Veterans' Guardianship Act (1943); T.C.A. 34-901 - 34-922
(1977). Revision, 1943.

Vital Statistics Act (1941); 53-401 - 53-458 (1977) Support
for this act was withdrawn in 1966 by the Conference.

Knowing the origins of these acts aids the researcher in
determining legislative intent. (See section 320). Texts of
Conference-approved acts with annotations are found in Uniform Laws Annotated (U.L.A.), now printed by West Publishing
Company, 1968-, supplemented. Still more background on these
acts can be found in the annual Handbook of National Conference of Commissioners on Uniform State Laws, 1914-. For
example, a difference between Tennessee's and a neighboring
state's interpretation of a uniform act may result because the
neighboring state enacted the suggested amendments/revisions

and Tennessee did not. The rationale for the acts and their amendments/revisions (if any) are included in the annual Handbooks.

§260   SPECIAL COMPILATIONS

Individuals, businesses and state governmental agencies interested in specific areas of the law have for many years compiled or reprinted "codes" of Tennessee law relevant to their interests. Prior to T.C.A. most were private compilations but, since its appearance, most are simply reprints of relevant T.C.A. sections (with some extra annotations) and are issued by a state agency.

A researcher desiring to know the present law on any of these subjects should be especially cautious in the use of special compilations because their issuance is unsystematic. Nevertheless, such compilations have merit because they are concise and may contain forms or other practice aids.

Some of these special compilations are listed in section 720; in addition to those, the following may be useful.

Compilation of Selected Laws on Children and Youth from the Tennessee Code Annotated. rev. 1974. Nashville: Commission on Children and Youth, 1974. 1 vol. looseleaf.

Workmen's Compensation Law, revised to July 1, 1973. Annotations, Accident Reporting Law and Discount Tables. Nashville: Department of Labor. Contains a unique subject matter annotation; however, the researcher should be mindful of changes, especially statutory.

[Year] Public School Laws of Tennessee, [Number] General Assembly, Compiled from Public Acts [Chapters]. Nashville: Department of Education. (annually). This pamphlet is merely a collection of the education-related laws passed by the most recent General Assembly.

Tennessee Laws Pertaining to Mental Health, Unofficial and Unannotated Edition. Nashville: Department of Mental Health, 1975. 1 vol. looseleaf.

Chapter III

Session Laws and Materials of Legislative Intent

Section 300   SESSION LAWS

Enactments of the General Assembly (both public and private acts) are published by the State in chronological order as approved by the Governor, appearing in bound form (together with a subject index) after the end of the legislative session. These are called session laws. From earliest times these have been published by the state or under state "authority," and are the primary sources for uncodified law.

Section 310   PUBLIC ACTS, PRIVATE ACTS AND RESOLUTIONS

A public act is the highest expression of legislative intent, and is a law general in nature, that is, typically embracing the whole of a subject and dealing with subject matter of common interest to the entire state. These criteria—intent, subject matter, and scope—are the factors determinative of whether an enactment is a public or private act. Mechanical tests to differentiate between public and private acts should not be used. For example, in construing a statute courts may disregard the description which denominated the law a "Public Act" and look to whether the enactment is private and local in form or effect, requiring local approval. Farris v. Blanton, 528 S.W.2d 549, 551 (Tenn. 1975). (See sections 800, and 850). Further, although most public acts are codified, this alone is not a satisfactory test to differentiate public and private acts because not all public acts are deemed appropriate for codification,[1] e.g., the Appropriations Bill.[2] Additionally, some public acts may be

1. A typical example is the act establishing a commission of members of the Sumner County Chapter of the Association for the Preservation of Tennessee Antiquities. The purpose of the commission is to advise the Tennessee Historical Commission on the purchase and restoration of "Crag Font," home of General James Winchester. Ch. 268 [1957] Tenn. Pub. Acts 896.

2. Despite its uncodified status, the Appropriations Bill deserves the

of a temporary or special nature, *e.g.*, raising a judge's secretary's salary. Moreover, public acts may be private acts in disguise such as the act construed in Farris v. Blanton (supra) which provided for run-off elections "in counties with a mayor as head of the executive or administrative branch of the county government," namely, Shelby County.

A private or local act (the term special act is sometimes used) is an enactment which is applicable to one or more, but not all, political subdivisions of the state. It is usually written in such a way as to apply only to a certain location, *e.g.*, Smith County, or may exclude a certain location from a general act. In the past, the technique of prescribing narrow population ranges, *e.g.*, "All cities having populations between 29,980 and 29,900" was popular, but now the general practice is to specify the city/county by name.

Private acts can have important legal consequences especially upon city and county governments. (See sections 800 and 850.) But they also often touch on the quaint and curious, such as those acts prohibiting beaver hunting in Sullivan County and prohibiting the use of firearms in raccoon hunting in Hamblen County. Ch. 84 [1974] Tenn. Priv. Acts 146; Ch. 84 [1973] Tenn. Priv. Acts 300.

The constitutionality of private acts is an endlessly litigated issue. The major challenges to their validity are: (1) the requirement of Article XI, section 8 that only general laws be passed, which trnaslates into a prohibition against unreasonable classifications, and (2) the requirement of Article XI, section 9 that acts local in form or effect be ratified at the local level. See Farris v. Blanton, 528 S.W.2d 549, 551 (Tenn. 1975).

The Tennessee Constitution makes no distinction between a bill and a resolution. It is generally thought, however, that resolutions are not included within the laws of the state; instead, they serve mainly to express the will of the majority of the house by which they are adopted. However, this is true only for simple resolutions, that is, those adopted by one house only.

close attention of the careful researcher because it discloses legislative intent. For example, the legislature often specifies its policy toward such matters as the percentage of state contribution toward state and federal sponsored health programs and the student-teacher ratio in public schools. Ch. 230, §§80, 83 [1973] Tenn. Pub. Acts 886. Moreover, the Appropriations Bill contains the Governor's appropriations veto message.

Joint resolutions, those submitted and passed in both houses in the same form have, according to one authority, "the force of law for certain limited purposes."[3]

An important early case suggested a test that looked to whether a joint resolution was "directory" rather than "mandatory" in nature. If mandatory, the resolution would become positive law if formally enacted. Richardson v. Young, 122 Tenn. 471, 536, 125 S.W.664, 677 (1909).[4] A better test, however, to determine whether a joint resolution rises to the dignity of law might adopt the three criteria distinguishing public from private acts mentioned above: intent, subject matter, and scope. This approach is necessary because the broad spectrum of legislative purposes expressed in resolutions militates against neat categories. Among these purposes are: (1) to name a bridge or highway, (2) to express condolences or congratulations, (3) to request a state or federal official to do or not to do something, (4) to provide for "housekeeping" details of the legislative session, and (5) to prompt in-depth study of public issues.

A final factor influencing the dignity of joint resolutions is the formality of their enactment. Joint resolutions are subject to the same constitutional provisions regulating the mechanics of enactment as are bills. The apparent exceptions to the requirement of gubernatorial approval are joint resolutions (1) on formal matters of legislative procedure, such as adjournment, (2) to propose specific constitutional amendments, and (3) to propose a referendum on calling a constitutional convention.

Finally, a list of interstate compacts to which Tennessee is a party is shown in the index to Tennessee Code Annotated. Another list, showing those which the state is eligible to join is in:

Interstate Compacts, 1783-1966. A Compilation. Chicago: Council of State Governments, 1966.

3. J. MYNATT, A BILL DRAFTING MANUAL FOR TENNESSEE 44 (1974).

4. *Cited in* Gilbreath v. Willett, 148 Tenn. 92, 105, 251 S.W. 910, 913 (1922); Huffins v. Gold, 154 Tenn. 583, 588, 288 S.W. 352, 354 (1926); Trapp v. McCormick, 175 Tenn. 1, 10, 130 S.W.2d 122, 125 (1939).

Section 315   BILL DRAFTING AIDS

Many good sources aid the researcher in bill drafting; this includes materials that assist in interpreting statutes. Foremost of these for the Tennessee draftsperson is:

Mynatt, James J. *A Bill Drafting Manual for Tennessee.* Nashville: Legislative Council Committee, 1974.

The better general books on this subject include:

Dickerson, Reed. *The Fundamentals of Legal Drafting.* Boston: Little, Brown & Co., and American Bar Foundation, 1965.

_____. *Legislative Drafting.* Boston: Little, Brown & Co., 1954.

_____. *The Interpretation and Application of Statutes.* Boston: Little, Brown & Co., 1975.

Sutherland, Jabez G. *Statutes and Statutory Construction.* 4th ed. (C. Dallas Sands, ed.) Chicago: Callaghan & Co., 1968-1972. 6 vols. supplemented. This is the standard reference book on this subject.

Law school casebooks and texts provide valuable insights; the better are:

Davies, Jack. *Legislative Law and Process in a Nutshell.* St. Paul, Minn.: West Publishing Co., 1975.

Nutting, Charles B., Sheldon D. Elliott, Reed Dickerson. *Cases and Materials on Legislation.* 4th ed. St. Paul, Minn.: West Publishing Co., 1969.

Read, Horace E., et al. *Materials on Legislation.* 3rd ed. Mineola, New York: Foundation, 1973.

A recent work has attempted to index sources of comparative provisions of state laws on specific subjects. For example, if a researcher needs an all-state list or digest of garnishment laws this index suggests CCH Consumer Credit Guide. This index is:

Schultz, Jon S. *Comparative Statutory Sources.* Buffalo, New York: Hein Co., 1973.

The standard sources of model or pattern state legislation are:

Council of State Governments. Committee of State Officials on Suggested State Legislation. *Suggested State Legislation,* 1941- (several volumes issued annually).

Uniform Laws Annotated. Master Edition. St. Paul, Minn.: West Publishing Co., 1968. 13 vols. supplemented. Interpretation of these acts is aided by research on the specific act in *Handbook of the National Conference of Commissioners on Uniform State Laws.* Chicago: National Conference of Commissioners on Uniform State Laws, 1892- (annual).

A storehouse of accurate and timely information about the activities of state governments, *e.g.*, consumer protection, constitutional revision, legislative trends, is found in:

The Book of the States. Lexington, Kentucky: Council of State Governments, 1935- (annual). Supplement volumes treat elective officials and administrators.

Bibliographies on state government or selected topics are helpful. These include:

Koslofsky, R., et al. *Selected Bibliography on State Government, 1959-1972.* Lexington, Kentucky: Council of State Governments, 1972.

Howell, Margaret A. *Bibliography of Bibliographies of Legal Materials.* 2 vols. Newark, New Jersey: The Author, 1969 (1969-1971 supplement).

Finally, the nation's law reviews should be consulted for articles on statutory drafting or tables and analyses of nationwide legislation. One law review is devoted entirely to this subject, *i.e.*, Harvard Journal on Legislation, but typical offerings include:

"Symposium on Statutory Construction," *Vanderbilt Law Review* 3 (1950): 365-584.

Menard, Jr., Albert R. "Legislative Bill Drafting," *Rocky Mountain Law Review* 26 (1954): 368-385.

Section 320   NORTH CAROLINA AND TERRITORIAL SESSION LAWS

North Carolina session laws relative to Tennessee were printed verbatim in the early compilations of North Carolina statutes. Note that these compilations were privately printed, consecutively arranged collections of session laws covering a given number of years, usually bound in one volume. (See section 200). Foremost of these are:

Iredell, James. *Laws of the State of North Carolina, 1715-1790.* Edenton: Hodge and Wills, 1791.

Haywood, John. *A Revisal of All the Public Acts of the State of North Carolina and the State of Tennessee.* Nashville: Bradford, 1809. Editions in 1812, 1815.

The "session laws" of territorial government prior to election of a general assembly were the gubernatorial promulgated ordinances (1790-94), followed by the first true session laws passed by the territorial general assembly (1794-1796). For discussion see section 120. Most of these enactments of a statewide nature are included in Haywood's Revisal, *supra* or the very useful:

Scott, Edward. *Laws of the State of Tennessee, including those of North Carolina Now in force in this State. From the year 1715 to the year 1820, inclusive.* 2 vols. Knoxville: Heiskell and Brown, 1821.

The session laws are:

Acts and Ordinances of the Governor and Judges of the Territory of the United States of America South of the River Ohio. Knoxville: Roulstone, 1793. 8 pp. (Issued between June 11, 1792 and March 21, 1793).

Acts Passed at the First Session of the General Assembly of the Territory of the United States South of the River Ohio. Knoxville: Roulstone, 1794. 101 pp. (This session convened August 25, 1794, and adjourned September 30, 1794).

Acts Passed at the Second Session of the first General Assembly of the Territory of the United States South of the River Ohio. Knoxville: Roulstone, 1795, 31 pp. (This session convened June 29, 1795, and adjourned July 11, 1795).

Section 325 STATE SESSION LAWS: 1796 TO PRESENT

A list of state session laws is shown in Appendix A.

Section 330   MATERIALS OF LEGISLATIVE INTENT—PRIMARY

Proper understanding and interpretation of statutes often requires research into sources that describe legislative intent. For a discussion of this procedure generally see:

> Note, (Glenden M. Fisher, Jr. and William J. Harbison) "Trends in the Use of Extrinsic Aids in Statutory Interpretation," *Vanderbilt Law Review* 3 (1950); 586-596.

> Folsom, Gwendolyn B. *Legislative History—Research for the Interpretation of Laws.* Charlottesville, Va.: University Press of Virginia, 1972. This book deals mostly with federal statutes.

The primary sources are the journals of the General Assembly and records of its debates.

Section 335   JOURNALS OF THE GENERAL ASSEMBLY:
1796 TO PRESENT

The Tennessee constitution requires each legislative house to keep and publish a journal of its proceedings. Issued daily since 1974 during the legislative session, (see section 344) these are issued in bound volumes after the legislature's adjournment. These journals were also kept under territorial government and a complete list to date is shown below. Note that the territorial journals, including the constitutional convention journal, were reprinted in Journal of the Territorial Councils of the Senate and House of Tennessee. Knoxville: Roulstone, 1794-1796. Reprint. Nashville: McKenzie and Brown, 1852. This reprint is the most readily available edition and is the source for territorial journals described below. Indeed, until 1971, the original imprints were presumed lost. See Dobson, John. The Lost Roulstone Imprints. Knoxville: Univ. of Tennessee Library, 1975.

A list of legislative journals since 1796 is shown in Appendix B.

Section 338   LEGISLATIVE DEBATES: RECORDINGS

Sometimes more illuminating than the journals are the mechanical recordings of legislative debates recorded by the State Library and Archives (Archives Section) beginning in 1955. In addition to the sessions, all hearings held in the chambers are recorded, as are budget hearings, if the Archives is notified. Committee meetings are also recorded on request. All legislative recordings have a minute-to-minute index. Arrangements can be made to have copies of the tapes or certified transcripts made.

Section 340   MATERIALS OF LEGISLATIVE INTENT AND SERVICES—CURRENT

Legislative matters relative to the current or most recent General Assembly are documented by the materials and services described in section 342, 344, 346, 348, and 349.

However, these materials/services are likely to change in some respect now that the Legislative Council (1954-1977) has been replaced by the Legislative Services Committee. (See section 352). The duties and publications of the old Council staff, to be performed by new Committee's Office of Legal Services and Office of Administration, are likely to be similar but not entirely alike those performed by the Council staff. *Continued references made here to "Legislative Council" will aid the researcher in tracing the materials/services until these are fully defined by the new offices.*

Section 342   LEGISLATIVE RECORD

The content and status of pending legislation is reported in the weekly tabloid, the Legislative Record, published since 1955 by the Legislative Council Committee during the legislative session. This document is cumulative for the pending legislative session. It is available upon subscription. Its features are: (1) committee memberships; (2) names and addresses of legislators; (3) initial action and most recent action regarding: (a) House bills, (b) Senate bills, (c) House Resolutions, (d) Senate Resolutions, (e) Joint Resolutions; (f) action (veto, etc.) by the Governor.

The Legislative Record is furnished at state expense to legislators who also receive copies of all general bills plus a daily list of bills and resolutions introduced, together with summaries of procedural actions taken by both houses. These materials are available to the general public by subscription. Moreover, the Council makes available to each legislator a weekly "sponsor index" which describes the status of all legislation sponsored by him through the preceding week. Copies are usually available upon inquiry but are not generally published. Likewise, each committee chairman receives a weekly list of bills and resolutions in his committee. Copies of the committees' calendars are available upon request from the committee office.

Section 344   UNBOUND HOUSE AND SENATE JOURNALS AND CHIEF CLERK'S INDEX

In recent years the Chief Clerk of the House has issued a daily pamphlet journal which summarizes the previous day's proceedings in both houses including voting records, but not including debates. Explanations of votes are included, however. These pamphlets are later collected and edited by the Chief Clerks of both houses and published in bound form. (See section 335).

Also, since 1974, the Chief Clerk of the House has kept an index of all bills that indicates the date on which each step of the enacting procedure was completed and the location of each bill in the process of becoming law. It is available on microfiche from the Legislative Council.

Section 346   UNOFFICIAL INDEX TO LEGISLATION INTRODUCED IN THE GENERAL ASSEMBLY

Since 1957 the staff of the Legislative Council Committee has published the *Unofficial Index to Legislation Introduced in the General Assembly* which is an index (arranged by bill number, by subject matter, and by code section amended) of all legislation (both public and private acts and resolutions) introduced in the General Assembly. In recent years an important feature of this publication has been the inclusion of the governor's veto messages. See section 640(b) for indexes of session laws.

Section 348   THE CONSTITUENTS "HOT LINE"

Since 1973 an information system, consisting of a toll-free telephone (1-800-342-8490), has been made available to the public as an aid for learning the status of pending legislation. Of course, this service is only available during the legislative session, but through it a constituent can gain access to information/services which are generally only available by subscription or free to legislators, such as the Legislative Record, unbound journals, and computer-printed reports. These are the "daily status report" (sometimes called the "bill history report") and the "daily subject index." Depending on how well the system is functioning and how busy the legislature is, these give up-to-date status information on legislation by bill or subject matter.

Section 349   PROPRIETARY REPORTING SERVICES

For at least a decade the activities of the legislature, as well as state government generally, have been the subject of a variety of proprietary reporting services. Sometimes partisan in nature, these services usually terminate after a few years but do provide valuable insights into the dynamics of lawmaking and government. The latest such service is The Tennessee Journal, published weekly by M. Lee Smith and Associates, Nashville. V. 1 January 6, 1975 —. Each issue comprises about four pages. See also, the Tennessee Attorneys Memo, section 432(a).

The best such service is the CCLC Legislative Newsletter, published weekly during the legislative session by the Coordinating Council on Legislative Concerns, Nashville. V. 1, 1974 —. Each issue comprises about eight pages.

Section 350   MATERIALS OF LEGISLATIVE INTENT—SECONDARY

Materials of legislative intent in the form of research studies and reports have originated in a variety of agencies, committees and commissions. Chief among these are the Legislative Council Committee (see section 352) and the Law Revision Commission (see section 354). Other sources include various committees of the General Assembly (often "special" or temporary) which focus on one topic, *e.g.*, taxation, education.

Although these documents are of uneven quality, some have great merit in amplifying a complex statute, especially where the studies/statutes were drafted by recognized scholars or practitioners. Examples include the studies of corporation, water pollution, and probate laws. See sections 354(b) and 360.

A special General Assembly committee of a more permanent nature is the Fiscal Review Committee created in 1967. T.C.A. §§ 3-701 to -708. Composed of legislative leaders, its purpose is to explore and review the fiscal affairs of the state and to make recommendations on the subject to the General Assembly proper or to its standing committees. See section 360.

Section 352   LEGISLATIVE SERVICES (COUNCIL) COMMITTEE

The Legislative Services Committee, until 1977 called the Legislative Council Committee,[5] through its staff called the Office of Legislative Administration and Office of Legal Services, will provide the legislature a range of services including legal research, subject surveys and analysis and bill drafting. The old Council issued a 16 page pamphlet, Legislators' Manual (latest edition 1975) which explained procedures for enacting bills and described the duties/services of the legislative support system generally. It also issued the Bill Drafting Manual. See section 315. The old Legislative Council also published (a) Final Reports (1954-1966) and (b) Topical Reports (1966-1977). See section 352 (a) and (b).

---

5. Ch. 89 [1977] Tenn. Pub. Acts. 165.
6. For a discussion of the services performed by similar bodies see Note, *State Legislative Services: An Overview*, 21 VAND. L. REV. 125 (1967).

Section 352(a)   FINAL REPORTS, 1954-1966

Until 1968 the Council submitted hard cover final or summary reports to the Governor and General Assembly that discussed matters ranging from boating laws to workman's compensation. These reports are excellent examples of legislative intent because they highlight shortcomings in the law and make recommendations. Shown below is a list of the early final reports showing some of the *major* topics studied. The careful researcher will want to examine the reports carefully because they include other reports on an array of issues, *e.g.*, recommendations regarding tax assessment, interstate compacts, and various departments of state government.

78th General Assembly, 1953-1954
   1. Legislative Procedures
   2. Retirement Systems
   3. School Program
   4. Rural Roads
   5. Commitment Policies

79th General Assembly, 1955-1956
   1. Indeterminate Sentence Law
   2. Juvenile or Family Courts
   3. Small Loan Businesses
   4. Laws on Hotel Inspection
   5. Lobbying
   6. Air Pollution

80th General Assembly, 1957-1958
   1. Election Laws
   2. Judiciary
   3. Divorce and Annulment
   4. Practice of Medicine
   5. Motor Vehicles (Uniform Motor Vehicle Code)
   6. Privilege Taxes

81st General Assembly, 1959-1960
   1. Billboard Regulation
   2. Boating Laws
   3. Judiciary
   4. Municipal Revenue
   5. Penal System
   6. Non-Profit Utility Systems

82nd General Assembly, 1961-1962
1. Alcoholism
2. Forestry Laws
3. Judiciary
4. Mentally Ill
5. Motor Vehicle Operation
6. Tax Assessments and Structure

83rd General Assembly, 1963-1964
1. Highway Beautification
2. Coal Industry
3. Department of Correction
4. Administration of Higher Education
5. Public Welfare
6. Revenue Collections

84th General Assembly, 1965-1966
1. Tax Problems
2. Structure of County Government
3. Child Labor Laws
4. State Teachers' Retirement System
5. Cancellation of Automobile Liability Insurance
6. Eminent Domain Laws

Section 352(b)   TOPICAL REPORTS, 1966 -

A variety of single topic reports were produced by the Council on its own initiative or through legislative resolution. Although some of these appeared in the final reports publications, since the late 1960's the practice has been to offer these topical reports *individually* in final form. The following is a *selected* list of Legislative Council Committee publications chosen here for their continuing relevance to the contemporary researcher.[7]

FINAL REPORTS:

Ad Valorem Tax	FR 1968-B5-op[8]
Administrative Procedures Act	FR 1973-B1
Aged and Chronically Ill	FR 1960-B13-op
Alcoholism	FR 1962-B1
Automobile Junkyards	FR 1964-B1

7. The Council has thrice catalogued its publications. The most recent is *Publications of the Tennessee Legislative Council Committee*, doc. No. P-1973. Nashville: Legislative Council Committee, 1973.

8. "op" indicates out of print.

56

Banking Laws	FR 1968-B6
Billboards Regulation	FR 1960-B1-op
Bloodbanks	FR 1964-B2-op
Boards and Commissions, State	FR 1970-Be
Boating Laws	FR 1960-B2
Building and Loan Association Laws	FR 1968-B7
Camping Trailer Safety	FR 1970-Br
Child Labor Laws	FR 1966-B1
Children, Mentally Ill and Emotionally Disturbed	FR 1962-B7
Children's Services, also 1974 (FR-1974-B1)	FR 1966-B2
Coal Industry	FR 1964-B3
College Entrance Tests & Testing Services	FR 1973-B2
Correction	FR 1964-B4-op
County Government	FR 1966-B3-op
Delinquent Youth Services	FR 1968-B1
Delinquent Youth Services, Part II (Juvenile Court System)	FR 1968-Bla
Domestic Relations Laws	FR 1970-B1
Development Disabilities	FR 1974-B2
Education, Distribution of State Funds (Grades 1-12)	
Education, Governance of	FR 1968-B8
Election Laws	FR 1973-B3
Electric Service, Rights of Cooperatives, and Municipalities	FR 1966-B4
Eminent Domain	FR 1968-B2
Fees and Charges	FR 1966-B5
Food, Food Handlers, Serving Facilities, Inspection of	FR 1970-B5
Forestry Laws	FR 1962-B2-op
Forestry School	FR 1960-B3-op
Game and Fish Commission	FR 1960-B4
Health Planning Agencies & "Certificate of Need" Legislation	FR 1973-B4

Higher Education	FR 1964-B5
Indigent Hospitalization	FR 1966-B6
Insurance, Cancellation, Failure to Write	FR 1966-B7
Insurance, Rating Procedures	FR 1962-B3-op
Insurance, State Self	FR 1966-B8
Interest Rates, Statutory	FR 1968-B10
Judiciary	FR 1960-B5-op
Judiciary (Case Loads of Chancery, Circuit and Criminal Courts)	FR 1962-B5-op
Legislative Apportionment	FR 1962-B5
Legislative Facilities, Procedures and Services	FR 1966-B9
Legislative Facilities, Procedures and Services	FR 1972-B1
Legislative Procedures	FR 1960-B6-op
Legislative Procedures	FR 1962-B7-op
Legislative Procedures	FR 1964-B9
Legislative Procedures	FR 1970-B6
Livestock Sales Records	FR 1960-B7
Library & Archives Programs, Administrative Location of	FR 1972-B5
Mechanics' and Materialmen's Liens	FR 1968-B11
Mentally Ill	FR 1964-B7
Mentally Retarded Public Offenders	FR 1970-B7
Milk Industry	FR 1960-B8-op
Milk and Milk Products, Regulatory Legislation	FR 1968-B3
Motor Vehicle Laws	FR 1972-B2
Motor Vehicle Operation	FR 1962-B8
Municipal Boundaries, Adjustment of	FR 1973-B6
Municipal Revenue	FR 1960-B10
Narcotics and Drug Abuse	FR 1970-B8
Noise and Air Pollution and Refuse Dumping	FR 1970-B9
Nurse Practice Act	FR 1966-B10

Nurses, Need, Supply and Education	FR 1968-B12
Nursing Homes for the Aged Mentally Ill	FR 1970-B10
Obsolete Laws	FR 1962-B9-op
Outdoor Advertising	FR 1964-B8
Parks and Recreational Facilities, Bond Financing	FR 1968-B12
Pay of Legislative Employees	FR 1972-B3
Penal System	FR 1960-B12
Public Employer, Employee Relations	FR 1970-B11
Presidential Elections, Right to Vote	FR 1970-B12
Public Library Services	FR 1960-B14-op
Public Utility Services	FR 1966-B11
Public Welfare	FR 1964-B9
Retirement Systems	FR 1968-B14
Residence Requirements	FR 1962-B10-op
Revenue	FR 1964-B10
Road Law, Model County	FR 1960-B9
Schools, Joint Operation of Local Public	FR 1970-B2
Security Measures for the General Assembly	FR 1972-B4
Small Loan Business, Regulation	FR 1968-B4
Social Problems—Job Training	FR 1973-B8(a)
—Housing and Slum Conditions	FR 1973-B8(b)
—Poverty & the Public Welfare System	FR 1973-B8(c)
State Salary Schedules	FR 1972-B5
State Salary Schedules & Fringe Benefits	FR 1973-B7
Sick Leave—Merit Salary	FR 1974-B6
Taxation: Certain Tax Problems	FR 1966-B112
Tax Assessments	FR 1962-B11
Tax Structure	FR 1962-B12-op
Teachers' Retirement	FR 1966-B15

Utility Systems, Non-profit	FR 1960-B11-op
Vocational Education Programs	FR 1973-B9
Water Resources and Related Lands	FR 1962-B13
Workmen's Compensation also, one for 1955	FR 1972-B6

Section 354   LAW REVISION COMMISSION

A fast changing society is in need of continuous revision of its laws. From 1963 to 1976 accomplishing this on a systematic basis was greatly assisted by the Law Revision Commission. The Commission was an independent, nonpolitical body composed of nine attorneys serving without compensation.[9] The Commission, through its full time director and paid researchers, undertook studies and made recommendations to the legislature on broad areas of the law such as corporations, elections, domestic relations, criminal and probate law. Studies were begun on its own initiative or by request of any one of the three branches of government. In 1976 the Commission was abolished, the position of executive director was assigned to the standing House and Senate Judiciary Committees, and the former commissioners asked to serve as an advisory committee to the standing committee staff. Ch. 832 [1976] Tenn. Pub. Acts 1256.

Section 354 (a)   GENERAL REPORTS

The Commission's general reports, summary in nature, outline the major needs for change and describe briefly the nature and source of proposed legislation. The following biennial reports have been published and like those of the Legislative Council are handy sources of legislative intent. See section 354(b).

84th General Assembly, 1966
Provides summaries of reports/recommendations regarding; 1. Organization of the Judiciary; 2. Rules of Civil Pro-

9. Sanford, *The Work of the Law Revision Commission*, 32 TENN. L. REV. 11 (1964).

cedure; 3. Rules of Criminal Procedure; 4. Practice before Administrative Agencies; 5. Corporation Laws.

85th General Assembly, 1967

Provides summaries of reports/recommendations regarding: 1. Criminal law; 2. Escheats; 3. Procedures before Administrative Agencies; 4. Rules of Civil Procedure.

86th General Assembly, 1969: none published

87th General Assembly, 1971

Describes work in process and recommendations regarding probate laws, domestic relations, criminal law and procedure.

88th General Assembly, 1973

Describes work in process and recommendations regarding probate laws, domestic relations, criminal law and procedure.

89th General Assembly, 1975

Makes recommendations regarding probate study/laws, domestic relations, criminal law and procedure.

Section 354(b)   TOPICAL REPORTS

The Commission's studies and reports on selected topics, if the suggested legislation is ultimately enacted, are probably the state's best source of legislative intent because each provides excellent analytical background of enacted or proposed legislation. A complete list of the Commission's studies is included in the Report to the 89th General Assembly, but shown below are those especially relevant to a contemporary researcher.

Administrative Law
   1.   *Administrative Law Study.* See section 700 generally.

Corporation Law
Several documents were published by the Commission on this subject. The better are:
   1.   *Section-by-Section Comment to General Corporation Act.* No date. 112 pp.
   2.   *Tennessee Corporation Law: The Need for Revision.* No date. 18 pp.
   3.   *Special Report to 85th General Assembly Concerning a Bill to Adopt a General Corporation Act, 1967*; 18 pp.

4.   Hartman, Paul. *Business Corporations Study.* 1964-65.

Criminal Law and Procedure

The Commission has prepared extensive draft revisions in this area during ten years of study. The more important documents are:

1.   *Tennessee Criminal Code and Code of Criminal Procedure.* Proposed Final Draft, November, 1973. 469 pp.
2.   *Tennessee Statutes Not in T.C.A. Title 39 Imposing Criminal Sanctions.* 1973. 79 pp.
3.   Miller, Charles H. *The Federal and Tennessee Rules of Criminal Procedure—A Comparison.* Knoxville: University of Tennessee, Government, Industry, Law Center, 1964. 100 pp.
4.   Dennis, Floyd. *A Post-Conviction Procedure Act for Tennessee.* 1966. 115 pp.

Election Law

1.   *Election Laws Work Document—Minimum Revision.* 1971. 192 pp.
2.   *An Elections Act Recommended to the 87th General Assembly with Section-by-Section Comments, 1972.* 223 pp.
3.   *Special Report to the 87th General Assembly Concerning a Unified and Coherent Treatment of All Elections.* 1972. 21 pp.

Escheat

1.   Overton, Elvin. *Study of Constitutional Problems and Policy Decisions in Drafting an Escheat Statute for Tennessee:* Knoxville: University of Tennessee, Government, Industry, Law Center, 1965. 72 pp.
2.   *Report Pertaining to Escheats, Unclaimed and Abandoned Property.* 1968.

Family Law

1.   *Tennessee Family Law Act—Tentative Draft, June 1973.* 65 pp.
2.   *Special Report to the 88th General Assembly on the Tennessee Family Law Act.* 1974. 71 pp.

Probate Law

1.   *Special Report to the 89th General Assembly on Probate Law Revision, 1976.* 14 pp.

2. *Proposed Final Draft, Tennessee Probate Code.* 1976.

Judicial System

1. *The Judicial System of Tennessee: A Background Survey.* 1966. 75 pp.
2. Wicker, William. *A Comparative Study of Civil Pleading, Practice and Procedure in the Tennessee Trial Courts of General Jurisdiction.* Knoxville: University of Tennessee, Government, Industry, Law Center, 1964. 152 pp.
3. Overton, Elvin E. *The Judicial System and its Administration in Tennessee—Potentialities for Reorganization and Improvement—A Comparative Study.* Knoxville: University of Tennessee, Government, Industry, Law Center, 1964. 88 pp. Reprinted in *Tennessee Law Review* 32 (1965): 501-572.
4. *Special Report to 85th General Assembly Concerning A Bill for Constitutional Convention on Article VI, the Judicial Department.* 1967. 31 pp.
5. Wicker, William. *Judicial Rule-Making as a Means to Procedural Reform.* Knoxville: University of Tennessee, Government, Industry, Law Center, 1964. 34 pp.
6. *Special Report to 87th General Assembly Concerning Certain Statutes on Civil Procedure and a Bill to Enact Certain Statutes Applicable to General Session Courts.* 1972. 24 pp.

Section 360   GENERAL ASSEMBLY COMMITTEE REPORTS

From the earliest days of the republic the General Assembly has from time to time established special committees to explore isolated issues on an *ad hoc* basis. Although a committee investigating an issue may exist and issue reports for many years, most of these committees are temporary entities. Sometimes, such committees are established to provide continuing service or oversight. Examples are the Legislative Council Committee and the Fiscal Review Committee. (See sections 352, 350).

Shown below are titles of *selected* documents published in recent years by these committees. A complete list of such reports published since 1954 is published in *A List of State Publications,* 1954 - (see section 744). A complete list of such reports published from 1836 to 1917 is published in *Analysis of Tennessee Collected Public Documents, 1836-1917* (see section 740).

Reports of the Fiscal Review Committee

1. Staff Report on Tennessee Uses of Federal Funds. 1968. 132 pp.
2. Staff Report on State Support for Local Government. 1968. 35 pp.
3. The Legislator's Role in Budgeting. 1968. 26 pp.
4. Report on the Medicaid Program. 1973. 22 pp.
5. Automatic Data Processing Equipment Costs: A. Report and Recommendations. 1970. 120 pp.

Special Committees of General Assembly

1. Report to the 88th General Assembly of the Special House Committee on Automobile Reparation Reform. 1974. 1 vol.
2. Report to the 88th General Assembly of the Senate Committee on Automobile Insurance Reform. 1974. 25 pp.
3. Report to the 87th General Assembly of the Joint Committee on Insurance and Banking. 1971. 97 pp.
4. Report to the 85th General Assembly of the Joint Committee on Constitutional Revision. 1968. 44 pp.
5. Report to the 88th General Assembly of the Joint Committee on Bank Holding Companies. 1973. 20 pp.
6. Report to the 88th General Assembly of the Special Public School Study Committee. 1973. 157 pp.
7. Report to the 88th General Assembly of the House Committee on Rural Roads. 1974. 36 pp.
8. Report to the House General Welfare Committee of the Subcommittee on Mental Retardation. 1972. 72 pp.
9. Report to the 88th General Assembly of the House Committee on Property Reappraisal Programs. 1974. 14 pp.

Special Study Commissions—Reports

1. Report to the Governor and the 88th General Assembly of the Local Government Study Commission. 1974. 63 pp.

2. White, Robert H. *Historical Background and Documented Survey of Legislative Apportionment in Tennessee.* Nashville: State Library and Archives. 1961. 47 pp.

3. Final Report to the Governor and the 88th General Assembly of the Tax Modernization and Reform Commission. 1974. 118 pp.

4. Maloney, Frank. *Final Report to the Commission of Public Health of the Study of the Water Pollution Control Laws of the Fifty States with Recommendations for Revision of the Tennessee Stream Pollution Control Law.* 2 vols. Nashville: Vanderbilt Law School, 1961.

Figure I.

The Tennessee Court System

(As of January 1, 1977)

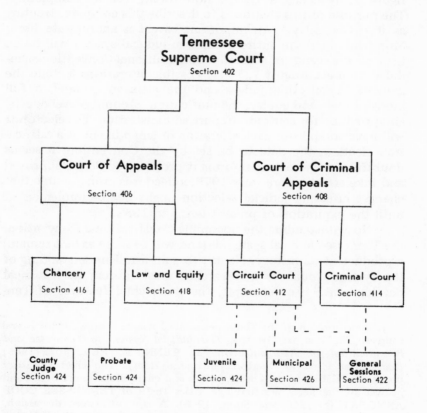

This is a **simplified** diagram of the court system, designed to show its chief features. Here, solid lines show **normal** routes of appeal and dotted lines indicate de novo appeal. Numerous optional routes of appeal may be available depending on such matters as the type of case (workmen's compensation cases may be appealed directly to the Supreme Court) and the type of court below (appeal may go from County Judges to either Circuit, Chancery, Court of Appeals, or Supreme Court depending on the type of case).

Chapter IV

TENNESSEE COURTS AND COURT REPORTS

Section 400   INTRODUCTION

A diagram of the Tennessee court system is shown in figure 1, revealing a system noteworthy for its complexity. The purpose of this chapter is to describe this complex structure as it exists today.[1] An important caveat is appropriate here: Modification of the entire Tennessee judicial system will be an issue on the agenda of a Limited Constitutional Convention scheduled to meet August 1, 1977. Possible alterations include the manner of selecting judges and the attorney general, a full merger of law and equity, the unification of county-level courts, and provision for centralized court administration. The electorate will have to approve each alteration or amendment at a ratification election, the date to be set by the Convention. It seems doubtful that whatever reforms it proposes could be approved and take effect before early 1979; indeed it is even possible that changes affecting judicial selection might not be implemented until the expiration of present terms in 1982.

Notwithstanding the upcoming Constitutional Convention, the Tennessee judicial system is (and will to some extent remain) a product of its history. Hence, to gain a full understanding of the system's nuances a researcher must fathom its historical development.[2] For example, the three chief features of Ten-

---

1. A description of the Tennessee judicial system is provided by several sources. The best is: Overton, *The Judicial System in Tennessee and Potentialities for Reorganization*, 32 TENN. L. REV. 501 (1965) [hereinafter cited as Overton, *Judicial System*]. The chief statutory provisions relating to the courts, judges and chancellors, court clerks, and justices of the peace are found in Titles 16-19 of TENNESSEE CODE ANNOTATED (1955 and Supp. 1976). A straightforward discussion, especially useful to laymen is that found in L. GREENE, D. GRUBBS, V. HOBDAY, GOVERNMENT IN TENNESSEE 156-174 (1975). [hereinafter cited as L. GREENE, GOVERNMENT IN TENNESSEE] Other descriptions include, THE JUDICIAL SYSTEM OF TENNESSEE. New York: Institute of Judicial Administration, 1971; F. LeCLERQ, PROFILE OF THE TENNESSEE COURT SYSTEM. Resource Plan. Corp. (1977).

2. Important developments in the court system are treated by historians

nessee's court system—an elected judiciary, the law-equity dichotomy, and strong legislative influence on courts' jurisdiction—are the products of political forces not easily identifiable today. For this reason the description of the courts will begin with their history.

Section 401   SUPREME COURT: 1790-1870

Tennessee's first "supreme court" was a three member Superior Court of Law and Equity.[3] Established by federal authority in 1790, its jurisdiction was largely patterned after existing North Carolina courts of the same name.[4] It had original jurisdiction in cases exceeding one hundred pounds and appellate jurisdiction in cases arising in courts of pleas and quarterly sessions (the justice of the peace courts). The judges were appointed by the President, their commissions continuing in force during good behavior.[5] Moreover, until 1794 they

in the standard works of Tennessee history, *e.g.*, S. FOLMSBEE, R. CORLEW, E. MITCHELL, HISTORY OF TENNESSEE (1960); and by legal writers as an important element in state constitutional development, *e.g.*, Laska, *A Legal and Constitutional History of Tennessee*, 6 MEM. ST. U. L. REV. 563 (1976), [hereinafter cited as Laska, *Legal and Constitutional History*]. *See also*, J. CALDWELL, CONSTITUTIONAL HISTORY OF TENNESSEE (1907). Other useful works include: P. Cason, History of Tennessee's Court System from its Beginning to 1834, August 1930 (unpublished thesis in the George Peabody College Library); [hereinafter cited as Cason, *History*]; W. BROEMEL, THE BEGINNING OF A COURT SYSTEM (1972).

3. Tennessee does not have a comprehensive analytical history of its Supreme Court. Discussions of Supreme Court history are generally descriptive and anecdotal. The better of these are: Marks, *The Supreme Court of Tennessee*, 5 GREEN BAG 120 (1893); J. GREEN, LIVES OF THE JUDGES OF THE SUPREME COURT OF TENNESSEE, 1796-1947 (1947); Williams, *The Genesis of the Tennessee Supreme Court*, 6 TENN. L. REV. 75 (1928) [hereinafter cited as Williams, *Genesis*]; Williams, *Phases of Tennessee Supreme Court History*, 8 TENN. L. REV. 323 (1944); Phillips, *Our Supreme Court Justices*, 17 TENN. L. REV. 466 (1942).

4. Superior Courts had been established for the Tennessee territory while it was under North Carolina jurisdiction. *See*, Burch, *Important Events in the Judicial History of Tennessee*, 15 TENN. L. REV. 24 (1938); Fink, *Judicial Activities in Early East Tennessee*, 7 E. TENN. HIST. SOC'Y PUBL. 38 (1935).

5. Cason, *History* at 20.

were also legislative officers because Territorial ordinances could
be enacted at the behest of the governor and concurrence of
any two judges.[6]

The first Tennessee constitution, drafted in 1796, did not
describe a judicial system. Rather, it provided that the judicial
power was vested "in such superior and inferior courts of law
and equity as the legislature shall direct."[7] Thus the Tennessee
practice of frequent legislative tinkering with the judiciary was
begun early in the state's political life.[8]

Again adopting the North Carolina model, the legislature
provided for three Superior Courts of Law and Equity with
jurisdiction as described above.[9] This was the first "supreme
court" established under state authority. This three member
court (which was not required to sit as a panel) was chosen by
the legislature and, at various times, included among its members David Campbell, Archibald Roane, Willie Bount, Andrew
Jackson, John Overton, and Hugh Lawson White—a constellation
of Tennessee leadership.[10]

Because of lack of harmony in the rulings of these judges
statewide, as well as delays brought on by allowance of antiquated technical defenses, the court was abolished in 1809,
In its place circuit courts were established and appellate jurisdiction was vested in the state's first truly supreme court, the
three-member Supreme Court of Errors and Appeals.[11] This

6. The first three judges were David Campbell, John McNairy and
Joseph Anderson. Williams, *Genesis* at 78.

7. Cason, *History* at 20.

8. The careful student of Tennessee judicial history can trace this
phenomenon in the massive work by Robert H. White, *Messages of the
Governors of Tennessee, 1796-1907.* 8 vols. (Nashville: Tennessee Historical Commission, 1952-1970) [hereinafter cited as WHITE, MESSAGES].
According to White, "The entire judicial system, from the lowly Justices
of the Peace composing the Quarterly County Court to the Judges of the
Supreme Court, was in the hands of the General Assembly from 1796 to
the adoption of the second constitution in 1835." 1 WHITE, MESSAGES
at 472.

9. Ch. 1 [1796] Tenn. Pub. Acts 9. 1 WHITE, MESSAGES 294.

10. Williams, *A Remarkable Bench: Campbell, Jackson and White,* 16
TENN. L. REV. 907 (1941); Green, *Judges Overton, Jackson and White,*
18 TENN. L. REV. 413 (1944).

11. As might be expected, the General Assembly kept tinkering with
the court. A third regular judge was added in 1815, a fourth in 1823, a
fifth in 1824, then reduced to four that same year, reduced to three in

court's two regular members[12] were chosen by the legislature to serve during good behavior. The third seat was to be occupied by a circuit judge sitting by special designation of the court. John Overton, who was later to sit on the Supreme Court of Errors and Appeals, compiled the first two volumes of this court's decisions—volumes one and two of Tennessee Reports.

These piecemeal attempts at overnight of the judicial system were unsuccessful, and by the early 1830's public confidence in the system was shattered.[13] The impeachment trials of two circuit judges[14] during 1829-1831 led to an intense political struggle. Serious attempts were made to abolish the court structure outright and begin anew—attempts that were nearly successful.[15] These episodes dramatized the tenuous existence of the courts, especially the Supreme Court of Errors and Appeals. The 1834 Constitution strengthened the position of the state's courts with an express provision vesting judicial power in a three-member Supreme Court (as it was to be called) that exercised appellate jurisdiction only.[16] The judges were selected by the legislature for twelve year terms. No more than one was to be elected from the same grand division of the state.

The pervasive doctrines of Jacksonian Democracy ("Any man can be a judge") led in 1853 to a constitutional amendment that has become a fixture of the Tennessee judicial system—the elected judiciary. The three Supreme Court judges, the Attorney General, circuit judges and chancellors, and local state's attorneys

1827, and finally increased to four in 1831. It remained a four-member court until the court was abolished in 1834.

12. The first two Judges were Hugh Lawson White and George W. Campbell.

13. Laska, *Legal and Constitutional History* at 603-605. For a brief discussion of the attempts at judicial reform see White, *Legislative Fathers of Our Judiciary*, 23 TENN. L. REV. 8 (1953); the drive for court reform, headed by Thomas Hart Benton, is well documented in: 1 WHITE, MESSAGES 295-315.

14. Anderson, *Impeachment and Trial of Judge N. W. Williams*, [1924] TENN. B. ASS'N. PROC. 204. W. Foster, Legislative Impeachment in Tennessee, August 1931 (unpublished thesis in the George Peabody College Library).

15. 2 WHITE, MESSAGES at 348-416.

16. Laska, *Legal and Constitutional History* at 604.

were henceforth to be elected by the people, not the legislature, for eight (not twelve) year terms.[17]

Section 402 - SUPREME COURT: 1870 -

Tennessee's present constitution, drafted in 1870, provided for a new five member[18] Supreme Court, elected by the people for terms of eight years, with no more than two members residing in any one of the grand divisions of the state.

Repeating language found in the 1834 Constitution, the 1870 draftsmen specified that the Supreme Court's jurisdiction "shall be appellate only, under such restrictions and regulations as may from time to time be prescribed by law; but it may possess such other jurisdiction as is now conferred by law on the present Supreme Court." Tenn. Const. art VI, section 2. The court is required to sit at Knoxville, Nashville, and Jackson.[19]

The only other important changes in the judiciary article made by the 1870 constitution were provision for selection of the Attorney General by the Supreme Court and specific reference to circuit and chancery courts, insulating them somewhat from legislative whim.

17. *Id.*

18. The schedule attached to the 1870 Constitution provided for six judges until a vacancy should occur after 1873, at which time the number should remain at five members. It also provided that incumbents in all judicial offices should vacate their places within thirty days after the time fixed for the election of their successor. The purpose of reconstituting the courts was to rid them of judges appointed during the Johnson-Brownlow-Senter administrations. Laska, *Legal and Constitutional History* at 643-646.

19. The general statutes relating to the Supreme Court are T.C.A. §§16-301 to -333 (Supp. 1976). For a good description of the workings of the court together with an overview of the appellate court system as seen by a former chief justice of the court see Prewitt, *The Judicial Structure in Tennessee*, 29 TENN. L. REV. 1 (1961).

Section 404   INTERMEDIATE APPELLATE COURTS: 1873-1925

A growing backlog of cases following the Civil War caused the legislature to establish two temporary appellate courts which operated from 1873 to 1885. Initially, a three member Arbitration Commission was given the power to hear cases at the request of both parties.[20] Its findings were reported to the Supreme Court which reserved the power to hear the case(s) itself. Otherwise, the Commission's holdings were final. In 1883 the Arbitration Commission (or Court as it was often called) was replaced with a Referees Commission that heard only those cases the Supreme Court referred to it.[21] This Commission reported back to the court its findings of facts and law; that is, the Commission did not render final judgments. The statutes establishing both of these commissions expressly forbade the publication of their findings and further provided that their reports were without precedential value.

Although these temporary courts were successful (several commissioners were later to serve on the Supreme Court), they did not immediately lead to establishment of a permanent intermediate appellate court. Public disenchantment with the court system was focused on the Supreme Court, leading to the "Judicial Clean Sweep of 1886."[22] A newly-elected Supreme Court, youthful and energetic, cleared its docket with dispatch.[23]

Section 404(a)   COURT OF CHANCERY APPEALS, 1895-1907

By 1895, the load of chancery appeals had become so great that the need for some screening was apparent. That year

20. Ch. 3 [1875] Tenn. Pub. Acts 5; The Commission had its origin in 1873. That year Justice A. O. P. Nicholson was severely injured in a fall from the capitol steps and two temporary commissioners were appointed to help him clear the Nashville docket. Res. 45 [1873] Tenn. Pub. Acts 221. Later, another panel was established to hear cases in West Tennessee, Ch. 69 [1877] Tenn. Pub. Acts 85; and still another in Knoxville. Ch. 180 [1879] Tenn. Pub. Acts 224.

21. Ch. 257 [1883] Tenn. Pub. Acts 342.

22. Marks, *The Supreme Court of Tennessee*, 5 GREEN BAG 283 (1893).

23. Green, *The Supreme Court of Tennessee in 1886*, 16 TENN. L. REV. 899 (1941).

the legislature established Tennessee's first true intermediate appellate court, a three member Court of Chancery Appeals. Its members were to be elected for eight year terms.[24] The court had equity jurisdiction only and was to be strictly appellate, its decisions reviewable by the Supreme Court only as to issues of law, not fact. A provision of the 1895 act allowed the Supreme Court to transfer equity cases to the new court's docket. By use of this device the bar grew to have confidence in the new court, and its opinions established precedents that are good law to this day. See section 444(a).

Section 404(b)   COURT OF CIVIL APPEALS, 1907-1925

In 1907 the legislature changed the name of the Court of Chancery Appeals to the Court of Civil Appeals and added two members,[25] thus creating a court of five judges. Its jurisdiction, still exclusively appellate, was enlarged to include appeals from circuit courts, but here began the legislative practice of limiting the appellate court's jurisdiction in certain types of cases. Cases involving the constitutionality of Tennessee statutes, contested elections, and state revenue, to name but a few, were to be appealed directly to the Supreme Court. Furthermore, the Supreme Court could no longer assign cases to this court, but mutual transfer of cases was provided by statute in 1909.[26] The decisions of this court, published in eight volumes, remain useful precedents today but are infrequently cited. See section 444(b).

Section 406   COURT OF APPEALS, 1925-

In 1925 the name of the Court of Civil Appeals was changed to the Court of Appeals by the legislature.[27] Four new members

24. Ch. 76 [1895] Tenn. Pub. Acts 113.
25. Ch. 82 [1907] Tenn. Pub. Acts 232.
26. Ch. 192 [1909] Tenn. Pub. Acts 690.
27. Ch. 100 [1925] Tenn. Pub. Acts 236. The general statutes dealing with the Court of Appeals are T.C.A. §§16-401 to -415 (Supp. 1976). *See*, Crownover, *The Tennessee Court of Appeals*, 15 TENN. L. REV. 144 (1938).

were provided, resulting in a nine-member court. The enlarged court was authorized to sit either in three-judge panels at Knoxville, Nashville and Jackson, or en banc. Additionally, members could be assigned by the presiding judge to other divisions in order to relieve congested dockets. The statute establishing the Court of Appeals provides that its jurisdiction shall be appellate only, and shall extend to all civil cases *except* (1) those where the constitutionality of a statute or city ordinance is the sole determinative question in the litigation, (2) cases contesting the right to hold public office, (3) workmen's compensation cases, (4) state revenue cases, (5) mandamus, (6) cases in the nature of quo warranto, (7) ouster suits, (8) habeas corpus cases, where the relator is being held under a criminal accusation or a rendition warrant issued by the Governor, and (9) cases that have been finally determined in the lower court on demurrer or other method not involving a review or determination of the facts, or (10) cases in which all the facts have been stipulated. T.C.A. §16-408. These ten excluded types of cases are appealed directly to the Supreme Court. However, this is not the exclusive list of matters which may be directly appealed. By law, many other cases, *e.g.*, teacher tenure suits (T.C.A. §49-1417), may be so appealed. No official list of such cases has been made, however, so the researcher must check the Code to insure that appeal is directed to the proper court.

When sitting in sections of three judges, the concurrence of two members is considered a decision of the whole court. T.C.A. §16-409. The decisions of the Court of Appeals are the backbone of modern Tennessee common law. See section 446.

Section 408   COURT OF CRIMINAL APPEALS, 1967-

In 1967 a new seven member intermediate appellate court, the Court of Criminal Appeals, was established to hear exclusively criminal appeals.[28] Its jurisdiction in criminal cases is restricted only when the sole question for determination involves the constitutionality of a statute or ordinance. Such

28. Ch. 226 [1967] Tenn. Pub. Acts 587. The general statutes relating to the Court of Criminal Appeals are T.C.A. §§16-441 to -453 (Supp. 1976).

cases may be appealed directly to the Supreme Court. T.C.A. §16-448 (Supp. 1976). The Court's membership was increased to nine in 1976, and like the Court of Appeals, it may sit in panels at Knoxville, Nashville and Jackson or en banc. A decision requires the concurrence of two of the three judges on a panel and is considered a decision of the whole court. T.C.A. §16-447 (Supp. 1976). See section 448.

Section 410   TRIAL COURTS

A detailed discussion of the history and jurisdiction of the state's trial courts (whether of general, special, or limited jurisdiction) is beyond the scope of this book.[29] The system is unnecessarily complicated because of several factors: (1) a constitution difficult to amend; (2) a political/legal system that respects the partisan political differences among the three grand divisions of the state; (3) a background of legislative (and executive) control of the judiciary, especially through the device of local legislation; and finally, (4) an attitude of caution and conservativism on the part of the public that has led to the survival of antiquated structures after their peculiar identity has been lost, *e.g.*, the chancery court. Moreover, a detailed discussion is likely to be misleading because, although the court system appears impervious to radical reform, it is nevertheless not fixed. Hence, the researcher should be aware of the *latest* legislative actions relative to his local jurisdiction as well as the specific earlier acts applicable to it.[30] Further, the researcher should be alert to the latest Supreme Court Rules, a relatively new development in Tennessee jurisprudence, that oversee the court system.[31] The following is a brief, general outline of the lower court system conditioned by the caveat that important differences exist between urban and rural areas and between different parts of the state.

It is generally understood that Tennessee has three levels of state courts: (1) *the appellate courts* (Supreme Court, Court of Appeals, Court of Criminal Appeals), described above; (2)

29. *See,* note 1, *supra.*
30. For a description of local or private acts see section 310.
31. For a description of Supreme Court rulemaking see sections 416(a), 500 and 520.

courts of general jurisdiction (primarily circuit courts and chancery courts, but including the law and equity courts as well); and the courts of special or *limited jurisdiction* (probate, juvenile, general sessions, municipal courts).

Section 412   CIRCUIT COURTS

Tennessee's court of general law (as opposed to equity) jurisdiction is the Circuit Court.[32] Each county is included in one of the state's twenty-nine circuits. In the populous counties—Shelby, Davidson, Knox and Hamilton—the county is co-extensive with the circuit and is served by several such judges, while in multi-county circuits there is generally only one circuit judge.[33]

The circuit court has general trial jurisdiction in all cases where such jurisdiction is not given to another court. In general, this means that circuit court *shares* jurisdiction in many civil cases, especially those of an equitable nature, with chancery court.[34]

Section 414   CRIMINAL COURTS

An outgrowth of circuit courts are the separate Criminal Courts that exist in the larger counties but also serve about thirty-five smaller counties, mostly in the eastern part of the state.[35] Where extant, they are usually coextensive with the particular judicial circuit. Their jurisdiction is generally limited

32. Overton, *Judicial System* at 507.
33. T.C.A. §§16-207 to -236 (Supp. 1976). A table of judicial circuits and chancery divisions by counties is shown *post* T.C.A. §16-251 and T.C.A. §16-255 (Supp. 1976).
34. As Overton explains, circuit court cannot act as a chancery court over the objection of the defendant, and in a few types of cases it has *exclusive* jurisdiction, *e.g.*, contest of the validity of a will. Overton, *Judicial System* at 508; T.C.A. §16-503.
35. Although created by special (local) acts these are circuit courts nonetheless. A table of the criminal courts according to judicial district and county is shown *post* T.C.A. §16-251 and T.C.A. §16-255 (Supp. 1976).

to criminal cases.[36]

Section 416   CHANCERY COURTS

Tennessee's other traditional court of general jurisdiction, Chancery, has primary jurisdiction in the field of equity.[37] Each county is served by at least one chancellor or law and equity judge (see section 418) with the state divided into seventeen regular chancery divisions that are not coterminus with the boundaries of the judicial circuits.[38]

The presence of dual court systems in Tennessee is the result of a century and a half of political development (see section 416(a)) and the distinctions, once sharp, have become blurred.[39] Circuit and chancery courts have concurrent jurisdictions with regard to certain matters, including divorce, workmen's compensation, interpretation of wills and adoptions.[40] Also, jurisdiction over certain of these matters is shared with some county courts and general sessions courts.

Section 416(a)   THE GROWTH OF EQUITY

Tennessee is one of the few states retaining, within its court structure, the distinction between law and equity. The reason, again, is largely the happenstance of history, not logic.[41]

36. Overton, *Judicial System* at 509-510.
37. *Id.* at 510-511.
38. T.C.A. §§16-601 to -626 (Supp. 1976). A table of chancery divisions by counties is shown *post* T.C.A. 16-251 and T.C.A. 16-255 (Supp. 1976).
39. The standard treatise on equity practice is GIBSON'S SUITS IN CHANCERY 2 vols. (5th ed. 1955), and it and *Tennessee Code Annotated* should be consulted regarding questions of equity jurisdiction. An interesting attempt to describe the jurisdiction of these courts, although now somewhat dated, but still valuable, is Bejack, *The Chancery Court*, 20 TENN. L. REV. 245 (1948). See section 510.
40. Perhaps the most important concurrent jurisdiction enjoyed by the chancery court is its power to hear all civil actions except those seeking unliquidated damages for injuries to persons, and unliquidated damages for injuries to property not resulting from breach of contract. T.C.A. §16-202 (1955).
41. The standard history of chancery court in Tennessee is GIBSON'S SUITS IN CHANCERY 2 vols. (5th ed. 1955) at 8-13.

The original "appellate" courts, both prior to and just after statehood, respected the merger of law and equity jurisdiction. In fact, they were called the Superior Courts of Law and Equity. The circuit courts, created in 1809, had equity jurisdiction. The first supreme court, the Supreme Court of Errors and Appeals, was given *exclusive* original equity jurisdiction in 1811 when the circuit courts that had such power were found inadequate. The circuit courts, however, regained concurrent equity jurisdiction in 1813. In 1821 the legislature provided that Supreme Court judges, sitting alone, were to hear *original* equity matters in newly-formed equity circuits. The Supreme Court, en banc, had appellate equity jurisdiction.

This scheme required an increase in the number of Supreme Court judges but, despite court expansion, resulted in judicial overwork. Therefore, in 1827, the legislature divided the state into two chancery divisions and named two chancellors to hear equity cases.[42] Appeals were made to the Supreme Court of Errors and Appeals. Since that time, fifteen more chancery divisions have been formed. See section 416.

Why did Tennessee opt for separate chancery courts? The answer is twofold. First, an absence of well-trained lawyers led to a poorly qualified judiciary, unable to handle complicated cases. This was because formal legal education was unfashionable until at least the 1870's, and the democratic principles of Jacksonian Democracy militated against a scholarly bar. But more important was the sheer volume and complexity of land litigation that arose during the first forty years of the state's existence. These suits were primarily equity cases, establishing precedents that had profound effect on the development of an agrarian economy.

So it developed that the state's better lawyers gravitated to the "other side" of the bar, both as practitioners and chancellors. New chancery divisions were established and became what the judicial historian, Justice Samuel Cole Williams, has called the "seed-plots for the production of appellate judges."[43]

As early as 1875, chancery courts began to gain some concurrent jurisdiction with the circuit courts in many matters.

42. Williams, *History of the Courts of Chancery of Tennessee*, 2 TENN. L. REV. 6, 18 (1923).
43. *Id.* at 20.

In the hundred years since, powers of the chancellor have been broadened so that, while the jurisdictions may not be strictly concurrent, they are largely overlapping. See sections 412 and 416.

A rule recently adopted by the Tennessee Supreme Court is likely to blur further the remaining distinctions between trial courts in the state, especially the distinctions between the various types of circuit courts. Acting under its inherent and statutory power to oversee the state's judicial system, the court's rule is designed to balance the caseloads of trial courts. Under the rule, the larger metropolitan circuits (and chancery divisions with which they are largely coterminus) are placed under the supervision of a presiding judge who is to supervise the assignment of cases. Further oversight of the system is provided by designation of five "appellate circuits," that is, a new apportionment of judicial circuits/chancery divisions, each such appellate circuit to be monitored by a specified Supreme Court Justice. Supreme Court Rule 45, October 23, 1975.

Section 416(b) COOPER'S TENNESSEE CHANCERY REPORTS

Today, as in the past, chancery opinions are not reported because chancery is a trial court, not an appellate court. However, an exception to this general rule is evident in a three-volume set of *nisi prius* opinions published between 1872 and 1878 by the distinguished Nashville chancellor, William F. Cooper, entitled Cooper's Tennessee Chancery Reports. Due to the great respect Chancellor (later Justice) Cooper earned as a scholar of equity jurisprudence, his opinions have been cited as competent authority for a hundred years. The cases were not reprinted elsewhere contemporaneously but were reprinted in 1956 by Dennis and Co. of Buffalo, New York.

Section 418 LAW AND EQUITY COURTS

Five counties are served by Law and Equity Courts which generally exercise concurrent civil jurisdiction with circuit and chancery courts. Because of their origins in private acts, the precise jurisdiction of such courts differs in some respects from each other, *e.g.*, the Dyer County court has both probate and juvenile jurisdiction, too; but these courts are the state's nearest examples of "merged" law-equity jurisdiction and have been favorably received by the bar because of their progressive nature. For example, such courts usually meet in continuous session.[44]

Section 420   COURTS OF SPECIAL OR LIMITED JURISDICTION

The lowest level of Tennessee courts are those of special or *limited* jurisdiction, with restricted territorial and subject matter jurisdiction. In most instances these are not courts of record, hence appeal is *de novo* in circuit or chancery court. While the specific jurisdiction of any given court may differ vastly, the following generalizations describe these courts as a whole.

Section 422   GENERAL SESSIONS

Most of the judicial functions of the justice of the peace system[45] have been transferred to the General Sessions Courts.[46] Although a few have concurrent jurisdiction with circuit or probate courts in some matters, their jurisdiction is limited in civil cases to suits involving no more than $5000 and in criminal cases, to misdemeanors (involving a sentence of not more than

44. The jurisdiction of these courts is now described by public acts. *See, e.g.*, Law and Equity Courts for Blount County (T.C.A. §16-211) and Dyer County (T.C.A. §16-227).

45. The county justices of the peace collectively are technically called the "court of pleas and quarterly sessions," that is, the *quarterly court* but is generally known as the "county court" or the "county quarterly court." It is the county legislative and administrative organ. It should not be confused with the "court of monthly sessions," that is, the *county judge*, discussed in section 424.

46. This, like virtually every other generalization about the judicial system is fraught with exceptions. For example, Anderson county is blessed with a Trial Justices Court, an interesting admixture having general sessions, juvenile and probate jurisdiction. *See also, Special Project, Judicial Reform at the Lowest Level: A Model Statute for Small Claims Courts,* 28 VAND. L. REV. 711 (1975).

11 months and 29 days).[47] The state's nearest equivalent of a "small claims" court, the overwhelming percentage of civil claims in this court are collection cases. On the criminal side, this court conducts preliminary examination to determine whether probable cause exists for further prosecution. Statewide it handles the bulk of state misdemeanor cases.

Section 424   COUNTY JUDGES, PROBATE COURTS, JUVENILE COURTS, DOMESTIC RELATIONS COURTS

The court of monthly sessions is a judicial body, being simply the County Judge, which has jurisdiction over probate matters and certain kindred subjects, such as guardianships.[48] The County Judge has concurrent jurisdiction with circuit and chancery courts in several probate-related cases, *i.e.*, sale or partition of a decedent's real property.[49] In Shelby and Davidson counties a court of record, Probate Court, handles the administration of estates and related matters.[50] See section 574. Jurisdiction over juveniles is shared, varying between counties, by (1) the County Judge, (2) general sessions court, (3) juvenile courts.[51] The latter exist as courts of exclusive juvenile

47. More precisely, such courts may not hear cases where the fine is greater than fifty dollars; nor may they sentence *to prison* for periods greater than a year. For discussion of general sessions jurisdiction, see the standard current treatise: W. HALL, THE GENERAL SESSIONS COURTS (1972). *See also,* Ellis, *The Jurisdiction of General Sessions Courts in Tennessee to Try and Determine Criminal Cases,* 36 TENN. L. REV. 458, (1969).

48. *See* T.C.A. §§16-701, 16-709. The best description of county legislative and judicial offices are in: THE COUNTY COURT IN TENNESSEE. (Nashville: Comptroller of the Treasury, 1974); and THE OFFICES OF THE TENNESSEE COUNTY JUDGE AND CHAIRMAN. (Nashville: Comptroller of the Treasury, 1974).

49. But only "routine matters" according to Dick v. Dick, 223 Tenn. 228, 443 S.W. 2d 472 (1969). D. RIZOR, PROBATE MANUAL FOR COUNTY JUDGES AND COURT CLERKS (1975). *See,* T.C.A. § 50-1118 (workmen's compensation).

50. Ch. 124 [1963] Tenn. Priv. Acts 394 (An act establishing a Probate Court for Davidson County).

51. *See,* COMPILATION OF SELECTED LAWS ON CHILDREN AND YOUTH, 1974 rev. (Nashville: Commission on Children and Youth, 1974). *See,* Note, *A Study of Domestic Relations, Juvenile and Family Courts in*

jurisdiction only in the urban counties. See section 576. Several populous counties have circuit courts separately known as Family or Domestic Relations Courts which attempt to handle the bulk of divorce cases.[52]

Section 426 MUNICIPAL COURTS

Municipalities enforce their ordinances through a variety of municipal officers, notably traffic court judges. Many of these officers are authorized to hear a variety of state law violations and have committing power to bind defendants over to a grand jury.[53]

Section 430 OFFICIAL COURT REPORTS

Since 1829 the Supreme Court has been required to give written opinions in all cases it decides except actions in which there is no defense. T.C.A. §27-120 (1955). This rule does not apply to denial of petition for rehearing, nor to denial of petition for writ of certiorari. Powers v. L. & N. Railroad Co., 183 Tenn. 526, 194 S.W.2d 241 (1946). Today, however, as in the past, not all written opinions are *reported*, that is, issued by the court marked "For Publication." Tennessee has adopted the policy of selective reporting, with the court approving for publication only those opinions that (1) establish a new rule of law or alter or modify an existing rule; or (2) involve a legal issue of continuing public interest; or (3) criticize existing law; or (4) resolve an apparent conflict of authority; or (5) update, clarify or distinguish a principle of law. A majority of the court participating in the decision must approve it for publication; dissents are published at the determination of the dissenting justice. Opinions not satisfying any of the above standards are marked "Not Designated for Publica-

Tennessee, 10 VAND. L. REV. 592 (1957). *See also,* K. TURNER, JUVENILE JUSTICE (1969).

52. Ch. 444 [1957] Tenn. Pub. Acts 138; *Family Courts: A Symposium,* 27 TENN. L. REV. 357 (1960).

53. France, *Effective Minor Courts: Key to Court Modernization,* 40 TENN. L. REV. 29 (1972); W. SWANNER, MUNICIPAL COURT GUIDE (1974).

tion." No opinion so designated shall be cited in any court unless a copy thereof shall be furnished to the court and to adversary counsel. (Supreme Court Rule 31, as amended, April 30, 1976; March 2, 1977). See sections 432, 433, 440 (intermediate appellate courts' unpublished opinions), 446, 448.

Researchers requiring unpublished opinions may locate them in bound form, chronologically arranged, in the clerk's office of the appropriate division. Also, they are available by subscription from the attorney general and are abstracted by unofficial reporting services. See section 432 (a). Noteworthy is the fact that the Supreme Court will entertain motions from the bar seeking to make public any specific unpublished opinion that the movant sincerely deems worthy.[54]

Section 432   SUPREME COURT REPORTS: TENNESSEE REPORTS; TENNESSEE DECISIONS

The opinions of the Tennessee Supreme Court (beginning with Volume 1 published in 1813 which reported cases for the years 1791 to 1813) are officially reported in the 225 volumes of Tennessee Reports. In 1972, the state stopped printing these official reports, ending with Volume 225, the last case being *French v. Shriver*, 225 Tenn. 727 (1972). Since that time Tennessee Supreme Court opinions have been *officially* reported in Tennessee Decisions.[55] This set is simply the name given to a duplicate printing (including page insertion) of all Tennessee cases published in the Southwestern Reporter, first and second series, since it began publishing Tennessee Supreme Court opinions in 1886 beginning with some cases published in Volume 84 of Tennessee Reports (16 Lea).[56]

54. Remarks of Mr. Justice William Harbison at Recent Legislation and Appellate Practice Seminar, Nashville. July 23, 1976.

55. *See*, 230 Tenn. at p. vi, 496 S.W. at p. vi (1974). Precisely, Tennessee Decisions/Southwestern Reporter became the official reports beginning with Sanders v. Forcum-Lannom, Inc., 225 Tenn. 637, 475 S.W.2d 173 (1972). This case, and the six following it in 225 Tennessee Reports (the last case being French v. Shriver, 225 Tenn. 727 (1972)) obviously have been *officially* reported. twice.

56. Precisely, the first case is Shelby Co. v. Mississippi and Tennessee Railroad Co., 84 Tenn. 401, 1 S.W. 32 (1886).

The Southwestern Reporter, first series, is complete in 300 volumes, ending in 1927.[57] The next year Southwestern Reporter, second series, was begun and is continuing. It is kept current by advance sheets issued weekly by its publisher, the West Publishing Company of St. Paul, Minnesota.

Now that the state has stopped printing separate official reports and West Publishing Company has become the official printer, forthcoming decisions will *not* require parallel notation. *See* 230 Tenn. at p. vi, 496 S.W.2d at p. vi (1974). For earlier decisions (those prior to volume 475 S.W.2d), however, a proper citation requires notation of both the official reports of appellate courts and the Southwestern Reporter. (Court of Appeals Rule 13, as amended, September 1, 1975).

A list of Tennessee Reports and Tennessee Decisions is shown in Appendix C.

Section 432(a) SLIP OPINIONS AND UNOFFICIAL REPORTING SERVICES

Since 1975 the Attorney General's office has reproduced the opinions of the Supreme Court and made them available to state and local governmental and law enforcement officials. These "slip opinions" have been made available to the public since December 1976 by subscription.

A new service designed to inform the bar quickly of recent appellate court decisions is Tennessee Attorneys Memo V. 1 January 5, 1976 —, published by M. Lee Smith and Associates, Nashville. This six page weekly newsletter attempts to summarize all actions of Tennessee appellate courts (including unreported decisions), the General Assembly, and executive agencies. The Tennessee Attorneys Memo, P. O. Box 3213, Arcade Station, Nashville, Tennessee 37219 615/242-7395, will, for a charge, provide: (1) a complete copy of any court opinion summarized in the Memo, (2) any General Assembly bill, amendment,

57. Precisely, Wilkens v. Reed, 156 Tenn. 321 (1927) is the last case reported in the first series, namely 300 S.W. 588. All of the cases appearing after it in volume 156 of Tennessee Reports appear in the first volume of Southwestern Reporter, second series. Of course, they do not appear in the same order as in Tennessee Reports.

public or private act, (3) any published opinion of the Attorney General, and (4) any executive agency rule or regulation. The Memo is successor to Tennessee Court Opinion Service 1 vol. May 19-December 29, 1975.

Another service providing timely summaries of appellate opinions of special interest to the trial bar is published by the Tennessee Trial Lawyers Association for its members. It is:

T.T.L.A. Opinions Service. Nashville: Tennessee Trial Lawyers Association, 1973. (monthly).

Finally, the Attorney General's office publishes a newsletter which contains an index to recent Attorney General opinions and provides abstracts of recent appellate cases. The information it contains is not to be considered an official opinion of the Attorney General nor an official report of court decisions. Available without charge to the bar it is:

Abstract. Nashville: Office of the Attorney General. V. 1, 1975— (bi-monthly).

Section 432(b) SUPREME COURT REPORTS—ANNOTATIONS

Tennessee cases of national importance are printed in full with complete nation-wide annotations in American Law Reports, published by Lawyers Cooperative Publishing Company. These reports are now in their third series. The publishers of A.L.R. have compiled the ALR Parallel Table from Official Reports to ALR (Rochester, Lawyers Co-op, 1951, 130 pp.) which provides a reference to the citation or annotation of state court cases in A.L.R. This volume covers 1-175 A.L.R. but pocket supplements cover later volumes. Shepard's Citations is more useful for this purpose, however. See sections 650 and 670. For citations to early cases printed in the forerunners of A.L.R. see section 438(a).

Section 433 PARALLEL CITATION TABLES

When the researcher has a case citation to an official Report but has only the Southwestern Reporter available (or vice versa) the use of a parallel citation table will aid in locating the desired case. The Tennessee Blue and White Book, published by West Publishing Company, is such a parallel citation table. In the blue section, all decisions reported in the Tennessee Reports from volume 85 (in addition to a few from volume 84) to date are listed by volume and page number with corresponding citations to the case as published in the Southwestern Reporter. Likewise, such tables show the same information for Tennessee Appeals Reports (beginning with volume 16) and Tennessee Criminal Appeals Reports (beginning with volume one). Conversely, the white portion of the book lists the volume and page numbers of all Tennessee cases (both Supreme Court and the two intermediate appellate courts) in the Southwestern Reporter giving parallel citations to the appropriate official reports.

A similar service is provided on a national scale by West Publishing Company in the National Reporter Blue Book, but its references run only from the state reports of each state to the National Reporter System and not the reverse. It consists of the original volume, four supplements (1936, 1948, 1960, 1970) plus an annual cumulative supplement.

Section 434   REVISIONS OF TENNESSEE REPORTS

In the early years of the state many of the Reports, like the statutes, were issued privately as a proprietary venture. This results in some confusion to the modern researcher when confronted with books and/or citations such as "23 Tennessee 131 (Cooper's edition)." Such books are *revisions* of the original Tennessee Reports.

The explanation of the need for these revisions can be traced to defects in the earliest reports. The first seven volumes of Tennessee Reports (Overton 1 and 2,[58] Cooke 1,[59] and

58. The cases were collected by Judge John Overton (1804-1816), but were edited and published by Thomas Emmerson (1807-1809, 1819-1822).

59. The "phantom volume" of Tennessee Reports, namely 3A (which was volume 2 of Cooke's Reports), appeared originally in 158 Tenn. Appendix (1929) and was reprinted and bound separately as 3A Tennessee Reports in 1940. These cases are not reported in Southwestern Reporter, but they are included in the Tennessee Digest. Ogden, *A Note on 3A Tennessee Reports,* 29 TENN. L. REV. 74 (1945). See section 438 (a).

Haywood 3, 4, 5,[60] and Peck 1) were issued by the judges themselves and lacked adequate headnotes. The first volumes issued by the first official Reporter (Martin & Yerger 1, and Yerger 1-10)[61] contained similarly inadequate headnotes. With the possible exception of volume 13 (Meigs 1), this deficiency continued in at least the next twenty-three volumes (Humphries 1-11, Swan 1-2, Sneed 1-5, Head 1-3, Coldwell 1), *i.e.*, 19-41 Tennessee Reports; these twenty-three volumes covering the years 1838 to 1860.

During the Civil War many courts were closed,[62] disrupting the judicial process. This resulted in a large backlog of cases during the era of Reconstruction. This backlog, together with the increase of litigation during that period, greatly overburdened the system of law reporting. Reporter Thomas H. Coldwell (1865-1870) was successful in issuing seven volumes with reasonable dispatch, and Joseph B. Heiskell (1870-1878) was able to do so through 1873. By that year the number of publishable opinions became so great (because an enlarged Supreme Court elected under the new 1870 Constitution sat in panels, doubling its output)[63] that Heiskell employed assistants to edit the cases beginning with Heiskell 5, (52 Tennessee Reports). These reports are:

60. Judge Haywood had published 2 volumes of North Carolina Reports (1789-1806) and this accounts for the numbering he gave his Tennessee Reports.

61. A few cases reported in Martin & Yerger 1 are re-reported in Yerger 1 and 2.

62. The Confederate Tennessee General Assembly had requested the courts to close, and later General Grant achieved the same result. The judicial process was not entirely stopped, however. *See,* W. ROBINSON, JUSTICE IN GREY, A HISTORY OF THE JUDICIAL SYSTEM OF THE CONFEDERATE STATES OF AMERICA (1941). The unfortunate West Humphreys, a federal District Judge (and former Attorney General and Reporter of Tennessee) was caught in the maelstrom. He was impeached and removed. Hall, *West W. Humphreys and the Crisis of the Union.* 34 TENN. HIST. Q. 48 (1975).

63. The Arbitration Commission and the Referees Commission greatly accelerated the Supreme Court's business. See section 404.

Heiskell Number	Ass't Reporter	Tennessee Reports Number	Term	Year Issued
4	None	51	1871	1873
5	W. B. Reese, Jr.	52	W. D. 1871	1874
6	Thomas H. Malone	53	E. D. Sept. 1871	1874
7	R. McP. Smith	54	M. D., Dec. 1871	1874
8	None	55	"1872-1876"64	1876
9	James C. Malone	56	W. D., April 1872	1876
10	Thomas H. Malone	57	W.D., Apr. 1872, and E.D., Sept. 1873	1878
11	W. B. Reese	58	E.D., Sept. 1872	1878
12	R. McP. Smith	59	W.D., April 1873 M.D., Dec. 1873	1878

Unfortunately, the scheme did not hasten the production of such reports and during the late 1870's several serial *unofficial* reports were issued. The most notable was that edited by Jere Baxter. See section 438(a).

Section 434(a)   TENNESSEE REPORTS, COOPER'S EDITION

Meanwhile, in 1871, Chancellor (later Justice) William F. Cooper began issuing a forty volume series of Tennessee Reports. Completed in 1881, this revision of Overton 1 through Coldwell 1 quickly became the paramount Tennessee Reports. Excellent notes and revised headnotes, coupled with Cooper's reputation as chancellor (see section 416(b)), insured the acceptance of this revision and it soon became the "official" Report.

Today reprints of the Cooper edition or the Shannon edition (see section 434(b)) are the Tennessee Reports found in every law library in Tennessee. No better evidence of the

---

64. This is a "special collection" of cases, all revenue related. Note that taxation, especially as it related to financing the state debt, was the critical political-legal issue of the time. Laska, *Legal and Constitutional History* at 641.

official nature of these Reports exists than this: The bench and
bar of Tennessee frequently cite the page numbers of the
revisions not the page numbers of the original Reports, in
pleadings, briefs and opinions. It is worth noting here that this
practice is wrong. Instead, the original page numbers which are
shown inserted and/or bracketed in the text of the revision should
be the page numbers in citations. Cooper did not delete cases.
He drafted original annotations following important cases,
However, but avoided invading the integrity of the cases themselves.[65] Headnotes were greatly expanded. Additionally, several
early Reports (appropriately labeled) were bound in single
volumes: Overton 1 and 2; Haywood 1, 2, and 3,[66] and Peck
1 with Martin & Yerger 1.

Cooper's revision ended with Coldwell 1 (41 Tennessee
Reports) and it is unfortunate that Cooper did not revise the
Reports for the Civil War and Reconstruction era[67] because
those Reports between Coldwell 2 (42 Tennessee Reports) and
Lea 1 (69 Tennessee Reports)—the years 1865 through 1878—
are the poorest in the state's jurisprudence.[68]

65. A leading example of Justice Cooper's annotations may be found in
Morgan v. Elam, 12 Tenn. 451 (1833), an important early case on married women's legal disabilities.

66. Haywood's Reports had been earlier reprinted and annotated by
M. M. Bigelow in 1870.

67. William F. Cooper (1820-1909) stands with Haywood, Shannon
and Williams as a major figure in Tennessee legal scholarship and advocacy.
Educated at Yale and privately tutored in law, he established a lucrative
practice in Nashville in 1846. He co-authored the first official Tennessee
Code in 1858 and saw his reward—election to the Supreme Court in 1861—
swept away by the Civil War. Following the war he became the state's
preeminent equity practitioner and was appointed Chancellor of the
important Seventh Chancery Division (Nashville) in 1872. While on the
bench he edited a revision of Tennessee Reports and issued Cooper's Tennessee Chancery Reports (3 vols.) a seminal work of his *nisi prius*
chancery opinions. Later, he edited an American edition of Daniell's
Chancery Practice and wrote several articles on equity practice for law
journals. He was elected to the Supreme Court in 1878 and performed
admirably. However, in 1886 vicissitudes of political life caught him
again. The quiet and scholarly Cooper relied on his reputation to insure
his re-election, but he fell victim to the "Judicial Clean Sweep of 1886."
Embittered, he moved to New York City and lived in semi-retirement
until his death.

68. According to Green, the reports from Coldwell 2 to 7 inclusive were

Heiskell's experiment with assistant reporters was carried a step further with the appointment of Jere Baxter as permanent assistant in 1878. Baxter had boot-strapped himself into the job by numbering the first three volumes of his Legal Reporter as 57, 58, 49, so as to follow the Cooper edition and Coldwell's reports consecutively. (See section 438(a)). The issuance of the official reports (Heiskell 10, 11, 12) bearing these numbers deranged this numbering. With his appointment as assistant reporter in 1878, Baxter adopted the official numbering as his own and issued nine volumes (60 to 68 Tennessee Reports) bearing his name but offered as *official* reports because they were "approved by the Reporter." These Reports were not arranged chronologically but covered the years 1872-78. Despite the overlap in years, these reports do not duplicate cases reported by Heiskell. In 1879, Reporter Benjamin Lea (1878-1886) assumed reporting responsibilities, and the practice of issuing official reports was continued until 1972. See section 432.

Section 434(b)   TENNESSEE REPORTS, SHANNON'S EDITION

In 1902-03, the indefatigable Robert T. Shannon[69] revised Cooper's edition of Tennessee Reports and continued his own revision through Pickle 17 (101 Tennessee Reports). Like

designated by lawyers of the day as "Coldwell's Fables" because they were the decisions of the Civil War-early Reconstruction Supreme Court (1865-1870). Green, *The Supreme Court in 1871*, 16 TENN. L. REV. 767, 769 (1941).

69. Robert T. Shannon (1860-1931) was, for nearly thirty years, the outstanding figure in Tennessee legal scholarship, the connecting link between Cooper and the present. He received his academic education at Vanderbilt and a legal education at Cumberland University at Lebanon, Tennessee. Establishing a practice in Nashville in 1892, he began an outpouring of legal scholarship that continued up to his death. Included in his works are: a supplement to the Milliken and Vertrees Code, annotated Constitution, his own massive Shannon's Annotated Code, a revision of Tennessee Reports, three volumes of unreported Tennessee cases, and finally, co-authorship of the State's second official code, the 1932 Tennessee Code. Shannon gave generously of his time, assisting the bar (especially the younger members) with legal research problems, and his death left a void that none could attempt to fill.

Cooper, he deleted no cases but expanded the headnotes and annotations (which he called citations).

Section 436   FEATURES OF THE SUPREME COURT REPORTS

Tennessee Reports contain useful information in addition to the opinions of the court. Each volume of these reports contains current lists, tables and other material such as:

Judges of the Supreme Court
Attorney General, Deputy, and Assistants
Court of Criminal Appeals Judges
Circuit Judges
Chancellors
Criminal Judges
Law-Equity Judges
District Attorneys-General and Assistants
Retired Judges, all levels
Table of Cases Reported
Attorneys Admitted During Term Reported

Older volumes of Tennessee Reports may contain somewhat different lists and tables, especially Rules of Court (see section 500) and memorials to lawyers and judges. For example, such volumes often contain tables of cases cited or distinguished. Rules, when included, are usually indicated on the spine of the official Reports and memorials are so indicated on the spine of Tennessee Decisions. An index to recent memorials is included in Tennessee Code Annotated (see section 230). For an index to earlier volumes (1-162) see 10 TENN. L. REV. 217 (1932). The Appendix to 176 Tennessee Reports (1940) contains a history of the Supreme Court and short biographies of the judges.

Every volume of Tennessee Reports contains an alphabetically arranged index. In the earlier volumes this indexing was a simple alphabetical scheme but, by volume 126, was improved so as to include an "analytical index"—brief statements of court holdings topically arranged. Also, each topic is divided into numbered sections for ease of finding it within the opinion. In the Southwestern Reporter these sections are assigned the appropriate West Key Number.

Each volume of the Southwestern Reporter includes reference tables of the following authorities cited in cases published therein:

Statutes construed, including the state Constitution; T.C.A.; Acts; U.S.C.A.; various Uniform Acts; Rules of Civil Procedure; Court Rules; A.B.A. Standards for Criminal Justice; Words and Phrases.

Section 438   THOMPSON'S AND SHANNON'S UNREPORTED CASES

In addition to the official Reports, two privately issued compilations of Supreme Court decisions are of such importance that they have risen to the dignity of official Reports. These are:

Shannon, Robert T. *Tennessee Cases with Notes and Annotations.* 3 vols. Nashville: Marshall & Bruce, 1898-99. Beginning in 1898, Shannon collected unreported decisions from the 1870's to that time. To these he added, edited, and annotated cases from *Thompson's Unreported Cases* and Jere Baxter's *Legal Reporter.* These were published in this three volume set that was popular because of its well-chosen and annotated cases. It is a necessary supplement to the official reports of the era 1847-1897. The set was reprinted by Dennis and Company of Buffalo, New York in 1957.

Thompson, Seymour D. *Unreported Tennessee Cases.* St. Louis: W. J. Gilber, 1878. Sometimes cited as *Thompson's Cases* or *Thompson's Unreported Cases,* this is a collection of unreported cases from 1847 through 1869. This curious book is replete with typographical errors and was supposedly "surpressed" for that reason. It remains useful nevertheless. This book was reprinted by Dennis and Company of Buffalo, New York in 1943.

Section 438(a)   MISCELLANEOUS SUPREME COURT REPORTS

Early Tennessee Supreme Court decisions not otherwise

reported can be gleaned from unofficial publications of a quaint and obscure nature. The usefulness of some of these precedents to the modern advocate is likely to be marginal. Yet they do much to explain the background of present law, especially issues of property law. These are:

Cooke, W. W. *Cooke's Reports.* Nashville: 1814, 1816, Judge Cooke, a member of the Supreme Court of Errors and Appeals, 1815-16, compiled in one volume certain cases that Judge Overton omitted in his two volumes of Tennessee cases (now 1 and 2 Tennessee Reports) and included certain relevant federal decisions. This work is now 3 Tennessee Reports. Cooke was gathering other cases at the time of his death in 1816, intending to publish these as a second volume. These cases were finally printed in 1929 by the State's Reporter in 158 Tennessee Reports, Appendix. These cases are also known as 3A Tennessee Reports, reprinted, Columbia, Missouri: E.W. Stephens Publishing Company, 1940.

Haynes, Milton A. *South-western Law Journal and Reporter.* 1 vol. Nashville: Cameron & Fall, 1844. This was Tennessee's first law review; its style and format is remarkably contemporary. Issued bimonthly in 1844, it contains numerous unreported cases (especially cases involving criminal and property law) and legal miscellany of the era. Apparently ahead of its time, the Journal expired after volume one. It was reprinted by Dennis and Company of Buffalo, New York in 1943.

Baxter, Jere. *Legal Reporter.* 3 vols. Nashville: Legal Reporter Printing House, 1878. Attorney General and Reporter Joseph B. Heiskell (1870-1878) was unable to issue the Reports promptly and enlisted the bar's aid in editing the last eight volumes bearing his name. Because of the need for such decisions, however, Jere Baxter began issuing a serial in 1877 that contained unreported decisions of the post-war years. Collected in these volumes, they are not in chronological order. Furthermore, when issued in book form they were spine-numbered consecutively to follow the Cooper edition, *i.e.*, 57, 58, 59. As best as can be determined these cases were not re-reported in either Baxter's reports or Heiskell's reports. See section 434(a). This set was reprinted by Dennis and Company of Buffalo, New York in 1957.

Trezevant, M. B. *Memphis Law Journal.* 2 vols. Memphis: S. C. Toof & Co., 1878-79. Similar in style and format to the above work by Baxter, this periodical contains unreported Supreme Court decisions. It expired after two volumes. This set was reprinted by Dennis and Company of Buffalo, New York in 1962.

McCall, H. G. *Southern Law Journal and Reporter.* 1 vol. Nashville and Birmingham: Tavel and Howell, 1879-80. Both the Legal Reporter and the Memphis Law Journal were merged into this publication. It too contains unreported decisions. Only one volume was issued.

Williams, Samuel Cole. *Re-Reported Tennessee Cases.* Jackson: McCowat-Mercer, 1916. Justice Williams published this pamphlet to aid the bar in finding Tennessee cases that had been re-reported in the national annotations of the time, namely American State Reports (Am. St. R.), Lawyers' Reports Annotated (L.R.A.: both original and New Series, N.S.), and American Annotated Cases (Ann. Cas.)—all now considered obsolete. These parallel citations cover the years 1886 to 1915 (85 to 133 Tennessee Reports) and are useful because the annotations usually included counsel briefs. After 1907 the parallel citation reference is to the Southwestern Reporter System.

Section 440   INTERMEDIATE APPELLATE COURT REPORTS

The present intermediate appellate courts, the Court of Appeals and the Court of Criminal Appeals, are required to issue written opinions only if the judgment of the inferior court is reversed and remanded. T.C.A. §27-122. In practice, both courts issue written opinions in most cases. As with Supreme Court opinions, however, not all such opinions are approved for publication. The intermediate courts generally follow the guidelines for publication adopted by the Supreme Court (see section 430). No opinion of these courts may be published until after the time has expired for the filing of a petition for the writ of certiorari. Further, if the Supreme Court grants the writ, or denies the writ of certiorari by concurring in the result only, the opinion of the intermediate appellate court may not be published. Citation of unpublished opinions of intermediate appellate courts should clearly indicate their status, e.g., *cert. denied, concur result only*, and a copy of such opinion should be given to the court to which it is cited and to adversary counsel. See section 430.

Section 444(a)   CHANCERY APPEALS REPORTS; CHANCERY APPEALS DECISIONS

The Court of Chancery Appeals (1895-1907) issued opinions printed in two sets of Reports. The first "official" decisions were printed in two volumes of cases collected by John Wright (one of the judges) entitled Tennessee Chancery Appeals Reports (1905). As best as can be determined, these cases were not reprinted elsewhere contemporaneously. These reports were reprinted in 1953 by Dennis & Co. of Buffalo, New York.

The West Publishing Company printed the other "unofficial" opinions of this court in the Southwestern Reporter, first series, beginning with volume 35 and continuing through volume 64. These cases did not appear in any official reports but were reprinted in 1953 by the same publisher in a separate eight volume set (including page insertion) entitled Tennessee Chancery Appeals Decisions. The appendix also contains a number of Supreme Court opinions that did not appear in the official reports.

Section 444(b)   COURT OF CIVIL APPEALS REPORTS

The decisions of the Court of Civil Appeals (1907-1925) are printed in an eight volume set entitled Tennessee Court of Civil Appeals Reports. The set contains only leading cases for the years 1909 to 1919. These were selected, edited and published by one of the court's judges, Joseph C. Higgins, with the court's approval. These cases were not reprinted elsewhere contemporaneously. Sometimes referred to as Higgins Reports, the editor's name should not be used in citation, *e.g.*, Howell v. Martin, 8 Tenn. Civ. App. 520 (1918). The set was reprinted in 1956 by Dennis & Co., of Buffalo, New York.

Section 446   TENNESSEE APPEALS REPORTS

The decisions of the Court of Appeals (as presently constituted in 1925) are printed in Tennessee Appeals Reports. Printed privately from opinions selected by the court, these are the official reports of this court, and clearly became such when the volumes began to be issued by the state in 1955. The state stopped issuing these reports with volume 63 in 1972. Since then the decisions have been officially published, like Supreme Court opinions, in Tennessee Decisions which is the duplicate printing of Tennessee cases from West's Southwestern Reporter, second series. The researcher should note carefully, however, that Southwestern Reporter, second series, did not begin publishing Court of Appeals decisions until the 1932-33 term (64 Southwestern Reporter, second series.) That is, none of the cases reported in the first fifteen volumes of Tennessee Appeals Reports are printed in Southwestern Reporter, second series. See section 432.

Section 448   TENNESSEE CRIMINAL APPEALS REPORTS

The decisions of this court were published by the state in four volumes beginning with the court's creation in 1967 until 1972. These reports are entitled Tennessee Criminal Appeals Reports. These were also printed in Tennessee Decisions, that is, Southwestern Reporter, second series. Current Criminal Appeals decisions are being printed in Southwestern Reporter, second series. See section 432.

Section 450   BRIEFS AND APPELLATE RECORDS

Original briefs and records of the state's appellate courts (Supreme Court, Court of Appeals, Court of Criminal Appeals) are kept in the offices of the clerks of the appropriate division where the case is heard.[70] However, the clerks have transferred most of these early briefs and records to the Archives Division, State Library and Archives. For example, the clerk in Nashville retains custody of Supreme Court materials since 1972; the earlier materials are at the State Library and Archives, indexed by style of the case and docket number. The same is generally true for clerks of the other divisions. Because the transfer policy is not uniform, communication with the clerks is necessary to determine actual holdings. Minutes of the appellate courts are also kept by the clerks. In the Middle Division, Supreme Court minutes dating back to 1854 and all intermediate appellate court minutes are in the clerk's office and are currently being microfilmed. A collection of early Supreme Court materials, such as trial and execution dockets and journals, is kept at the State Library and Archives.

Finally, the Tennessee Trial Lawyers Association maintains a brief bank on selected areas of law, e.g., medical malpractice, products liability, for the benefit of its members. Originated in 1974 this bank is affiliated with that of the American Trial Lawyers Association.

Section 460   COURT CALENDARS

The Supreme Court must hold one session each year in each grand division of the state: the second Monday in September at Knoxville, the first Monday in December at Nashville, and the first Monday in April at Jackson. (T.C.A. §16-204). However, the Court actually meets oftener, e.g., four times per year at Nashville in 1976. Docketing of cases is not centralized, however. The calendar (docket) for each appellate court

---

70. The names and addresses of the Division clerks are: John A. Parker, Clerk, Supreme Court Building, 719 Locust Street, S.W., Knoxville, Tennessee 37901; Ramsey Leathers, Clerk, 100 Supreme Court Building, Nashville, Tennessee 37219; Mrs. Jewel Redden, Clerk, Supreme Court Building, Jackson, Tennessee 38301.

(Supreme Court, Court of Appeals, Court of Criminal Appeals) is arranged by each court through the clerk of the appropriate division (Eastern, Middle, Western). Although counsel are notified well in advance of hearing dates, the official Docket for the upcoming session of each court is printed in pamphlet form and usually distributed to counsel and interested parties a few weeks prior to the session. This pamphlet gives information as to actual day of hearing, names of counsel, and origin of cases.

Section 470 EXECUTIVE SECRETARY TO THE SUPREME COURT

The Executive Secretary to the Supreme Court is the chief court administrator for the state's judicial system. Created in 1963, the Executive Secretary is the chief financial officer of the judicial system in addition to being charged with "improving the administration of justice" by performing general supervisory duties and by sponsoring training sessions and research projects. The Executive Secretary serves at the pleasure of the Supreme Court. T.C.A. §§16-324 to -329 (Supp. 1976). He publishes an Annual Report (copies of which are available through the Executive Secretary's office) as well as a newsletter for the state judiciary, entitled Tennessee Judge. He also compiles aids for the judicial system such as a Court Reporter's Manual and a Court Clerk's Manual.

Section 480 APPELLATE COURT NOMINATING COMMISSION

A variation of the Missouri plan for the selection of judges became effective in Tennessee in 1971 with the creation of the Appellate Court Nominating Commission "to assist the governor in finding and appointing the best qualified persons available for service on the appellate courts." T.C.A. §17-701 (Supp. 1976). In 1974 the legislature removed the Supreme Court from this screening process. This eleven-member commission of laymen and lawyers, including representatives elected by practicing lawyers and appointees of the governor and legislative leaders, nominates three persons to any vacancy in the intermediate appellate courts. From the nominees the governor selects a candidate who serves, subject to voter approval in a subsequent uncontested election.[71]

Section 490   JUDICIAL STANDARDS COMMISSION

In 1971 a Judicial Standards Commission was created to investigate complaints against judges and to inquire into an individual judge's fitness to perform his duties. This nine-member commission composed of judges, lawyers, and laymen makes its recommendations to the general assembly which may impeach or remove/retire any judge. T.C.A. §§17-801 to -816 (Supp. 1976). Another responsibility of the Commission is to issue opinions as to what conduct may violate the Canons of Judicial Ethics. Supreme Court Rule 43; adopted December 2, 1974.

71. The procedure was generally approved in State ex rel. Higgins v. Dunn, 496 S.W. 2d 480 (Tenn., 1973). For a good discussion of the difficulties the State has had with the procedure see L. GREENE, GOVERNMENT IN TENNESSEE at 166-167.

Chapter V

COURT RULES AND COURT PRACTICE AIDS

Section 500 COURT RULES

The steps by which a case progresses through the Tennessee courts are outlined by the *rules of procedure*. Generally, these are of five types: (1) appellate rules, including rules governing admission to and regulation of the bar; (2) rules of civil procedure for trial courts of general jurisdiction; (3) rules of criminal procedure for trial courts of general jurisdiction; (4) local civil and criminal rules for courts of general jurisdiction; and (5) civil and criminal rules for courts of limited or special jurisdiction, *e.g.*, general sessions courts. Recently, trial and appellate rules for Tennessee courts have been compiled and published by West Publishing Company in Tennessee Rules of Court-1976 Desk Copy. This compilation includes:

Timetable for Lawyers

Proposed Rules of Civil Procedure—Amendments (see section 540).

Proposed Rules of Criminal Procedure (see section 550).

Index, Rules of Civil Procedure

Supreme Court Rules (see section 520 and 530)

Court of Appeals Rules (see section 530)

Court of Criminal Appeals Rules (see section 530)

Code of Judicial Conduct

Code of Professional Responsibility (see section 530)

U.S. District Court Rules, Western District (see section 538)

U.S. District Court Rules, Eastern District (see section 580)

Rules of Appellate Procedure—Federal (see section 580)

U.S. Court of Appeals—Sixth Circuit (see section 580)

As described below, court rules have evolved from a heritage of statutory and common law procedure—but this process is not finished. Indeed, many Tennessee courts do not have a coherent, unified body of procedural rules. The researcher is therefore thrown back to primary sources (statutes and case law). To ease this burden, many authors writing on substantive law, *e.g.*, wills and estate administration, often include treatment of relevant procedural aspects. Such works (treatises and practice aids) will be described here according to the appropriate court. Other treatises and practice aids on substantive law subjects are described in section 920.

Section 510   COURT RULES AND PROCEDURE—PRE-1970

Although modern rules of civil procedure have greatly overturned the old ones (see section 520) and progress is being made in revising appellate and criminal procedural rules (see section 596 and 550), the legal researcher should have some familiarity with old rules (or at least their sources), largely because such knowledge will often clarify many older cases and statutes.

Earliest "rules" of procedure were drawn from the common law—that is, the forms of action that developed from centuries of precedents in both law and equity cases.[1] The forms of action, like the substantive law, were modified by statutes so that in time it became impossible to look to any one source for such rules. This led some states, but not Tennessee, to flirt with codification of pleading. Ironically, one of the probable reasons procedural reform was slow in coming to Tennessee was the influence of Cumberland University Law School (1847-1961). Precisely, its curriculum was designed around one book, an important handbook of procedure, Caruthers' History of a Lawsuit. First published in 1852, the book enjoyed eight editions/revisions and became not only the standard textbook on the subject, but also was frequently cited as the authority on procedure by Tennessee courts as well as the courts of other states. Today the book's importance is greatly diminished, but it is not entirely obsolete (as some lawyers maintain) because the book provides important background information about the growth and development of Tennessee jurisprudence.

Only the last (8th) edition is cited today but older cases refer to earlier editions; therefore the following list names them all.

Abraham Caruthers. *History of a Law Suit in the Circuit Court of Tennessee, Addressed to the Law Student.*

1. Higgins, *Forms of Action in Tennessee,* 11 TENN. L. REV. 256 (1933).

Lebanon, Tennessee: Office of the Banner of Peace, 1852. 173 pp.; Abraham Caruthers. *History of a Law Suit in The Circuit Court of Tennessee.* 2nd ed. Nashville: W.F. Bang & Co., 1856. 184 pp.; Abraham Caruthers, *History of a Lawsuit.* Nashville: A.A. Stitt, 1860, 670 pp.; This is actually a revision of the 1856 second edition, but may be considered the "first edition" of the work published under this title. Abraham Caruthers. *History of a Lawsuit.* 2nd ed. Cincinnati: Robert Clarke & Co., 1866. 670 pp. Caruthers died in 1862. This is one of several reprints of the 1860 edition. *Caruthers' History of a Lawsuit.* (Andrew B. Martin, ed.) 3rd ed. Cincinnati: Robert Clarke & Co., 1888. 688 pp.; *Caruthers' History of a Lawsuit.* (Andrew B. Martin, ed.) 4th ed. Cincinnati: Robert Clarke & Co., 1903. 639 pp.; *Caruthers' History of a Lawsuit.* (Andrew B. Martin, ed.) 5th ed. Cincinnati: W.H. Anderson & Co., 1919. 709 pp.; *Caruthers' History of a Lawsuit.* (Sam B. Gilreath, ed.) 6th ed. Cincinnati: W.H. Anderson & Co., 1937. 814 pp.; *Caruthers' History of a Lawsuit.* (Sam B. Gilreath, ed.) 7th ed. Cincinnati: W.H. Anderson & Co., 1951. 1033 pp.; *Caruthers' History of a Lawsuit* (Sam B. Gilreath and Bobby R. Aderholt, ed.) 8th ed. Cincinnati: W.H. Anderson & Co., 1963. 1059 pp.

In addition to Caruthers' History of a Lawsuit, there were several other treatises on procedure that were more elaborate, usually treating the subject in more detail and including forms. For these reasons they still contain a surprising amount of "good" law. These are:

Higgins, Joseph and Arthur Crownover. *Tennessee Procedure in Law Cases.* Charlottesville: Michie Company, 1937. 1263 pp. This book is still in print and although largely superseded is not without value.

Smithson, Noble. *Treatise on Civil Procedure in Tennessee.* Nashville: Marshall & Bruce, 1903. 1653 pp. A second edition was published by the Baldwin Book Company in 1916.

Morison, J.H.S. *The Rules of Pleading as Adapted to Courts of Law in Tennessee, with Forms.* St. Louis: F.H. Thomas Law Book Co., 1907. 554 pp.

Parks, James G. *A Manual of the Law of Pleading.* Knoxville: Ogden Brothers, 1894. 217 pp.

As described earlier, equity jurisprudence had a growth separate from the law in Tennessee. See section 416(a). Accordingly, it is not surprising that the rules of equity procedure would be treated separately by the bar and legal writers. Here again, one book has dominated the subject—Gibson's Suits in Chancery. This book, in its 5th and latest edition, retains more of its vitality than Caruthers' because of the broader scope of its subject matter, namely, the "substantive" rules of equity. It is: Henry R. Gibson. *A Treatise on Suits in Chancery.* Knoxville: Ogden Brothers & Co., 1891. 1188 pp; Henry R. Gibson. *A Treatise on Suits in Chancery.* 2nd ed. Knoxville: Gant-Ogden Co., 1970. 1203 pp. This edition was reprinted by the Baldwin Book Company in 1916. *Gibson's Suits in Chancery.* (Joseph Higgins and Arthur Crownover, Jr., ed.) 4th ed. Cleveland, Ohio: Banks-Baldwin Company, 1937. 1346 pp.

The latest edition is *Gibson's Suits in Chancery.* (Arthur Crownover, Jr.) 5th ed. 2 vols. Charlottesville, Virginia: Michie Company, 1955-1956. Two other equity treatises were also available, although neither enjoyed the reputation of Gibson's. They were:

Clark, George L. *Equity: Tennessee Edition.* Columbia, Mo.: Stephens Publishing Co., 1920. 722 pp.

Hicks, Wesley J. *The Tennessee Manual of Chancery Pleading and Practice.* 2nd ed. (Hardin P. Figuers, ed.) Nashville: Marshall & Bruce, 1883. 620 pp.

A valuable recent summary of Tennessee chancery practice was published by the College of Law, University of Tennessee. It is:

Broughton, Jr., Len G. et al. *Chancery Practice.* Knoxville: University of Tennessee, College of Law, Continuing Legal Education, 1976.

Section 520   COURT RULES AND PROCEDURE: 1970-

It is now generally recognized that the Tennessee Supreme

Court has both the statutory *and* inherent power to oversee and control the judicial system. T.C.A. §§16-112 to -118; 16-330 to -333 (Supp. 1976) This includes such matters as adopting rules of procedure (see sections 540, 550), balancing caseloads (see section 416(a)), setting standards for admission to and expulsion from the bar (see section 530), and more recently, controlling the bar generally, including the power to unify it. Cantor v. Brading, 494 S.W.2d 139 (Tenn. App. 1973) (cert. denied); Barger v. Brock, 535 S.W.2d 337 (Tenn. 1976). The present rule is certainly correct; it is worth noting, however, that this rule has not always been so firmly fixed and that tension on this issue has existed between the judicial and the legislative branch since the earliest days of the republic. Moreover, there have been periods during which the legislature dominated the court and largely pre-empted this area, and there have also been times when the court was simply reluctant to exercise such control. The chief issues of contention have been admission to the bar[2] and rules of procedure.[3]

Section 530   APPELLATE AND BAR ADMISSION RULES

The rules of appellate procedure are currently under study by the Advisory Commission on Rules. Changes, therefore, may be expected in the near future. See T.C.A. §16-118. See section 596.

Supreme Court rules are kept in the office of the court clerk in Nashville, are usually published in the advance sheets of Southwestern Reporter, and later appear in the bound volumes of Tennessee Decisions. The spine of the appropriate volume will usually indicate the inclusions of rules, as was the practice when the rules were published in the official reports, *i.e.*, Tennessee

2. As early as 1823 the Supreme Court was trying to raise educational standards for bar admission applicants. Such effort was met by a legislative resolution challenging its action. 2 R. WHITE, MESSAGES OF THE GOVERNORS OF TENNESSEE 59-60 (1954). One hundred and fifty years later the issue of court vs. legislative power over bar admissions was still being litigated. Belmont v. Board of Law Examiners, 511 S.W.2d 461 (Tenn. 1974). Cantor v. Brading, 494 S.W.2d 139 (Tenn. App. 1973) (cert. denied).

3. *See* note 4 *infra.*

Reports, etc. All Supreme Court rules must be published in T.C.A. These appear in volume 5A (1977). They also appear in West's Tennessee Rules of Court, 1976 at 131-200.

Bar admission rules are found in volume 5A of T.C.A. See also, West's Tennessee Rules of Court, 1976 at p. 150-164.

The rules and regulations of the Board of Law Examiners appear in the Official Compilation of Rules and Regulations published by the Secretary of State. Tennessee lawyers must conduct themselves according to the Code of Professional Responsibility, shown in volume 5A of T.C.A. See also, West's Tennessee Rules of Court, 1976 at p. 237-308.

The rules of the Court of Appeals and the Court of Criminal Appeals likewise appear in volume 5A of T.C.A. and similarly appear in Southwestern Reporter (Tennessee Decisions) as they are announced.

Section 540   RULES OF CIVIL PROCEDURE

A quarter century of attempted procedural reform succeeded in 1970 when Tennessee adopted new rules of civil procedure patterned generally after the Federal Rules.[4] The new rules were the first promulgated under T.C.A. §16-114 which gave the Supreme Court power to prescribe court rules subject to the approval, as expressed by joint resolution, of the General Assembly. Such rules must be published in Tennessee Code Annotated. They appear in volume 5A (1977). See T.C.A. §16-115. They also appear in West's Tennessee Rules of Court, 1976 at p. 1-129. Proposed amendments are shown on p. XVII-XLIV.

4. Wicker and Coffey, *Shall the Supreme Court of Tennessee be Given the Power to Regulate by Rules of Court all Evidence and Procedure?* 17 TENN. L. REV. 168 (1943). *See also,* Wicker, *Judicial Rule-Making as a Means to Procedural Reform.* Knoxville: Government-Industry-Law Center and the Law Revision Commission, 1964. 34 pp.; Wicker, *A Comparative Study of Civil Pleading, Practice and Procedure in the Tennessee Trial Courts of General Jurisdiction.* Knoxville: Government-Industry-Law Center, 1964. 152 pp.

For interpretation of the Tennessee Rules of Civil Procedure, the bar has come to rely on the first treatise on this subject. It is:

> *Tennessee Practice.* Vols. 3 & 4 (Rules of Civil Procedure). St. Paul: West Publishing Co., 1970. supplemented. This set contains Advisory Committee comments.

The value of this set will be further enhanced by use in conjunction with a recent work by Professor Harold Bigham of Vanderbilt Law School. It is:

> *Tennessee Practice.* Vols. 5 & 6 (Civil Procedure Forms). St. Paul: West Publishing Co., 1977.

An excellent one-volume form book also includes commentary on the rules. Recently published, it is:

> Cooper, Gary A. *Tennessee Forms for Trial Practice.* Norcross, Georgia: Harrison Co., 1977.

Because the rules were patterned after the federal rules, the Tennessee Supreme Court has said that decisions rendered under federal rules are persuasive in interpreting state rules. Moredock v. McMurry, 527 S.W.2d 462, 463 (Tenn. 1975). For sources of federal rules interpretation, see section 580.

Of special value to the bar is a 1974 symposium on the rules published in an entire issue of the Memphis State Law Review. Following an introductory article, each rule is described and analyzed in detail, effectively making the periodical a handbook of civil procedure. See Special Issue—Tennessee Rules of Civil Procedure. 4 Mem. St. U.L. Rev. 211 (1974).

Other handy references to the rules of civil procedure are the works of Chancellor Hendry. These are:

> Hendry, Earl. R. *Hendry's Manual of Tennessee Civil Procedure, Annotated.* 2 vols. Nashville: McQuiddy Printing, 1974. A useful feature of this work is inclusion of an "Indexer," that is, a cross index which correlates the rules with the many T.C.A. procedure-related sections still in force, *e.g.*, venue.
>
> _____. *Hendry's Handbook on Tennessee Discovery and Depositions.* Nashville: McQuiddy Printing, 1975.

Finally, an excellent recent summary of pre-trial preparation has been prepared by the College of Law, University of

Tennessee. It is:

> Paine, Donald, et al. *Tennessee Civil Procedure: Preparation for Trial.* Knoxville: University of Tennessee, College of Law, Continuing Legal Education, 1976.

Section 550   RULES OF CRIMINAL PROCEDURE

Both the substantive and procedural rules of Tennessee criminal law are scattered throughout Tennessee Code Annotated and the court reports because they are the product of nearly two centuries of piecemeal legislation and court decision.

Attempts have been made to reform this area of the law. In 1973 the Law Revision Commission offered the General Assembly the final draft of its Tennessee Criminal Code and Code of Criminal Procedure. Nashville: Law Revision Commission, 1973. 469 pp. This document culminated a ten-year effort at criminal law reform but was not enacted into law.

In 1975 the Advisory Committee (Commission) on Criminal Rules drafted rules which were approved by the Supreme Court and were placed before the General Assembly for ratification. (See section 596). As with the Law Revision Commission code, these rules were not approved by the General Assembly. The proposed rules, patterned after the federal rules of criminal procedure, are a great improvement over the present situation and it may be expected that they will meet with legislative approval in the near future. Alternatively, the Supreme Court has indicated it may adopt the rules under its inherent powers. Worth noting is proposed Rule 57 requiring that copies of local rules be furnished the executive secretary of the Supreme Court and that such rules be printed or reproduced for distribution to the bar and public. These proposed rules are:

> *(Proposed) Tennessee Rules of Criminal Procedure.* In advanced sheets, 537 S.W.2d 155, prefatory pages 1-106. (July 13, 1976). Copies available for inspection at the Supreme Court clerk's office in Nashville.

The proposed rules also appear in West's Tennessee Rules of Court, 1976 at p. XLV-CXXI.

Until procedural reform similar to that described above is

accomplished, the researcher must look to the primary sources (statutes and case law), but may be assisted to some extent by the following sources:

A. *Caruthers' History of a Lawsuit.* 8th ed. p. 855-906.

B. Every year since 1968 Professor Joseph Cook of the University of Tennessee, Knoxville, College of Law, has written a critical survey of Tennessee criminal law. Published annually in the *Tennessee Law Review*, this is an excellent treatment of both substantive and procedural aspects of criminal law.

C. *Tennessee Law of Criminal Procedure.* Knoxville: University of Tennessee, Public Law Research and Service Program, 1976. 1 vol.

D. *Basic Prosecutor's Manual.* Nashville: District Attorney General's Conference, 1976. 1 vol. looseleaf. A preliminary draft has been forwarded to all district attorneys. Revisions and supplementation should be forthcoming.

E. *Tennessee Sheriff's Manual.* Nashville: County Technical Advisory Service and the Tennessee Law Enforcement Planning Agency, 1974. 1 vol. looseleaf. This manual is being revised at this time.

F. Swanner, Will D. *Municipal Court Guide.* Knoxville: Municipal Technical Advisory Service, 1974. 178 pp. This is an excellent discussion of the powers of municipal courts. It includes forms.

G. Beene, Joe F. *General Sessions Clerks: Criminal Cases.* Knoxville: University of Tennessee: Public Law Research and Service Program, 1974. 1 vol.

H. *Tennessee Law of Crimes.* Knoxville: University of Tennessee, Public Law Research and Service Program, 1976, 1 vol.

I. Canale, Jr., Phil et al. *Pretrial Preparation of Criminal Cases.* Knoxville: University of Tennessee, College of Law, Continuing Legal Education, 1976.

J. Barrett, Jr., Lionel, et al. *Defense of Drug Cases.* Knoxville: University of Tennessee, College of Law, Continuing Legal Education, 1976.

Section 560   LOCAL RULES

Trial courts of general jurisdiction have power to make local rules that supplement the Rules of Civil Procedure and/or statutory rules so long as such rules are not inconsistent with the law. Richie v. Liberty Cash Grocers, Inc. 63 Tenn. App. 311, 471 S.W.2d 559 (1971). An example of such a rule would be one requiring motions to be heard on a specific day of the week.

Local rules are generally not published. Rather, they are kept on file by the appropriate court clerk who publicly posts the latest rules. From time to time the larger metropolitan circuits will publish their rules that are available without charge to attorneys. Examples are:

> *Rules of Practice in the Chancery Court of Davidson County, Tennessee.* 1975. 19 pp.

> *Rules of Practice and Procedure in the Criminal Court of the Tenth Judicial District of Tennessee (Davidson County).* 1963. 11 pp.

> *Rules of Practice for the Circuit Courts of General Jurisdiction of the Tenth Judicial Circuit of Tennessee at Nashville.* 1976. 16 pp.

Because local rules are constantly revised, the researcher should make a diligent effort to secure the *latest* rules.

Section 570   RULES FOR COURTS OF LIMITED JURISDICTION

The rules for courts of limited jurisdiction are statutory, so Tennessee Code Annotated and the case law must be consulted for such rules. That is, for cases falling within their exclusive jurisdiction, these courts do not look to modern rules such as the Tennessee Rules of Civil Procedure. When these "other courts" (county judge, probate, juvenile, domestic relations, and general sessions) are exercising the jurisdiction of circuit or chancery courts, however, they must apply the Tennessee Rules of Civil Procedure. But whenever any general sessions court exercises the powers conferred on it by a *public* rather than private act, whether or not such jurisdiction is concurrent with that of circuit or chancery courts, the Rules do *not* apply.[5]

Courts of limited jurisdiction sometimes prescribe local rules that generally are not published. Copies are made available, however, by the appropriate court clerk, *e.g.*, *Rules of Practice in the Probate Court of Davidson County, Tennessee*. 1974. 5 pp.

The statutory and case law origin of procedure in courts of limited jurisdiction has led to inclusion of this subject in many of the treatises or practice aids dealing with the substantive law before courts of this nature. Therefore, such sources are shown below in sections 572 to 578.

Section 572   DOMESTIC RELATIONS/FAMILY LAW

For discussion of domestic relations courts see section 424. Domestic relations local court rules sometimes appear as part of the rules of courts of general jurisdiction in the circuit. Otherwise, they are available from the appropriate court clerk.

The statutory procedures for cases of the type usually handled by these courts are best described in the following publications, but a researcher using books of this type should be attentive to changes made in the law since these books were published. See also section 576.

Trimble, Benson. *Tennessee Divorce Authorities*. Charlottesville, Va.: Michie Company, 1966. 637 pp.

————. *Tennessee Adoption Authorities with Forms.* Charlottesville, Va.: Michie Company, 1968. 213 pp. Note that adoption is a matter of circuit and chancery court jurisdiction.

Cohen, Alfred E. *Divorce and Alimony in Tennessee with Forms.* Charlottesville, Va.: Michie Company, 1949. 562 pp. This book is of primarily historical interest.

Section 574   PROBATE COURTS, COUNTY JUDGES/PROBATE LAW

For a discussion of the jurisdiction of probate courts and

5. *Symposium-Tennessee Rules of Civil Procedure*, 4 MEM. ST. U.L. REV. 219 (1974).

county judges, see section 424. As explained above, probate courts (or county judges) may promulgate local rules, but the source of both substantive and procedural law in this matter must be gleaned from the appropriate statutes and case law. Several valuable treatises and practice aids are helpful. These are:

> *Pritchard's Law of Wills and Administration of Estates in Tennessee* (Harry Phillips, ed.) 3rd ed. Cincinnati: W.H. Anderson Company, 1955. 2 vols. supplemented. This is the leading treatise on this subject and a revised edition is forthcoming. The first edition was published in 1894, a second revised edition (J.B. Sizer ed.) was published in 1925.

> Higgins, Joseph. *Administration of Estates in Tennessee.* Charlottesville, Va.: Michie Company, 1943. 714 pp. This was the leading treatise until the publication of *Phillips' Pritchard on Wills.* It remains useful.

For other probate, estate, and will related materials see section 920.

Section 576   JUVENILE COURTS/JUVENILE LAW

For discussion of juvenile courts generally see section 424. Juvenile judges sometimes issue local rules. These may be secured from the appropriate clerk or secretary. Because juvenile court practice and procedure is mostly statutory, Title 37 of T.C.A. should be consulted first by the researcher. Statutes relating to children, however, are scattered throughout the code. The Commission on Children and Youth has prepared an unofficial compilation of such statutes in:

> *Compilation of Selected Laws on Children and Youth from the Tennessee Code Annotated.* 2nd ed. Nashville: Commission on Children and Youth, 1973. rev. 1974. 1 vol. looseleaf.

Valuable treatises on Tennessee juvenile law, that include forms are:

> Turner, Kenneth A. *Juvenile Justice: Juvenile Court Problems, Procedures and Practices in Tennessee.* Charlottesville, Va.: Michie Company, 1969. 282 pp.

Tennessee Law of Children. Knoxville: University of
Tennessee. Public Law Research and Service Program,
1976. 260 pp.

Section 578   GENERAL SESSIONS COURTS

For discussion of general sessions courts see section 422.
The jurisdiction and procedure of the general sessions courts is
largely statutory. See T.C.A. section 16-1101 to -1136 (Supp.
1976) and pertinent private acts. Judges of the general sessions
court may adopt local rules under the supervision of the Supreme
Court and the legislature. T.C.A. §§16-112, -114, -115, -1120.
Where such rules are in force they may be secured from the
court clerk. In practice, the legal researcher is wise to first consult the chief handbook for general sessions practice and procedure. It is:

Hall, William W. *The General Sessions Court.* Charlottesville, Va.: Michie Company, 1972. 658 pp. with
1973 expanded index.

Other sources include: Beene, Joe F. *General Sessions Clerks:*
Criminal Cases. Knoxville: University of Tennessee, Public Law
Research and Service Program, 1974. 1 vol. Plaas, Hyman, Otis
H. Stephens and James J. Glass, *The Function of the Judge in*
the General Sessions Court of Knox County, Tennessee. Knoxville: Bureau of Public Administration, University of Tennessee,
1973. 251 pp.

Section 580   FEDERAL COURT RULES AND PRACTICE

There are three trial-level federal courts in Tennessee,
namely, District Courts for the Eastern, Middle, and Western
Districts fo the state. Counties comprising these districts are
described in 28 U.S.C.A. § 123. The Eastern District holds
court, as necessary, in Knoxville, Greeneville, Chattanooga,
and Winchester. The Middle District likewise sits in Nashville,
Cookeville, and Columbia, while the Western District may sit
at Memphis, Jackson, and Dyersburg.

The decisions of federal courts in Tennessee, plus those of
the Sixth Circuit Court of Appeals, are printed in Federal

Supplement and Federal Reporter (first and second series) respectively; both published by West Publishing Company.

An unofficial reporting service provides monthly edited summaries of Sixth Circuit opinions and will also provide unedited copies. Available on subscription this service is:

> *Sixth Circuit Review.* Louisville, Kentucky: Sixth Circuit Review. Vol. 1, 1973-

Cases in federal courts are conducted according to federal procedural rules. These rules, together with valuable commentary, are described in Title 28 U.S.C.A. Rules (3 vols., including Federal Rules of Evidence) St. Paul: West Publishing Co.: 1968; and in these sources:

> Wright, Charles A., Arthur R. Miller, and Edward A. Cooper. *Federal Practice and Procedure.* St. Paul: West Publishing Co., 1970. 15 vols. supplemented.

> Moore, James W. *Moore's Federal Practice.* 2nd ed. New York: Matthew Bender, 1971-. 27 vols. supplemented.

> Volz, Marlin M., ed. *West's Federal Practice Manual.* 2nd ed. St. Paul: West Publishing Company, 1970. 7 vols. supplemented.

> *Cyclopedia of Federal Procedure.* 3rd ed. Chicago: Callaghan, 1965. 20 vols. supplemented.

Federal district courts may also promulgate local rules. These are kept on file at the clerk's office. An attempt is made to collect all such rules for Tennessee courts in Federal Local Court Rules. 2 vols. Chicago: Callaghan & Co., 1972. Because the service has not been successful in including all rules, *e.g.*, the six person civil jury rule in the Middle District, the researcher should ask the clerk for the latest rules. Local rules of the Western and Eastern Districts are shown in West's Tennessee Rules of Court, 1976 at p. 309-344; and Administrative Orders relative to Magistrates' powers are shown at p. 345-387.

Rules for the United States Court of Appeals for the Sixth Circuit, which includes Tennessee, may be found in Federal Local Court Rules. 2 vols. Chicago: Callaghan & Co., 1972. These supplement the Federal Rules of Appellate Procedure that may be found in the sources described above or in Title 28 U.S.C.A. (United States Code Annotated) Rules at p. 367-381; 172-181, published by West Publishing Company, 1968, supplemented. These rules also appear in West's Tennessee Rules of

Court, 1976 at p. 389-435. See also, Phillips, Appellate Review in the Sixth Circuit, 2 Mem St. U.L. Rev. 1 (1971); Moore, James W, Allan D. Vestal, Philip B. Kurland, Moore's Manual-Federal Practice and Procedure. 2 vols. New York: Matthew Bender, 1962-.; Moore, James W., Louis R. Frumer, Irwin Hall, Moore's Manual-Forms. 4 vols. New York: Matthew Bender, 1964-. Federal Bar Association. Practitioner's Handbook for Appeals to the United States Court of Appeals for the Sixth Circuit. Cincinnati: Cincinnati Chapter of the Federal Bar Association, rev. 1975. 68 pp.

Bankruptcy is the subject of federal jurisdiction, and this court is guided by its own rules. Moreover, the bankruptcy judges may prescribe local rules which are available from their offices upon request. Bankruptcy rules, together with valuable commentary, are described in Title 28 U.S.C.A. (United States Code Annotated) § 2075 Rules at p. 127-401. (Supp. p. 40-52) as well as these sources:

> Bare, Clive, et. al. *Consumer Bankruptcy for the General Practitioner.* Knoxville: Univ. of Tenn., College of Law, Continuing Legal Education, 1975.

> Laube, William T., W.J. Hill, Lawrence P. King. *Collier Bankruptcy Manual.* 2nd ed. 4 vols. New York: Matthew Bender, 1954-.

> Duesenberg, Richard W., et al. *Collier on Bankruptcy.* 14th ed. 21 vols. New York: Matthew Bender, 1974-.

> Ryan, Edward J., Harvey R. Miller, Michael L. Cook. *Collier Forms Manual.* 2nd ed. 2 vols. New York: Matthew Bender, 1963-.

Section 590   JUDICIAL CONFERENCE AND JUDGES CONFERENCE

The Judicial Conference, created in 1953, is composed of all judges of courts of record paid by the state. T.C.A. §17-401. The judges are required to meet in conference once a year (expenses paid by the state) in order to consider "matters pertaining to their official duties" and specifically to prescribe rules of official conduct for judges (see section 490). The conference may also draft suitable legislation for the "more effective suppression of crime" and submit its recommendations to the General Assembly. The Conference speaks through its officers and six-member executive committee. Its reports and recommendations are on file with the Executive Secretary of the Supreme Court. In 1970 a General Sessions Judges Conference was established to perform, generally, the same function for these judges as the Judical Conference does for the state-paid trial judges. T.C.A. §§17-601 to 17-604 (Supp. 1976).

In 1976 the legislature established a Trial Judges Association, a voluntary association open to all trial judges and chancellors whose salary is paid wholly by the state. The group is to meet annually for consideration of matters pertaining to the rights and duties of trial judges. In light of an existing Judicial Conference, the nature and future of this Association is unclear. Ch. 795 [1976] Tenn. Pub. Acts 1093.

Section 592   DISTRICT ATTORNEY GENERAL'S CONFERENCE

In 1961 a District Attorney General's Conference was established whereby the district attorneys general were required to meet in conference (expenses paid by the state) and to consider "matters pertaining to their official duties" and specifically to suggest laws and rules of procedure as may be necessary to the "more effective suppression of crime," and submit these to the general assembly. T.C.A. §§8-713 to -725 (Supp. 1976). The bulk of the administrative duties of the conference are assumed by a full-time Executive Secretary who functions much as does the Executive Secretary to the Supreme Court, i.e., he is the chief fiscal officer and administrator of the district attorneys. He also acts as liaison to other branches of government and performs educational and information services such as publishing a Basic Prosecutor's Manual that includes uniform criminal procedure forms.

Section 594   JUDICIAL COUNCIL

In Tennessee, Dean Roscoe Pound's campaign for judicial reform resulted in creation of the state's first Judicial Council in 1943.[7] T.C.A. §§16-901 to -910 (Supp. 1976). This seven-teen-member council of judges, legislative officials, and prac-ticing lawyers is charged with making a continuous survey and study of the judicial system, collecting and analyzing statistics relating to the judicial system, and suggesting ways of simplifying judicial procedure. Many years it makes an Annual Report to the governor and Supreme Court. The Council is modestly funded and, in recent years, much of its fact-gathering work has been performed through the Executive Secretary of the Supreme Court who is an *ex officio* member of the council. Such data appears in the Executive Secretary's Annual Report.

Section 596   ADVISORY COMMISSION ON RULES

A 1965 act established a nine-member Advisory Com-mission on Rules, charged with advising the Supreme Court regarding the rules of practice and procedure. This Commission played a key role in adoption of the Tennessee Rules of Civil Procedure. Currently, the Commission is studying revisions of appellate rules. T.C.A. §16-118 (Supp. 1976).

The above statute was amended in 1975 to provide for an Advisory Commission on Rules of Criminal Practice and Proced-ure. The rules suggested by this Commission were approved by the Supreme Court but have not, as yet, been adopted by the General Assembly. (See section 550). T.C.A. §16-118 (Supp. 1976).

7. Coffey, *The Judicial Council Movement,* 16 TENN. L. REV. 960 (1941); Hooker, *The Need for a Judicial Council in Tennessee,* 17 TENN. L. REV. 149 (1942); Pound, *Judicial Councils and Judicial Statistics,* 17 TENN. L. REV. 153 (1942); Tipton, *The Judicial Council in Tennessee,* 19 TENN. L. REV. 65 (1945).

Chapter VI

ANNOTATIONS, DIGESTS, INDEXES, AND CITATORS

A researcher of Tennessee law is provided with a variety of tools that aid in finding the law or linking law sources together. These include annotations, indexes, digests, and citators.

Section 600   ANNOTATIONS

Precisely, an annotation is a short commentary about a subject designed to explain its meaning. In legal writing, however, the term is broader, and researchers recognize three types of annotations: (1) Those that analyze an important *legal issue* by focusing on a leading case (or cases) dealing with that issue. See section 432(b). (2) Those that describe and analyze the *legislative history* of a statute. See section 220. (3) Those that describe and analyze the *judicial interpreattion* given a statute by the state's courts. This third meaning is the most important in everyday research and is the reason ours is an annotated code: Tennessee Code Annotated. However, early annotations were an important aspect of legal research, too.

Early Tennessee annotations were crude and merely adjuncts to the statutes. The state's early compilations were largely private proprietary ventures and emphasis was placed on the statutory material, not the annotations. But as the state's law (statutory and common) developed greater importance, importance began to be attached to the rationale and process of jurisprudence. Reviewing Section 200, it appears that even the better of the early compilations (Code of 1858, p.21; Thompson and Steger's Code, p. 22; Milliken and Vertrees' Code, p.23) were deficient in annotations.

Shannon's Code of 1896, p.24, dramatized the importance of annotations; each code that followed included an increasing array of such material. Today, the main body of statute-related annotations are found in Tennessee Code Annotated. See section 220. It should be noted, however, that the work of early annotators, especially Shannon, should not be ignored even though T.C.A. purports to have incorporated his work. Research in obscure areas of Tennessee law can uncover some remarkably thorough annotations in early codes. For example, the T.C.A. annotation for the topic "Attorney-General and Reporter" refers to Shannon's Annotation of the Constitution, where the researcher discovers an extended treatment of the origins and statutes relating to this office—not well treated in T.C.A., unfortunately.

In short, the early annotations should be consulted where later ones seem incomplete, and for the purposes of ascertaining the earliest origins and interpretations of statutes and cases.

Early annotations include:

Shannon, Robert. *Annotations on Tennessee Decisions with Table of Cases and Citations.* 5 vols. Nashville: Marshall and Bruce, 1905-07. Supplement, 1915. A second edition in six volumes was published by Callaghan and Company in 1929. Because of the alphabetical arrangement of cases this set has only marginal value as an annotation.

Shannon, Robert T. *The Constitution of the State of Tennessee, Annotated.* 1 vol. Nashville: Tennessee Law Book Publishing Company, 1915.

Shannon provided a separate index for the annotations in his Code of 1917 (and 1918). See section 200.

Section 610   DIGESTS

The tool most frequently used to find case law on a given topic is the digest. In a sense it is simply a master index to case law. Precisely, it is a compilation of synopses (or headnotes) of legal points taken from the cases topically arranged (criminal law, etc.).

Tennessee, which does not have an encyclopedia of its law, is served by two digests, the West Company's Tennessee Digest and Michie Company's Michie's Digest of Tennessee Reports.

Section 610 (a)   WEST'S TENNESSEE DIGEST

Currently the more popular of the two digests because its Key Number System follows that of the Southwestern Reporter, this digest was published in 1947 by West Publishing Company of St. Paul. It now consists of twenty-eight bound volumes which are kept up to date by annual pocket-part supplements plus an annual pamphlet supplement. The set covers official Tennessee Supreme Court and appellate court Reports as well as federal and U.S. Supreme Court decisions arising in Tennessee. The set purports to digest all Tennessee reported cases since 1791, not merely those reported in Southwestern Reporter. Volume twenty includes a table of cases and a table of words and phrases.

Access to the Digest is gained by the use of the descriptive word index that comprises volume one (in two books).

Section 610 (b)   MICHIE'S DIGEST OF TENNESSEE REPORTS

The revised edition of an earlier digest (§ 630), Michie's Digest of Tennessee Reports was published in 1936 by the Michie Company of Charlottesville, Virginia. It consists of eighteen volumes which are kept current by pocket parts, the last issued in 1974. The set covers official state appellate and federal decisions relating to the laws of the state. Law reviews of the state's schools are also referenced. An alphabetical table of cases appears in volume seventeen. As with any digest, it is approached through the general index, volume eighteen.

Section 620   AMERICAN DIGEST SYSTEM

West Publishing Company's Century Digest and the succeeding Decennial Digests (General Digest), attempt to cover all American cases from 1658 to date. Tennessee cases are included under the appropriate Key Number. These volumes have tables of cases; case finding by subject matter is aided by reference to the appropriate Key Number.

Section 630   EARLY DIGESTS—TENNESSEE

Tennessee has had a digest of its Reports since early days. Close examination reveals that they were (or attempted to be) quasi-encyclopedias or annotations. Their usefulness today is very limited; the better have been subsumed into contemporary digests. The early digests are:

Holman, James T. *Digest of the Reported Cases Ruled and Adjudged in the Courts of Tennessee.* Nashville: W. Hassell Hunt and Co., 1835.

Meigs, Return J. *Digest of All the Decisions of the Former Superior Courts of Law and Equity and of the Present Supreme Court of Errors and Appeals.* 2 vols. Nashville: W. F. Bang and B. R. McKennie, 1848.

Vollintine, H. *Digest of the Decisions of the Supreme Court of Errors and Appeals in the State of Tennessee.* Philadelphia: C. Sherman and Son, 1858.

King, Henry C. *The Tennessee Digest.* 4 vols. Boston: Little, Brown, and Company; Memphis: Cleaves, Smithwick, and Hatcher, 1869.

Milliken, W. A. *Digest of All the Decisions . . . By Return J. Meigs.* 2nd ed. 3 vols. Clarksville: Neblett and Titers, 1881. This was an updated revision of the above work.

Marks, A. D. *Index-Digest of the Decisions of the Supreme Court of Tennessee.* Nashville: Marshall and Bruce, 1889. This was a supplement to the above work. Also, it contains an alphabetical table of Tennessee cases and notation where cited.

Taylor, Lytton. *Index-Digest of the Tennessee Reports.* Nashville: Albert B. Tavel, 1888.

Shannon, Robert T. *Digest of Decisions of the Supreme Court of Tennessee.* Nashville: Marshall and Bruce, 1899.

Webb, James A. *Digest of All Published Decisions by Courts of Tennessee and All Federal Decisions.* 3 vols. St. Louis: F. H. Thomas Company, 1899. The spine reads Webb and Meigs' Tennessee Digest. This work was supplemented three times: first by Joseph

Wheless in 1917 and twice by T. D. Crawford in 1923 and 1925.

Michie, Thomas J. ed. *Encyclopedic Digest of Tennessee Reports.* 12 vols. Charlottesville: Michie Company, 1906-08. This set was supplemented by three sequentially numbered volumes in 1914, 1918, and 1923. In 1928-29 a three volume cumulative supplement was issued, followed by a final supplement issued in 1934. It is now subsumed into Michie's Digest of Tennessee Reports. See section 610(b).

Shannon, Robert T. *Shannon Tennessee Annotation and Digest.* 2nd ed. (see section 600).

Crawford, T. D. *Digest of Tennessee Decisions.* 7 vols. St. Louis: Thomas Law Book Company, 1929. This was a revision of the Webb and Meigs Digest, as supplemented. This work was supplemented cumulatively in 1934, 1937 and 1940. This work appears to have been subsumed into the West Tennessee Digest.

Section 640   INDEXES TO STATUTES, SESSION LAWS, REPORTS

Section 640(a)   STATUTES

The chief index to current statutes is the three-volume General Index at the end of Tennessee Code Annotated. Included in T.C.A. is a parallel reference table to acts in earlier codes. See section 230. Naturally, each of the early codes discussed in section 200 has an index of its own.

Section 640(b)   SESSION LAWS

Session laws are indexed in the bound volume in which they appear, and unless such laws are codified or are private acts (see 640(c) below), they are not officially indexed. See section 310. However, an unofficial index of legislation introduced each year in the General Assembly is available. See section 346.

In recent years M. Lee Smith & Associates, publishers of

Tennessee Attorneys Memo have published an Index to [Number] General Assembly, which contains a list of public chapter numbers and bill numbers showing code sections thus amended. See section 432(a).

Section 640(c)   INDEX TO PRIVATE ACTS

Local or private acts, as they are called, are an important part of Tennessee law despite a constitutional amendment restricting them. (See sections 310, 800-810). Currently, there are two indexes to private acts. Although technically these duplicate each other, this is not precisely the case. Rather, the two indexes augment each other owing to what has been seen as certain shortcomings in the first. These indexes are arranged by county or town and also by subject matter.

> *Index to the Private Acts of Tennessee.* Indianapolis: Bobbs-Merrill Company, 1962. Supplemented annually.

> *Private Acts of [Name] County.* Nashville: County Technical Assistance Service, 1975-. (See Section 850).

Section 640(d)   INDEX TO REPORTS

The state had an early alphabetical index to reports. It is:

> Hunter, Benjamin and Myer, William G. *Index to the Tennessee Reports.* St. Louis: Gilbert Book Company, 1875. A second volume supplementing the first was published in 1882.

Today, digests perform the function of these early indexes. See section 610.

Section 650   CITATORS — SHEPARD'S TENNESSEE CITATIONS

A citator is a tool that enables the researcher to discover whether a given case is still "good law"—whether, for example, it was followed or overruled in later decisions. This service is performed today by Shepard's Tennessee Citations published by Shepard's Citations, Inc., of Colorado Springs, Colorado. Published in two volumes, it is kept up to date by advance sheets (bound in white paper) and cumulative quarterly supplements (red paper). In recent years Shepard's has expanded its scope beyond case and statute citation into areas such as ordinance and court rule citation. See section 840. Consequently, it contains a wealth of reference material for the reseracher's use.

One volume of Shepard's Tennessee Citations is labeled "Cases" and includes cases through 1971. It cites cases that appear in:

A. Tennessee Reports

B. Shannon's Tennessee Cases

C. Tennessee Chancery Reports

D. Appellate Reports: Chancery Appeals, Civil Appeals, Tennessee Appeals Reports

E. Southwestern Reporter (Tennessee cases), first and second series

F. United States Reports, including Lawyers' Edition and Supreme Court Reporter

G. Federal materials: Federal Cases, Federal Reporter, Federal Supplement, and Federal Rules Decisions

H. Numerous law reviews, including Memphis State, Tennessee, and Vanderbilt law reviews

I. American Law Reports, first and second series

The second volume, also published in 1971, is called the "Statute Edition" and gives citations to:

A. United States Constitution

B. United States Code, including Supplement

C. United States Code Annotated

D. Federal Code Annotated, now United States Code Service

E. United States Statutes at Large

F. United States Treaties and Other International Agreements

G. Federal Court Rules

H. Tennessee Constitution, 1870

I. Superseded Tennessee Codes: Code of 1932, Williams' Tennessee Code, Michie's Tennessee Code, code sections no longer in Tennessee Code Annotated

J. Tennessee Code Annotated, including replacement volumes and supplements

K. Table of Tennessee Acts by Popular Names or Short

Titles
L. Tennessee Acts, 1796-1970 (not codified when cited)
M. Municipal Charters (Home Rule)
N. Index to Municipal Charters (Home Rule)
O. Ordinances
P. Index to Ordinances
Q. Tennessee Court Rules

The supplement to Shepard's Citations keeps the set current. For example, the supplement gives citations to recent Tennessee cases, recent replacement volumes and supplements of T.C.A. The supplement now includes citations to the American Law Institute's Restatements and to Tennessee Jury Instructions.

Section 660   CITATORS—EARLY

Prior to the publication of Shepard's, Tennessee was served by a local citator, now largely obsolete. It is:

Wheless, Joseph. *Tennessee Citations*. St. Louis: F. H. Thomas Company, 1913. This citator includes all state Supreme Court and appellate court cases in alphabetical order and gives a reference to later cases in which the case was cited. Note that, according to Wheless, *thousands* of citation errors such as non-existent citations, mistakes of names, and incorrect citation numbers have been made in Tennessee Reports and other Tennessee reported cases throughout the years.

Section 670   SHEPARD'S SOUTHWESTERN REPORTER CITATIONS

Shepard's Southwestern Reporter Citations, 3rd ed., was published in 1950 in one massive volume (3325 pp.) by Shepard's Citations, Inc. of Colorado Springs, Colorado. It is kept up to date by a 1950-1971 bound supplement and quarterly supplements (bound in red paper) and advance sheets (white paper). It lists citations from the Southwestern Reporter, first and second series, given in other elements of the National

Reporter System, and aforementioned Supreme Court decisions, and the American Law Reports, all three series, and Federal cases. The chief advantage of this set is that it gives nationwide coverage through the National Reporter System with cases grouped according to jurisdiction. First are grouped opinions of the Tennessee courts included in Southwestern Reporter, then opinions of the Federal courts followed by opinions of other state courts included in Southwestern Reporter in alphabetical order; then opinions of all other state courts included in the National Reporter System, arranged in alphabetical order; finally there are given citations to A.L.R.

As explained above, a table of Tennessee acts by popular name or short title can be found in Shepard's Tennessee Citations. These are also included in Shepard's Acts and Cases by Popular Names, Federal and State (Colorado Springs, Colorado, Shepard's Citations, Inc., 1968, and a red paper-covered current supplement). A special feature of this book is the citations to important Tennessee cases by popular name, for example, Evolution Teaching Case, or Reapportionment Cases.

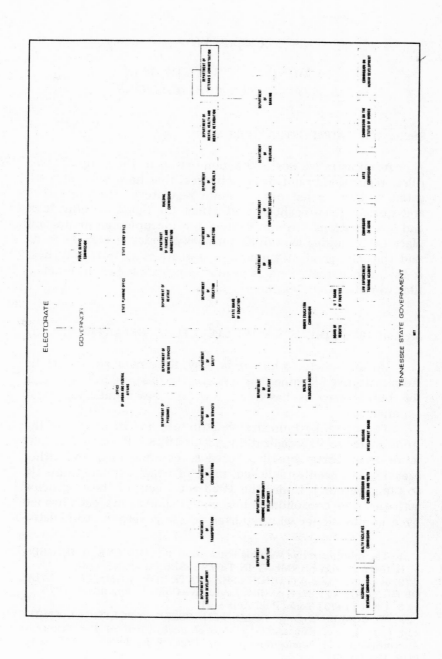

TENNESSEE STATE GOVERNMENT

Chapter VII

ADMINISTRATIVE LAW AND
STATE AGENCY PUBLICATIONS

Section 700 ADMINISTRATIVE LAW

Administrative law is the name given to the body of laws, rules, regulations (and daily activities) that have been promulgated and/or carried out by state regulatory, administrative, and quasi-judicial agencies that affect the rights of individuals and corporations. Administrative law occupies an important place in Tennessee as well as nationally; today it may be fairly said that the greatest amount of law affecting our daily lives is that which fuels (and is produced by) what has been called the Administrative Machine.[1]

Section 710 ADMINISTRATIVE STRUCTURE—DEPARTMENTS

Unfortunately, while it is easy to generalize about the Administrative Machine it is not easy to describe it.[2] Although the bureaucracy is based on law, the law is not logic but experience.

The present administrative structure had its origins in the Administrative Reorganization Act of 1923.[3] Prior to that time more than forty boards, bureaus, commissions, and other agencies had been established, most of which reported directly to the governor.[4] Under the 1923 act, many of these agencies' activities were consolidated into eight departments, each headed by a commissioner who reported to the governor. Administra-

1. The Administrative Machine is discussed in L. GREENE, D. GRUBBS, V. HOBDAY, GOVERNMENT IN TENNESSEE (1975) 128-133.
2. A better attempt is TENNESSEE STATE GOVERNMENT:MANUAL OF ORGANIZATION. Nashville: Legislative Council Committee, 1970.
3. Ch. 7 [1923] Tenn. Pub. Acts 8-44.
4. W. COMBS AND W. COLE, TENNESSEE, A POLITICAL STUDY 114 (1940). *See,* Rouse, *The Historical Background of the Tennessee Administrative Reorganization Act of 1923,* 8 E. TENN. HIST. SOC. PUB. 104 (1936).

tive reorganization has continued since that time, especially in the 1930's;[5] the effect of such reorganization has been a net *increase* in the number of departments and a parallel increase in the number of boards and commissions that exercise varying degrees of administrative authority.

Although their duties and even their names vary from time to time, various departments carry out the major functions of state government. See Title 4, Tennessee Code Annotated. These departments are listed below together with the *major* titles in Tennessee Code Annotated that describe their functions.

1. *Agriculture:* Titles 43, 44, 52
2. *Banking:* Title 45
3. *Conservation:* Title 11
4. *Correction:* Title 41
5. *Economic and Community · Development:* Title 4
6. *Education:* Title 49
7. *Employment Security:* Title 50
8. *Finance and Administration:* Title 9
9. *General Services:* Title 12
10. *Human Services:* Title 14
11. *Insurance:* Title 56
12. *Labor:* Title 50
13. *Mental Health and Mental Retardation:* Title 33
14. *Military:* Title 7
15. *Personnel:* Title 8
16. *Public Health:* Title 53
17. *Revenue:* Title 67
18. *Safety:* Titles 4, 38, 59
19. *Transportation:* Titles 4, 42, 54
29. *Tourist Development:* newly established, Ch.468 [1976] Tenn. Pub. Acts 177.
21. *Veterans Affairs:* Titles 4, 7

Section 712 ADMINISTRATIVE STRUCTURE—COMMISSIONS, BOARDS, COUNCILS, AND COMMITTEES

Although the names of only sixteen boards or commissions appear on the official state organization chart, there are at least one hundred and eighty commissions, boards, councils, and committees in the executive branch.[6]

5. W. COMBS AND W. COLE, TENNESSEE, A POLITICAL STUDY 126-142 (1940).
6. J. PICKERING, A STUDY OF TENNESSEE STATE EXECUTIVE BRANCH BOARDS, COMMISSIONS, COMMITTEES, AND COUNCILS 1 (1976). This is the best study of such agencies to date. A Legislative Council Committee report in 1970 was able to locate only about one

At least thirteen commissions, such as the Tennessee-Missouri Bridge Commission,[7] are either defunct or inactive[8] while at least as many wield, or have the potential for wielding, considerable influence. These include the Public Service Commission, Wildlife Resources Agency (formerly the Game and Fish Commission), Alcoholic Beverage Commission, Higher Education Commission.

The names and duties of these boards and commissions are too numerous to list here, but they may be understood best by functional categorization.[9] Accordingly, twenty-six have major administrative responsibility, while thirty-two have secondary administrative responsibility. Forty-two have regulatory powers, while forty serve only an advisory role. Twelve are quasi-judicial bodies, while six seek to promote area development. Nine are interstate bodies.

A full list of all executive-related state commissions, boards, etc., including a description of their duties, is included in: Pickering, John W., *A Study of Tennessee State Boards, Commissions, Committees and Councils.* Nashville: State Planning Office, 1976. Throughout the years the bar has come to rely on the annual Tennessee Blue Book (Nashville: Secretary of State, 1975-76) as the "official" list of departments and important commissions. The Blue Book is particularly useful because it describes agencies' subdivisions and provides names of officials. Another list, giving addresses of sixty-four important departments/commissions and boards is shown in the Memphis State University Law Review, Vol. 6, No. 2 (1976), 367-369. Finally, another such directory is: *Governmental Guide: Ten-*

---

hundred and sixty agencies but this included the judiciary-related boards and commissions as well. *See,* STUDY ON BOARDS AND COMMISSIONS Nashville: Legislative Council Committee, 1970. Readily discoverable judiciary-related agencies are the Board of Law Examiners, T.C.A. §29-101; Code Commission, T.C.A. §1-101; Law Library Commission, T.C.A. §10-515; Judicial Council, T.C.A. §16-901; Advisory Committee to the Supreme Court on Rules, T.C.A. §16-118; Supreme Court Building Commission, T.C.A. §16-1324.

7. Ch. 167 [1949] Tenn. Pub. Acts 512.

8. *See* J. PICKERING, note 6 *supra,* at 10. Taps was not blown for a sentimental favorite, the Board of (Confederate) Pension Examiners until 1971. T.C.A. §4-341 (repealed), Ch. 29 [1971] Tenn. Pub. Acts 74.

9. *See,* J. PICKERING, note 6 *supra,* at 10.

nessee Edition. Madison, Tennessee: Governmental Guides Inc. (annual). It lists names and addresses of state officials including judges. Another edition, listing education officials is available.

Section 720   FINDING CURRENT ADMINISTRATIVE LAW

The task of locating sources of state administrative law was greatly lessened by the passage of two acts in 1974, the Uniform Publications Act,[10] and the Uniform Administrative Procedures Act.[11] Prior to this time, the reseracher seeking current regulations governing a particular subject was forced to contact the appropriate agency for the latest regulations. Quite often, the researcher would be presented with an unorganized sheaf of papers to which was appended the agency's enabling legislation and a "helpful" note explaining that the offeror thinks the documents are complete—but that, of course, the regulations are undergoing revision at the present time. Other agencies published their rules and regulations in a more systematic way but subject to the same caveats. Examples of typically available rules and regulations, oftentimes included in the agency's annual report include:

Real Estate Commission, *The Tennessee Real Estate Broker License Act of 1973; Rules, Regulations and Code of Ethics.* 1973. 51 p.

Board of Cosmetology, *Tennessee Cosmetology Law; Sanitary Rules and Regulations.* 1973. 24 p.

Department of Education, *Rules, Regulations, and Minimum Standards for Education of Handicapped Children.* 1974. 13 p.

Department of Personnel, *Civil Service Commission Rules and Regulations for Administering Title 8, Chapters 30-32, T.C.A.* 1974. 40 p.

Another continuing source of agency rules and regulations is the loose leaf services, especially in the areas of tax law and labor law. See section 900.

10.Ch. 491 [1974] Tenn. Pub. Acts 219; Ch. 370 [1975] Tenn. Pub. Acts 1970, T.C.A. §§4-508 to -511; 4-534 (Supp. 1976).

11. Ch. 725 [1974] Tenn. Pub. Acts 945. T.C.A. §4-502 *et seq.* (Supp. 1976).

Section 722   ADMINISTRATIVE LAW SOURCES: 1974-

The Administrative Procedures Act of 1974 and its companion, the Uniform Publications Act of 1974, are the primary vehicles for insuring fair and orderly agency actions respecting individual's rights. These two acts should be read together and are generally referred to as, simply, the Administrative Procedures Act, (or A.P.A.). They seek to establish guidelines for: (1) promulgation and publication of rules, (2) practice before agencies, especially adjudicatory hearings and/or investigations, and (3) judicial and appellate review. Because the Act is likely to be amended in the future, a detailed discussion is not warranted here. The Administrative Procedures Act was the subject of a valuable symposium comprising an entire issue of the Memphis State University Law Review, Vol. 6, No. 2 (1976) at p. 143-401. Articles in this issue were written by knowledgeable lawyers and judges (including Tennessee Supreme Court Justice Harbison) on the following issues relating to the Act: legislative history, scope, rulemaking, publication, prehearing procedure, hearing procedure, judicial and appellate review, and proposed amendments.

For research purposes, an important feature of the A.P.A. are its provisions which suggest the development of precedents based on the decisions of agencies in contested cases. Read in concert with the Public Records Law, T.C.A. §§15-304 to -307 (Supp. 1976) these provisions allow public access to written final orders, decisions and opinions. See Levinson, "Contested Cases Under the Tennessee Uniform Administrative Procedures Act," Memphis State University Law Review 6 (1976): 215-251, at 242, 243. Finally, the A.P.A. contains a provision whereby an interested party may petition an agency for a declaratory ruling; these too should be available for inspection on request. T.C.A. §§4-513 (Supp. 1976).

Section 724   TENNESSEE ADMINISTRATIVE REGISTER

The Administrative Procedures Act outlines the steps by which a rule becomes effective, i.e., it must be approved as to its legality by the Attorney General.[12] An important mandatory

12. These steps, which include legislative review of rulemaking, are likely

step (for legal research purposes) is the requirement that proposed rules be published in the Tennessee Administrative Register which is the state counterpart of the Federal Register, and, as such, contains other matter such as notices of rulemaking, hearings, proposed amendments, and emergency rules.[13] The Tennessee Administrative Register has been published monthly since July 1975 by the Secretary of State and is available from the Administrative Procedures Division, Department of State, 976 Capitol Building, Nashville, 37219.

Section 726   OFFICIAL COMPILATION, RULES AND REGULATIONS OF THE STATE OF TENNESSEE

Beginning in 1975, as mandated by the A.P.A., the effective rules and regulations of all state agencies have been and/or are now being published in the Official Compilation, Rules and Regulations of the State of Tennessee, presently consisting of six loose-leaf volumes, available from Administrative Procedures Division, Department of State; 976 Capitol Building, Nashville, 37219. The Compilation contains all such rules and regulations except those which have been adopted verbatim from federal rules, in which case a citation is given to the proper issue of the Federal Register or the proper section of the Code of Federal Regulations. Also, in the case of a few particularly voluminous publications which have been adopted verbatim by an agency, (e.g., fire codes adopted by the Department of Insurance) and that are easily available from other sources, such publications are not reprinted but a citation is given to the proper edition of that publication along with a statement of how those books can be obtained.

The rules are arranged by agency and the agencies listed in alphabetical order; the rules are not indexed although they are numbered according to a control number, paragraph and section system. New rules, amendments and repeals are published as

to be altered but are ably described in Stiles, *Rulemaking Under the New Tennessee Uniform Administrative Procedures Act*, 6 MEM. ST. U. L. REV. 171 (1976).

13. *See*, Beasley, *Publication Under the New Tennessee Unfiorm Administrative Procedures Act and the Public's Right to Know*, 6 MEM. ST. U. L. REV. 187 (1976).

replacement pages and mailed monthly as part of the Tennessee Administrative Register.

Section 728   EXECUTIVE ORDERS

The executive orders and proclamations of the governors prior to Winfield Dunn were not centrally collected. Locating them, if at all possible, entails examination of the governors' papers, usually in the custody of the State Library and Archives. A few major proclamations, however, are included in the session laws, Tennessee Code Annotated, or White's Messages of the Governors, 1796-1907.

Beginning with the Dunn administration (1974), major administrative policy statements, especially those resting on a legislative grant of administrative discretion, have been made in the form of Executive Orders. Example: Order Dispatching the National Guard to the Tennessee State Prison in Nashville. Executive Order No. 24, September 16, 1975. These orders are kept on file in the governor's office and copies are on file at the State Library and Archives. Major proclamations are treated as explained above. No official index compilation is made of minor proclamations.

Section 730   OPINIONS OF THE ATTORNEY GENERAL

As the state's chief legal officer, the Attorney General represents the state in all litigation involving state agencies or officers, gives legal advice (in the form of written opinions) to all departments and/or state officers representing them, represents the state in criminal appeals, and oversees the investigations and litigation relative to the duties of various departments. T.C.A. §§8-603; 8-609. The Attorney General is also the official Reporter of decisions; that is, it is his duty to gather and publish the opinions of the Supreme Court. T.C.A.§§8-612 to -614.

The precise legal status of the Attorney General's opinions is unclear, but by longstanding custom such opinions are presumed binding as to the actions of agencies and/or officials. Regarding the impact of such opinions on an individual's rights, the Court of Appeals has stated what appears the rule nationally, namely, that opinions of the Attorney General may be persuasive but are in no way binding authority and do not have the effect of court decisions. Whaley v. Holly Hills Memorial Park, 490 S.W.2d 532 (Tenn. App. 1972) *cert. denied.*

In declaratory judgment actions assailing the constitutionality of a statute, the Attorney General must be "served with a copy of the proceeding and be entitled to be heard." T.C.A. §23-1107 and Tenn. R. Civ. P. 24.04. This provision was designed to afford the Attorney General opportunity to argue on behalf of the validity of the challenged act. However, the Attorney General is sometimes placed in an awkward position when called to defend an act which he has previously opined was unconstitutional. Such was his predicament in the landmark case of Cummings v. Beeler, 189 Tenn. 151, 223 S.W.2d 193 (1949), which upheld an act calling for a limited constitutional convention. Language in two recent cases seems to offer guidance in this situation. Initially, the Attorney General seems to be on the same plane as other subordinate state officials or agencies (*e.g.*, State Board of Claims) in that he lacks standing to challenge the constitutionality of an act unless personally affected thereby. Norman v. State Board of Claims, 533 S.W.2d 719 (Tenn. 1975); Z. D. Atkins, et al. v. Middle Tennessee Utility District, unpublished opinion, Tennessee Supreme Court at Nashville. June 14, 1975. In its opinion on a petition to rehear in the Atkins case, the court observed that the Attorney General is not required to defend the constitutionality of a statute in all circumstances, but if he chooses not to, the Attorney General should afford the Governor the opportunity to employ special counsel to do so.

Unpublished opinions probably have the same efficacy as published ones and are filed by T.C.A. title and section numbers. Single copies are available upon request. Moreover, a large quantity of unpublished opinions for the years 1933 to 1972 remain in the archival files of the Attorney General's office in the custody of the State Library and Archives. These records (but not the opinions themselves) are catalogued by year, subject matter, and case.

Prior to 1971, only sporadic attempts were made to publish the opinions of the Attorney General. These opinions, like unpublished ones, may be of some interest to researchers. These are:

Year	Title	Attorney General	Paging
1875	Opinion of Attorney General J. B. Heiskell, 1875	J. B. Heiskell	4 p.
1899-1912	Opinions of the Attorney General	George W. Pickle Charles T. Cates	Bound letter-file, in State Archives, 133 p.
1902-1914	Index-Digest of the Opinions of the Attorney General rendered to the Comptroller from September 1902, to June 1914. Made by Robert T. Shannon for Comptroller George P. Woollen. Nashville: McQuiddy Printing Co., 1914	Charles T. Cates Frank M. Thompson	96 p.
1926-1930	Opinions of the Attorney-General of Tennessee from September, 1926 to December, 1930. (Contains "History of Attorney-General's Office" p. ix-xix)	L. D. Smith History p. ix-xix Opinions p. 1-1479 Index p. 1481-1581	xix, 1581 p.
1930-1931	Opinions of the Attorney-General of Tennessee, from October 1, 1930 to September 30, 1931.	L. D. Smith Opinions p. 1-763 Index p. 765-805	805 p.
1931	Employment and contract between members of the legislature and the State	L. D. Smith	32 p.
1931	Peddlers tax	L. D. Smith	11 p.
1932	Opinions of the Attorney-General, State of Tennessee, 1932 Revenue Bill, Volume I. Compiled by Roy C. Wallace, Comptroller of the Treasury.	L. D. Smith	124 p.
1946	Right of the Legislature to Call a Limited Constitutional Convention, Opinion of the Attorney General of Tennessee to the Constitutional Revision Commission. Roy H. Beeler, Attorney General, May 16, 1946.	Roy H. Beeler	27 p.

The opinions are now published in:

1971-	Opinions of the Attorney General of Tennessee. Nashville: Attorney General, 1971- (five loose-leaf volumes to date). Issued monthly, indexed, with cumulative annual index.		

Since 1975 the office of the Attorney General has made available to the bar an index of recent opinions in a newsletter called Abstract. See section 432(a).

See section 845 for city attorney opinions.

Section 740   PUBLIC DOCUMENTS, 1836-1954

Between 1836-1917 a variety of acts, usually the general appropriations act, required that reports of all agency heads be filed with the Governor at least biennially. These reports are readily available today because the practice was to attach them as the Appendix to the House and/or Senate journals. The reports are an important source of valuable descriptive and statistical information about the state. They contain regular reports from public officials such as the Governor, the Secretary of State, the Comptroller, and the Treasurer. Also included are an extraordinary number of reports regarding other matters, *e.g.*, the penitentiary, state-chartered banks, educational institutions, and a host of special General Assembly reports that deal with matters as diverse as state boundary-line disputes, attempted impeachments, and the statue of Andrew Jackson.

Many of these reports are annual reports but they were published at least biennially from 1836 to 1917 except for the years 1861-1864 and 1901. Prior to 1836 such reports were incorporated in the text of the House and Senate journals. Some reports of this nature have been so included since then but the great bulk, especially for the years 1836 to 1917, were placed in the Appendixes. Moreover, most *important* state documents for the period 1796 to 1907 are included in the monumental Messages of the Governors of Tennessee, 1796-1907.

The index to these reports remains unpublished. It is: *Analysis of Tennessee Collected Public Documents, 1836-1917*. Nashville: State Library and Archives, Library Division, 1960. 145 pp. An earlier index describing the somewhat incomplete holdings of the University of Tennessee, Knoxville, Library is: Frances Gass, Eleanor Goehring, Mary L. Ogden, comp. *Guide to Reports of State Departments and Institutions Found in the Appendix Volumes of Tennessee House and Senate Journals.* Knoxville: University of Tennessee Library (unpublished typescript), 1936. 26 pp.

Research has failed to discover a master list or index of state publications for the period 1918 to 1953. However, such a list/index is available for the years 1900 to 1938 in the thesis prepared in 1940 by the well-known Tennessee librarian Frances Cheney. It is: Cheney, *Historical and Biographical Study of the Administrative Departments of the State of Tennessee*. June 1940. (unpublished thesis, Columbia University Library.) For titles of reports and documents published between 1938 and 1955, the researcher may be able to find such information in Harbison and Tilley, Index to Information Available from State Agencies. Nashville: State Planning Commission, 1955.

Section 742   PUBLIC DOCUMENTS, 1954-

At the request of the Secretary of State, the officer in charge of each agency publishing a report or document must transmit at least two copies of such publication to each of the state depository libraries, namely, the State Library and Arch-ives, the University of Tennessee, Knoxville Library, the Memphis Public Library and Information Center, and the Memphis State University Library. T.C.A. §§12-607 to -612. For a list of research libraries generally, see section 970. For list(s) of current state publications, see section 744.

Section 744   LIST OF TENNESSEE STATE PUBLICATIONS

Although there is presently no cumulative list or index of state publications, a highly useful document for gaining access to state-published materials is A List of Tennessee State Publications. 1954-. An annual publication of the State Library and Archives, it records, by agency, the titles of publications of state agencies and institutions that are "issued for publication" and are received by the Library during the ensuing year. It has been published annually since 1954 except for 1965 and 1966 and copies are available from the Library and Archives.

Another list of such documents is: U. S. Library of Congress, Processing Department: *Monthly Checklist of State Publications.* Washington: G.P.O., 1910- (monthly). This is a record of state documents issued during the last five years which are currently received by the Library of Congress from the states. Monographs and periodical publications are listed. The Checklist is indexed annually.

The 1975 General Assembly established a state publications committee with power to regulate the publishing of state agency reports, especially those printed at facilities not operated by the state. The committee is charged with maintaining a master index of all state publications that is to include the name of the publication, issuing department, number of copies printed, a general list of distribution, and estimated cost of printing and distribution. Ch. 694 [1976] Tenn. Pub. Acts 700.

Section 750   SERVICES AND HOLDINGS OF THE STATE LIBRARY AND ARCHIVES

The State Library and Archives located at 403 Seventh Avenue North, Nashville, is a premier resource for legal research, especially primary documentation such as manuscripts, land records, and state agency records. Its services and holdings are described in: *The State Library and Archives, An Introduction* (pamphlet) Nashville: State Library and Archives, 1975.

The Library. The official State Library, its quarter-million volumes emphasize history, political science and law, all of which are highly useful to researchers. The book collection is well catalogued and a researcher is ably served by the capable staff. In addition to the book collection, the Library has a collection of Tennessee newspapers covering some two hundred cities. See, *A Cumulative List of Microfilmed Tennessee Newspapers in the Tennessee State Library and Archives.* Nashville: State Library and Archives, 1969.

State Archives. The Archives section preserves public and private records important to Tennessee. These include:
1)   Legislative recordings (see section 338);
2)   Transcripts or microfilms of county records;
3)   Bills, memorials, petitions to the General Assembly;
4)   Land records, usually indexed. These are: a) North Carolina Grants, 1783-1800, b) Tennessee Grants, 1806-1927, c) Hiwassee and Ocoee Districts, d) Survey certificates.

Important manuscripts are in the custody of the Manuscripts Section which is attempting to microfilm its holdings. Two important tools aid the researcher in locating manuscripts. These are: Bauch, ed. *Guide to the Microfilm Holdings of the Manuscripts Section, Tennessee State Library and Archives.* 2nd ed. Nashville: Library and Archives, 1975. Owsley, *Guide to the Processed Manuscripts of the Tennessee Historical Society.* Nashville: Library and Archives, 1969. See generally, *Manuscripts in the Tennessee State Library and Archives.* (pamphlet) Nashville: Library and Archives, 1975; *Land Records in the Tennessee State Library and Archives,* 1975.

Records Management Section. The records management section of the Department of Finance and Administration, in conjunction with the State Library and Archives and the Public Records Commission, is responsible for the processing, preservation and/or disposal of contemporary state and county public records. Generally, these records remain under the jurisdiction of the agency that produced them and access is subject to agency specified restrictions. Permission must usually be obtained from the appropriate agency before third parties may have access to such records. There is no generally available masterlist of such records now in storage and/or being microfilmed. However, the section has published a Records Disposition Manual which is kept current. This manual is designed to guide agencies in their recordkeeping duties and provides an indirect method of learning the nature of available records. See also, T.C.A. §§15-304 to -307; 15-401 to -406; 15-501 to -513, and appropriate regulations regarding disposition and access to public records generally.

Section 752   SERVICES AND PUBLICATIONS OF STATE PLANNING OFFICE

The State Planning Office (formerly Commission) provides analyses of regional planning problems, prepares a comprehensive state plan, and receives other plans produced in the state. The local planning division provides technical assistance to counties and municipalities through studies and draftsmanship of such items as land use plans, subdivisions and zoning regulations or ordinances.

Of special usefulness to legal researchers is the Office's library located in room 660 Capitol Hill Building, 301 7th Avenue N., Nashville, 37219, that is open to the public. Its collection, including Planning Office publications and other agency publications, reflects the comprehensive nature of planning. The library publishes a monthly acquisitions list and has issued bibliographies of Planning Commission studies. The latest is Publications of the Tennessee State Planning Commission, 1950-1968. 75 p. A sample of the Office's publications include:

1. *Land Use Mapping in Tennessee.* 1974.
2. *Directory of State Statistics for Local Areas in Tennessee: A Guide to Sources.* 1970.
3. *State Financial Assistance to Local Governments.* 1973.
4. *Tennessee State Government: Policy Development and Implementation.* 1970.

Section 754 PUBLICATIONS OF THE COMPTROLLER

The Office of the Comptroller performs a variety of service functions for the state generally or for the General Assembly, usually of an auditing or financial nature. One of its divisions, the Office of Local Government, seeks to coordinate activities and services between state agencies and local government.[14] In recent years this office has prepared descriptive studies of agencies of local government which provide excellent background for the legal researcher. These are:

1. *State of Tennessee Local Government Bond Laws,* 2nd ed., 1975.
2. *The County Assessor of Property in Tennessee.* 1975.
3. *The County Board of Equalization in Tennessee.* 1975.
4. *The Office of the Tennessee County Judge and Chairman of the County Court.* 2nd ed., 1974.
5. *The Office of the County Trustee in Tennessee.* 2nd ed., 1974.

14. *See,* J. SMITH, THE OFFICE OF LOCAL GOVERNMENT: ITS FUNCTIONS AND ORGANIZATION. (1975).

6. *The Office of the County Sheriff in Tennessee.* 2nd ed., 1974.
7. *The Quarterly County Court in Tennessee.* 3rd ed., 1974.
8. *The Office of the County Register in Tennessee.* 2nd ed., 1975.
9. *The Offices of the County Medical Examiner and County Coroner in Tennessee.* 2nd ed., 1974.
10. *The Office of the County Court Clerk in Tennessee.* 2nd ed., 1974.
11. *Search Warrants in Tennessee.* 1973.
12. *Clerks of Courts in Tennessee.* 2nd ed. 1973.
13. *Succession to Vacancies in County Offices.* 1973.
14. *County Officials Surety Bond Laws.* 1972.

Section 756   REPORTS OF THE PUBLIC SERVICE COMMISSION

The Public Service Commission has, since 1955, published an annual report. From 1879 until that date its reports were biennial and issued by predecessor commissions variously called the Railroad Commission (which derived from the office of "Road Commission" created in 1858) and the Railroad and Public Utilities Commission, 1919-1955[15]. The Commission has promulgated and published rules and regulations governing public utilities, railroads, motor carriers, including practice and procedure rules and ad valorem tax assessments. *Tennessee Railroad Commission:* Reports were issued annually from 1919 through 1954 except for 1937-1944. *Public Service Commission:* An annual report has been issued since 1955. Reports are available from the Commission; copies of such reports are available at the State Library and Archives.

15. Anderson, *Tennessee's Railroad and Public Utilities Commission,* 16 TENN. L. REV. 974 (1941).

Chapter VIII

LOCAL GOVERNMENT LAW

Section 800 MUNICIPAL CORPORATIONS

Until 1953 municipalities (cities or towns) were entirely creatures of the state. That is, their governmental powers flowed from their individual charters of incorporation, granted by private state act, that could be significantly altered and even abolished by legislative enactment.[1] In 1953, the Constitution was amended to provide, among other things, that private (or local) acts required the approval of the local governing body by two-thirds vote (or majority referendum) in order to be effective.[2] Today, the vast majority of Tennessee municipalities are still governed under state charters, although there exist through the provisions of general acts (or home rule, see section 342 below) optional standard forms of municipal government. These are: mayor-council, council-manager, and commission forms.[3] The great variety in types of municipal governments found in Tennessee virtually defies any detailed description.[4]

Material in Tennessee Code Annotated concerning municipal corporations is indexed on pp. 521-557 of volume 14 (1974) of T.C.A. Private acts directly relating to cities have not been codified but were indexed in 1962, supplemented annually in Index to the Private Acts of Tennessee. Indianapolis: Bobbs-Merrill, 1962. Private acts addressed to counties usually affect

---

1. *See*, L. GREENE, D. GRUBBS, V. HOBDAY, GOVERNMENT IN TENNESSEE 189-213 (1975) for a thorough discussion of municipal government in Tennessee. [Hereinafter L. GREENE, GOVERNMENT IN TENNESSEE.]

2. For a discussion of the amendments that affected state-local relations, see Laska, *Legal and Constitutional History of Tennessee, 1772-1972*, 6 MEM. ST. U. L. REV. 661-662. [Hereinafter Laska, *Legal and Constitutional History.*]

3. These forms are provided by general law (TCA §§6-101 to -3808) and are described in three publications of the Municipal Technical Advisory Service. *Mayor-Council Charter Draft.* 1962. 38 pp.; *Tennessee Mayor-Alderman Charter.* 1970. 48 pp.; *Tennessee Uniform Commission-Manager Charter.* 1971. 58 pp.

4. L. GREENE, GOVERNMENT IN TENNESSEE at 193-198.

cities also, thus reference to the compilation of private acts by county is suggested. See section 850.

Section 810 HOME RULE AND CITY-COUNTY CONSOLIDATION

The 1953 amendments to the Constitution also provided for "home rule" for municipalities, that is, allowed for general legislation which could permit the citizens of a municipality to propose and be governed by a local charter.[5] Moreover, the 1953 amendments also provided for consolidation of city and county governments.[6] Neither of these has been utilized to a great extent but, where established, they have been successful.[7]

To date, there are only thirteen home rule municipalities although Nashville largely achieves that result through metropolitan government. The cities are: Chattanooga (1972), Clinton (1954), East Ridge (1954), Etowah (1964), Johnson City (1955), Knoxville (1954), Lenoir City (1954), Memphis (1963) Oak Ridge (1962), Red Bank (1956), Sevierville (1954), Sweetwater (1955), and Whitwell (1958). A thorough analysis of home rule government is: Hobday, Victor C. *An Analysis of the 1953 Tennessee Home Rule Amendments.* 2nd ed. Knoxville: Municipal Technical Advisory Service, 1976.

Section 820 ORDINANCES—LARGER CITIES

Municipalities may enact ordinances (including zoning plans) under the authority granted them in their charters, as amended, or, if organized under general law, derive their legislative power from that source. T.C.A. §6-202.

There is no general statutory requirement that all municipalities *codify* their ordinances, and uncodified ordinances are typically collected according to number in an ordinance book

---

5. Laska, *Legal and Constitutional History* at 662. The state's authority on home rule discusses the issue in V. HOBDAY, AN ANALYSIS OF THE 1953 TENNESSEE HOME RULE AMENDMENTS. 2d ed. 1976. [Hereinafter cited V. HOBDAY, TENN. HOME RULE AMENDMENTS.]

6. L. GREENE, GOVERNMENT IN TENNESSEE at 262.

7. *See* V. HOBDAY, TENN. HOME RULE AMENDMENTS at 73.

(or minute book) by the city recorder (or manager) of the municipality. Municipalities following the mayor-council form of government, however, must codify their ordinances at least every ten years. T.C.A. §6-213. Larger cities have been doing this for many years; codified ordinances for such municipalities are generally available. Examples are:

> *Charter, Related Private Laws, Code of Laws of Metropolitan Government of Nashville and Davidson County, Tennessee.* 2 vols. Charlottesville, Va.: Michie City Publications Co., 1967. Supplemented since 1972 by Municipal Code Corporation, Tallahassee, Florida.

> *Zoning Ordinances for Metropolitan Nashville and Davidson County, effective December 24, 1974.* Nashville: Metropolitan Planning Commission, 1974. 1 vol. looseleaf. supplemented.

> *Charter and Related Laws. Code of Ordinances. City of Memphis, Tennessee.* 3 vols. Tallahassee, Florida: Municipal Code Corporation, 1967. supplemented.

> *City Code of Chattanooga, Tennessee. Charter and General Ordinances of the City.* Tallahassee, Florida: Municipal Code Corporation, 1968. supplemented.

The Municipal Corporation Company has also published codes for these cities: Bolivar, Clarksville, Jackson, Kingsport, Knoxville, McMinnville, Mrufreesboro, Newport, Oak Ridge, Signal Mountain, Sparta, Sullivan County, Trenton, Tullahoma, Winchester. The Michie Company has published codes for: Cleveland, Johnson City, and Morristown.

Section 825   ORDINANCES—SMALLER CITIES

Ordinance codification for smaller cities has become a major project of the Municipal Technical Advisory Service which, to date, has codified and provided annual updating revisions for one hundred seven cities. Arrangements can be made with MTAS to secure individual copies. Codified ordinances have been prepared for:

Alamo	Englewood	Loudon	Ripley
Alcoa	Erin	Madisonville	Rockwood
Algood	Erwin	Manchester	Rogersville

Ardmore	Fairview	Mason	Savannah
Ashland City	Fayetteville	McEwen	Selmer
Athens	Franklin	McKenzie	Sevierville
Baxter	Gallatin	Middleton	Shelbyville
Brownsville	Germantown	Milan	Smithville
Camden	Greeneville	Minor Hill	Smyrna
Centerville	Harriman	Monteagle	Soddy Daisy
Chapel Hill	Hartsville	Monterey	Somerville
Clinton	Henderson	Moscow	South Fulton
Collegedale	Humboldt	Mt. Pleasant	South Pittsburg
Columbia	Huntland	Munford	Spring City
Cookeville	Huntingdon	New Johnsonville	Springfield
Covington	Jacksboro	New Tazewell	Spring Hill
Crossville	Jefferson City	Norris	Surgoinsville
Dandridge	Jellico	Obion	Sweetwater
Dayton	Kingston	Oliver Springs	Tennessee
Dechard	Lafayette	Onedia	Ridge
Dickson	Lafollette	Paris	Union City
Dover	Lake City	Parsons	Wartrace
Dresden	Lebanon	Petersburg	Watertown
Dyersburg	Lenoir City	Pulaski	Waverly
Dyer	Lewisburg	Red Bank	Waynesboro
East Ridge	Livingston	Ridgely	White Bluff
Etowah	Maryville	Rutherford	White Pine

Section 830   MUNICIPAL TECHNICAL ADVISORY SERVICE

Since 1952 the Municipal Technical Advisory Service, affiliated with the University of Tennessee, has provided a variety of technical, consultive and field services to municipalities in all areas of municipal administration.

MTAS has its own special library located in Knoxville and it contains more than 20,000 books and reports, including an extensive newspaper clipping file that is usually available to serious researchers but not the public generally.

Section 835   MTAS PUBLICATIONS

The Municipal Technical Advisory Service has produced an array of high quality documents and reports throughout the years. Titles may be gleaned from A List of State Publications (see section 744) and a selected list of titles in print is found in the MTAS 1974-1975 Annual Report, p. 27.

The chief MTAS publications meaningful to the legal researcher are:

1. *Directory of Tennessee Municipal Officials.* (annual)
2. *Annexation Handbook for Tennessee Cities and Towns.* 3rd ed. 1975.
3. Snoderly. *Easement Acquisition by Tennessee Cities.* 1968.
4. *Mayor-Council Charter Draft.* 1962.
5. Swanner. *Municipal Court Guide.* 1974.
6. Martin. *Registration of Motor Vehicles by Tennessee Cities.* 1962.
7. Overby. *Sample Code of Ordinances for Small Cities and Towns in Tennessee.* 1973.

The MTAS also publishes an annual booklet, Ideas for a Better City, several documents relating to fiscal administration, and since 1973, nine technical reports on subjects ranging from cable television to annexation law. All are listed in the 1974-1975 Annual Report, p. 27.

Section 840   JUDICIAL INTERPRETATION OF ORDINANCES

Tennessee city ordinances are the subject of increasing judicial interpretation. Such cases now appear as digest notes in a new indexing service, Shepard's Ordinance Law Annotations. 6 vols. Colorado Springs, Colorado: Shepard's Citations, 1969-. The cases are arranged by state and city, by case name, and by subject matter. The set is supplemented annually.

Section 845   CITY ATTORNEY OPINIONS

Opinions of city attorneys are unpublished but individual

opinions are usually made available upon request. Nashville has a systematic compilation. It is: *Opinions of the Department of Law. Metropolitan Government of Nashville and Davidson County, Tennessee.* Tallahassee, Florida: Municipal Code Corporation, 1971. 2 vols. supplemented.

Section 850   COUNTY GOVERNMENT

County government, like municipal government, is a creature of state law—only to an even greater degree.[8] Its general features are outlined in the Constitution, Article VII, sections 1, 2, 4; Article X, sections 4, 5; Article XI, sections 9, 17; described generally by public law (see pp. 1-175 of volume 2A (1971) of T.C.A.); and embellished by private acts.

Private acts, which not only affect the governmental system (*e.g.*, describe the jurisdiction of courts), but also set substantive law, are still very important although their influence (and quantity) has waned in recent years. See section 310.

The primary source for the private acts are the session laws. See section 310. More useful is the ninety-five volume compilation of private acts (collected by counties) recently published by the County Technical Assistance Service, *e.g.*, Private Acts of Shelby County. 2 parts. 1975. The compilation is arranged by subject headings, provides considerable legislative history of each county's private acts, and will be updated and revised by CTAS. Another tool for access to private acts is Index to the Private Acts of Tennessee. Indianapolis: Bobbs-Merrill, 1962. Supplemented. See sections 310, 640(c) and 800.

Section 860   COUNTY LEGISLATIVE-ADMINISTRATIVE ACTIVITIES

The official county legislative-administrative body, generally

---

8. County government is described in L. GREENE, GOVERNMENT IN TENNESSEE at 226-245. Two other studies provide much good descriptive information. Jack E. Holmes, Walter N. Lambert, Nelson M. Robinson, *The Structure of County Government in Tennessee.* Nashville: Legislative Council Committee, 1966. Barrett R. Joyner and James M. Smith, *County Government in Tennessee.* Nashville: Comptroller of the Treasury, 1976.

called the county quarterly court, is an instrumentality of state government and derives all of its powers from the above-described state laws.[9] T.C.A. §5-528. Although recent years have seen an increase in the activities performed by counties as they take on the duties performed by urban services districts, the actual legislative power of the county quarterly court is minimal. It is concerned largely with fiscal matters, that is, making appropriations to carry out the county's responsibilities, chiefly in the areas of education, highways, and welfare. T.C.A. §5-901.

The county quarterly court's activities and resolutions are typically entered in memorandum form in the court's minutes, kept by the county court clerk. Most counties have at least a crude subject matter index of their court's minutes, and the resolution documents are usually kept on file by the clerk also. Under state law all such records must be made available for public inspection. T.C.A. §15-304.

Section 870   COUNTY TECHNICAL ASSISTANCE SERVICE

Established in 1973, the County Technical Assistance Service, affiliated with the University of Tennessee, provides the same technical and consultative services to counties as MTAS provides to municipalities

The organization has published several documents useful to legal researchers, the most notable is its compilation of private acts by county (see section 850). Other meaningful publications include:

1. Rizor. *Probate Manual for County Judges and County Court Clerks.* 1975. 76 pp.
2. *Directory of Tennessee County Officials.* (annual)
3. *Boards, Committees, and Commissions of County Government in Tennessee.* 1975. 120 pp.
4. *The Local Sales Tax—Handbook for Local Officials.* 1976. 11 pp.

The CTAS has also produced a series of nine shorter technical reports, *e.g.,* Election Campaigns for County Offices: Dis-

---

9. The functions of the court are described in Holmes, et al., *Structure of County Government, supra* note 8, at 71-88.

closure Statements, Technical Report No. 8 (1976). It anticipates publishing a newsletter in the near future.

Chapter IX

LOOSE-LEAF SERVICES, TREATISES, PERIODICALS AND MISCELLANEOUS PUBLICATIONS

Section 900   LOOSE-LEAF SERVICES

The legal researcher's need for a topical collection and explanation of the law on a given *subject*, especially a collection that is current, has led to development of loose-leaf services. Arranged in binders so that new material (which may appear weekly, bi-weekly or monthly) can be inserted easily, these services include all relevant types of law: statutes, decisions, agency regulations. Information is organized by paragraph numbers rather than official references. This requires the researcher to make careful use of the index and/or "finding aids" provided with each service. For example, Prentice Hall's Federal Taxes contains a single volume general index; other volumes in the set, *e.g.*, Estate & Gift Taxes often include a separate index, cross reference tables, case and ruling tables.

Loose-leaf services follow a similar format but each has special features so the researcher should first consult the "How to Use this Service" instructions in the front of each service.

The leading publishers of loose-leaf services are the Bureau of National Affairs (BNA), Commerce Clearing House, Inc. (CCH), and Prentice—Hall, Inc. (P-H). Shown below is a list of the more important of these services; those specifically including Tennessee-related material are indicated with an asterisk.

Blue Sky Reporter (CCH)
Consumer and Commercial Credit Service (P-H)
Consumer Credit Guide (CCH)*
Corporation Law Guide (CCH)*
Environment Reporter (BNA)*
Family Law Reporter (BNA)
Food, Drug and Cosmetic Reporter (CCH)
Government Employees Relations Report (BNA)
Labor Law Reporter, (State Laws) (CCH)*
Labor Relations Reporter (BNA)*
Products Liability Reporter (CCH)

Professional Corporations Guide (P-H)*
Secured Transactions Guide (CCH)*
Securities Regulation Service (P-H)
State and Local Taxes (Tennessee) (P-H)
State Tax Reporter (Tennessee) (CCH)*
State Tax Guide (P-H)*
Trade Regulation Reporter (CCH)*
Unemployment Insurance Reporter (CCH)*

Special mention should be made of an important loose-leaf service that reports up-to-date actions of the United States Supreme Court and important decisions/actions of federal courts and agencies, United States Law Week (BNA).

Section 910   FORM BOOKS

Many of the treatises described throughout this book include forms useful to the legal researcher-draftsperson, *e.g.*, Gibson's Suits in Chancery. Another source of forms is the loose-leaf services, especially those that deal with tax, securities, and commercial law. Further, multi-volume treatises often contain forms and special multi-volume form books are now available, *e.g.*, Modern Legal Forms. West Publishing Co., 1938-, and Rabkin and Johnson, Current Legal Forms, with Tax Analysis. Matthew Bender, 1948-. All of these sources are appropriate for Tennessee lawyers when used carefully.

Tennessee has been served by a form book from the earliest time. The most recent offering, devoted solely to civil procedure forms, is by Professor Bigham, described in section 540. For over a quarter century the bar has utilized an important form book. It is:

> Gore, Thomas P. *Gore's Forms for Tennessee, Annotated*, 3rd ed. Charlottesville, Va.: Michie Company, 1970. 4 vols.

Recent years have seen the appearance of three more excellent Tennessee law-related form books. These are:

> Watson, Robert H., Jr. comp. *The University of Tennessee Legal Clinic's Handbook of Forms.* rev. 1974. Knoxville: University of Tennessee Legal Clinic, 1974. 218 pp.

Cooper, Gary A. *Tennessee Forms for Trial Practice.* Norcross, Georgia: Harrison Co., 1977. Able commentary and well-chosen forms make this an outstanding one-volume trial practice form book.

Summers, Jerald H., comp. *TTLA Office Form Manual and Procedures.* Nashville: Tennessee Trial Lawyers Association, 1974.

Section 920 TREATISES AND PRACTICE AIDS

A treatise is a text written by a scholar that usually covers only one area of substantive law (*i.e.*, contracts, constitutional law) and/or provides an overview of the law generally, or examines a type of law practice (*i.e.*, chancery practice). These latter books/materials may sometimes be referred to as "practice aids," especially when their scholarly level is not high.

Multi-volume treatises of wide circulation such as Williston on Contracts or Davis on Administrative Law occupy an important place in legal research, and their appearance has largely preempted the need for such books written with a Tennessee perspective. Local books were important in Tennessee in the 19th century; foremost among these was Caruthers' History of a Lawsuit and Gibson's Suits in Chancery. See section 510. Moreover, good books of this type are still an asset to the contemporary legal researcher. Earlier sections of this handbook described such offerings concurrent with the discussion of the court system and court rules/substantive law. See sections 572, 574, 576, 578.

The following is a list of treatises, local and national in scope, that should be useful to the Tennessee researcher. This list is not exhaustive and books helpful for locating other sources are listed in section 930.

Accounting:

Sellin, Henry. *Attorney's Handbook of Accounting.* New York: Matthew Bender, 1971.

Administrative Law: See chapter VII.

Cooper, Frank E. *State Administrative Law*. Indianapolis: Bobbs-Merrill, 1965. 2 vols.

Davis, Kenneth C. *Administrative Law Treatise*. St. Paul, Minn.: West Publishing Co., 1958. 4 vols. supplemented.

Agency:

Seavey, Warren A. *Handbook of the Law of Agency*. St. Paul, Minn.: West Publishing Co., 1964.

Automobiles:

Blashfield, Dewitt C. *Automobile Law and Practice*. (Frederick D. Lewis, ed.) St. Paul, Minn.: West Publishing Co., 1965. 17 vols. supplemented.

Bankruptcy: See section 580.

Civil Procedure: See chapter V.

Commercial Law: See Uniform Commercial Code.

Constitutional Law: See sections 170, 180.

Tennessee Code Annotated, Vol. 1 (for United States Constitution).

United States Constitution. *The Constitution of the United States of America, Analysis and Interpretation*. Washington, D.C.: U.S. Government Printing Office, 1973. Supplement.

Contracts:

Williston, Samuel. *Treatise on the Law of Contracts*. 3rd ed. (Walter H.E. Jaeger, ed.) Mount Kisco, N.Y.: Baker, Voorhis and Co., Inc., 1957-1969. 15 vols. supplemented.

Copyright: See Patent, Copyright and Trademark.

Corporations:

Tennessee does not have a modern treatise on corporate law, but the need for one has greatly diminished since passage of the General Corporation Act of 1968. See discussion, section 250, under "Business Corporation Act."

Today, the researcher should consult the national treatises, for example:

American Bar Foundation. *Model Business Corporation Act Annotated*. 2d ed. St. Paul, Minn.: West Publishing Co., 1971. 3 vols. supplemented.

Cavitch, Zolman. *Business Organizations with Tax Planning.* New York: Matthew Bender, 1968-, looseleaf.

Fletcher, William. *Cyclopedia of the Law of Private Corporations.* Chicago, Ill.: Callaghan and Co., 1933-1957. 27 vols. supplemented.

Henn, Harry G. *Handbook of the Law of Corporations and Other Business Enterprises.* 2nd ed. St. Paul, Minn.: West Publishing Co., 1970.

Israels, Carlos L. *Corporate Practice.* 3rd ed. New York: Practicing Law Institute, 1974.

O'Neal, F. Hodge. *Close Corporations.* Chicago, Ill.: Callaghan and Co., 1971. 2 vols. loose-leaf.

O'Neal, F. Hodge. *Oppression of Minority Shareholders.* Chicago, Ill.: Callaghan and Co., 1975.

Pantzer, Kurt F. and Richard E. Dear. *Drafting of Corporate Charters and Bylaws.* 2nd ed. Philadelphia, Pa.: Joint Committee on Continuing Legal Education, ALI/ABA, 1968.

Rohrlich, Chester. *Organizing Corporate and Other Business Enterprises.* 5th ed. New York: Matthew Bender, 1975. loose-leaf.

Older treatises on Tennessee corporation law (now obsolete) may still be useful in explaining the common law tradition and early statutory development of corporate law, which included *municipal* corporations.

Vartanian, P.H. *The Law of Corporations in Tennessee.* Charlottesville, Va.: Michie Company, 1929.

Watts, James L. *Corporation Laws of Tennessee.* Nashville: Marshall & Bruce, 1907.

Creditors' Rights:

Lincoln, J. William, et al. *Creditors' Rights and Remedies.* Knoxville: Univ. of Tenn., College of Law, Continuing Education, 1976.

Criminal Law: See section 550.

Perkins, Rollin M. *Criminal Law.* 2d ed. Mineola, N.Y.: Foundation Press, 1969.

Wharton, Francis. *Wharton's Criminal Evidence.* 13th ed. (Charles E. Torcia, ed.) Rochester, N.Y.: Lawyer's

Co-op. 1972. 4 vols. supplemented.

Wharton, Francis. *Wharton's Criminal Procedure*. 12th ed. (Charles E. Torcia, ed.) N.Y.: Lawyer's Co-op., 1976. 4 vols. supplemented.

Divorce: See Family Law; see also section 572.

Education:

Hughes, Larry W. and Robert J. Simpson, eds. *Education and the Law in Tennessee*. Cincinnati: W. H. Anderson, 1971.

Elections:

Working with the Tennessee Election Code—an Instruction Manual. Nashville: University of Tennessee, Center for Government Training, 1973.

Equity: See section 510 for Tennessee treatises.

National treatises include:

Pomeroy, John. *A Treatise on Equity Jurisprudence as Administered in the United States of America*. 5th ed. (Spencer W. Symons, ed.) San Francisco, Calif.: Bancroft-Whitney, 1941. 5 vols.

Estate Planning: See Wills and Estate Administration.

Evidence:

An important new treatise on evidence authored by Professor Paine has recently appeared. It is:

Paine, Donald F. *Tennessee Law of Evidence*. Indianapolis: Bobbs-Merrill, 1974. supplemented. This work supersedes an earlier treatise: Lee, Oscar O. *Tennessee Evidence*. Charlottesville, Va.: Michie Company, 1949.

Jones, Burr. *Jones on Evidence, Civil and Criminal*. 6th ed. (Spencer A. Gard, ed.) Rochester, N.Y.: Lawyers Co-op., 1972. 4 vols. supplemented.

McCormick, Charles T. *Evidence*. 2nd ed. St. Paul, Minn.: West Publishing Co., 1972.

Family Law: See section 572 for Tennessee materials.

Clark, Homer. *The Law of Domestic Relations*. St. Paul, Minn.: West Publishing Co., 1968.

Nelson, William T. *Divorce and Annulment with Selected Forms*. 2nd ed. (James M. Henderson, ed.) Chicago: Callaghan and Co., 1961. 4 vols. supplemented.

Federal Practice and Procedure: See section 580.

General Sessions Courts: See sections 422 and 578.

Insurance:

> Couch, George. *Cyclopedia of Insurance Law.* 2nd ed. (Ronald Anderson, ed.) Rochester, N.Y.: Lawyer's Co-op. 1959-1969. 24 vols. supplemented.

Juvenile Law including Adoption: See sections 424, 572, and 576.

Jury Instructions:

A special commission was appointed by the Supreme Court in 1973 to draft model or pattern jury instructions, both civil and criminal. Its work is expected to be published by West Publishing Company sometime in 1977.

Other present offerings include:

> Smith, Wallace J. *Tennessee Jury Instructions: Civil and Criminal Cases.* 2 vols. Charlottesville, Va.: Michie Company, 1963. 1970 supplement, civil volume.

Labor Law: See section 900.

> Forkosch, Morris. *A Treatise on Labor Law.* 2nd ed. Indianapolis, Ind.: Bobbs-Merrill, 1965.

> Kheel, Theodore. *Business Organizations: Labor Law.* New York: Matthew Bender, 1972. 8 vols. looseleaf.

Legal Ethics: See section 530.

> American Bar Association. Committee on Ethics and Professional Responsibility. *Formal and Informal Opinions.* Chicago: American Bar Association, 1975. looseleaf. See also, *Informal Ethics Opinions.*

Municipal Law: See sections 820, 825; see also Corporations.

> Antieau, Chester. *Municipal Corporation Law.* New York: Matthew Bender, 1955. 5 vols. looseleaf.

> McQuillin, Eugene. *The Law of Municipal Corporations.* 3rd ed. (Clark Nichols, ed.) Chicago, Ill.: Callaghan and Co., 1949-1965. 21 vols. supplemented.

Patent, Trademark and Copyright:

> Costner, Thomas and Harold Einhorn. *Business Organizations: Patent Licensing Transactions.* New York: Matthew Bender, 1968. 2 vols. looseleaf.

> Nimmer, Melville. *Nimmer on Copyright: A Treatise on*

the Law of Literary, Musical and Artistic Property and Protection of Ideas. New York: Matthew Bender, 1975. 2 vols. looseleaf.

Products Liability:

Hursh, Robert D. and Henry J. Bailey. *American Law of Products Liability.* 2nd ed. Rochester, N. Y.: Lawyers Co-op., 1975-1976. 6 vols.

Property, including Future Interests, Leases and Zoning:

Four sources are helpful in researching Tennessee law; these are:

Gore, Thomas P. *Gore on Real Property and Abstracting (with forms).* Charlottesville, Va.: Michie Company, 1939.

Griffith, Charles E. and Ogden Stokes. *Eminent Domain in Tennessee.* Knoxville: Institute for Public Service, University of Tennessee, 1972.

_____, *Collection of Delinquent Real Property Ad Valorem Taxes.* Knoxville: Institute for Public Service, University of Tennessee, 1973.

Institute for Practicing Lawyers on Real Property. Memphis: Memphis and Shelby County Bar Association, 1963. 1 vol. transcript.

National treatises include:

Casner, A. James. *American Law of Property.* Boston, Mass.: Little, Brown & Co., 1952. 7 vols. supplemented.

Friedman, Milton R. *Friedman on Leases.* 2 vols. New York: Practising Law Institute, 1974. supplemented.

Powell, Richard R. and Patrick J. Rohan. *Powell on Real Property.* New York: Matthew Bender, 1968. 7 vols. looseleaf.

Rohan, Patrick J. and Melvin Reskin. *Real Estate Transactions.* New York: Matthew Bender, 1976. 10 vols. looseleaf.

Rose, Jerome G. *Landlords and Tenants.* New Brunswick, New Jersey: Transaction Books, 1973.

Simes, Lewis M. *Handbook on the Law of Future Interests.* 2nd ed. St. Paul, Minn.: West Publishing Co., 1966.

Yokeley, Emmet C. *Zoning Law and Practice.* 3rd ed. Charlottesville, Va.: Michie Company, 1965. 4 vols.

supplemented.

Securities:

Loss, Louis, *Securities Regulation.* 2nd ed. Boston, Mass.: Little, Brown and Co., 1961. 6 vols. supplemented.

Statutory Construction: See section 315.

Taxation, Business:

Bittker, Boris L. and James Eustice. *Federal Income Taxation of Corporations and Shareholders.* 3rd ed. Boston, Mass.: Warren, Gorham and Lamont, 1971. supplemented.

Ness, Theodore and Eugene Vogel. *Taxation of the Closely Held Corporation.* New York: Ronald Press, 1972.

Willis, Arthur B. *Partnership Taxation.* New York: McGraw-Hill, 1971.

Taxation, Estate and Gift:

Kahn, Douglas A. and Earl M. Colson. *Federal Taxation of Estates, Gifts and Trusts.* 2nd ed. Philadelphia, Penn.: American Law Institute, 1975.

Harris, Homer. *Handling Federal Estate and Gift Taxes.* rev. ed. (Joseph Rasch, ed.) Rochester, N.Y.: Lawyers Co-op., 1972. supplemented.

Taxation, Income:

Chommie, John E. *The Law of Federal Income Taxation.* 2nd ed. St. Paul, Minn.: West Publishing Co., 1973.

Mertens, Jacob. *The Law of Federal Income Taxation.* Chicago, Ill.: Callaghan and Co., 1942. 22 vols. looseleaf.

Ratkin, Jacob and Mark Johnson. *Federal Income, Gift and Estate Taxation.* New York: Matthew Bender, 1942. 16 vols. looseleaf.

Torts: See also *Products Liability.*

Louisell, David and Harold Williams, *Medical Malpractice.* New York: Matthew Bender, 1960. 2 vols. looseleaf.

Prosser, William L. *Handbook of the Law of Torts.* 4th ed. St. Paul, Minn.: West Publishing Co., 1971.

Trial Practice:

Hunter, Robert S. *Federal Trial Handbook.* Rochester, New York: Lawyer's Co-op., 1974.

Schweitzer, Sydney C. *Cyclopedia of Trial Procedure.* 2nd ed. Rochester, N.Y.: Lawyers Co-op., 1970. 10 vols. supplemented.

Trusts:

Bogert, George G. *The Law of Trusts and Trustees.* 2nd ed. St. Paul, Minn.: West Publishing Co., 1965.

Uniform Commercial Code:

Tennessee does not have a localized treatise on the U.C.C.; but see a collection of forms and commentary by Bigham and White:

Tennessee Practice. Vols. 1 & 2 (Uniform Commercial Code-Forms). St. Paul: West Publishing Co., 1967. supplemented.

Other nationwide treatises or reporting services include:

Anderson, Ronald A. *Anderson on the Uniform Commercial Code.* 2nd ed. Rochester, N.Y.: Lawyers Co-op., 1970. 4 vols. cumulative supplement.

Bender's Uniform Commercial Code Services. New York: Matthew Bender, 1967-. 20 vols. supplemented.

Ezer, Mitchel J. *Uniform Commercial Code Bibliography.* Philadelphia: ALI-ABA Joint Committee on Continuing Legal Education, 1972. supplemented.

Nordstrom, Robert J. *Handbook of the Law of Sales.* St. Paul, Minn.: West Publishing Co., 1970.

White, James J. and Robert S. Summers. *Handbook of the Uniform Commercial Code.* St. Paul, Minn.: West Publishing Co., 1972.

Williston, Samuel. *Williston on Sales.* 4th ed. (A. Squillante & J. Fonseca, eds.) Rochester, N.Y.: Lawyers Co-op., 1973. 3 vols. supplemented.

Wills and Estate Administration: See section 574.

Other Tennessee sources include:

Bigham, W. Harold, ed. *Tennessee Will Manual Service.* Louisville, Ky.: Blakemore & Gathright, 1964. 1 vol. looseleaf. supplemented. This book is provided as a service to the Tennessee bar by certain Tennessee banks, *e.g.,* Third National Bank (Nashville) and First National Bank of Memphis.

Rizor, David. *Probate Manual for County Judges and County Court Clerks in Tennessee.* Nashville: County Technical Assistance Service, 1975.

National treatises include:

Casner, A. James. *Estate Planning.* 3rd ed. Boston: Little, Brown & Co., 1961. 2 vols. cumulative supplement, 1975.

Page, William H., William J. Bowe and Douglas H. Parker, *Page on the Law of Wills.* Cincinnati, Ohio: W. H. Anderson Co., 1960. 9 vols. supplemented.

Workmen's Compensation:

Stone, S. C. and R. R. Williams. *Tennessee Workmen's Compensation—With Forms.* Charlottesville, Va.: Michie Company, 1957. supplemented in 1965.

Larson, Arthur. *The Law of Workmen's Compensation.* New York: Matthew Bender, 1952. 7 vols. looseleaf.

Other Law-Related Texts:

McSweeney, E. *Tennessee Personal Injury Fact Digest.* Nashville: Fact Digest Co., 1949. Obsolete.

The Law of Automobiles in Tennessee. 1938 edition. Charlottesville, Va.: Michie Company, 1938. 728 pp. Supplemented through 1944. Now obsolete. Successor to Vartanian, P. H. *The Law of Automobiles in Tennessee.* 1929.

McSweeney, E. *Tennessee Automobile Fact Digest.* Nashville: American Rule Co., 1940. 53 pp. Supplemented through 1944. Obsolete.

Tennessee Women and the Law. Nashville: Vanderbilt Women Law Students Association, rev. 1976.

Kain, William C. *The Constable's Guide, with Forms.* Knoxville: Jesse A. Rayl, 1859.

————. *The Tennessee Justice and Legal Advisor: A Compendium of the Law for the Use of Business Men and Magistrates in Tennessee.* rev. ed. Nashville: R. H. Howell, 1883.

————. *The Tennessee Officer: A Practical Treatise on the Powers, Duties, Rights and Liabilities of Officers in the State of Tennessee.* Knoxville: Ogden Brothers & Co., 1893.

Rogers, Jesse L. *The Magistrates Manual and Legal Advisor.*
7th rev. ed. (Ray Stuart ed.) Nashville: Marshall &
Bruce, 1942.

McGuire, G. G. W. *McGuire's Tennessee Justice: Or,
Magistrate's Guide.* Nashville: Bang, 1860.

Holman, James T. and Preston Hay: *Form Book.* Nashville: S. Nye & Co., 1837.

Tillman, Lewis, Jr. *Legal Essays.* Knoxville: Ogden Bros.,
1878.

Rooker, George F. *The Courts of Davidson County.* rev.
ed. Nashville: Circuit Court Clerk, 1975.

Higgins, Joseph C. *Essays in Jurisprudence and Allied
Subjects.* Nashville: Marshall & Bruce, 1917.

Junior Bar Conference of Memphis. *Monographs on the
Practice of Law in Tennessee.* Charlottesville, Va.:
Michie Company, 1953.

**Section 930   REFERENCE BOOKS, BIBLIOGRAPHIES
AND LEGAL WRITING BOOKS**

The most important reference books to the legal researcher
are the legal encyclopedias. These are:

American Jurisprudence, Second Series. San Francisco, Ca.:
Bancroft-Whitney, 1962-. 83 vols. supplemented. Re-
placing *American Jurisprudence.* 1936-1948. 62 vols.

Corpus Juris Secundum. Brooklyn, N.Y.: American Law
Book Co. and St. Paul, Minnesota: West Publishing
Co., 1941-. 142 vols. supplemented.

Standard legal dictionaries include:

Ballentine's Law Dictionary. 3rd ed. (William S. Anderson
ed.) Rochester, N.Y.: Lawyers Co-op. 1969.

Black's Law Dictionary. Revised 4th ed. St. Paul, Minn.:
West Publishing Co., 1968.

The legal researcher needing more extensive listings of
treatises and law-related materials by subject should consult:

Kavass, Igor I. "Guide to Law Book Selection for Establishment of Small Law Libraries or Bar Association
Libraries in Tennessee." (forthcoming) in *Tennessee*

Bar Journal.

Moody, Margaret M. and Cerul L. Ade. *Annual Legal Bibliography (Harvard Law School).* Cambridge: Harvard Law School Library, 1961- annual.

Sloane, Richard, ed. *Recommended Law Books.* Chicago: American Bar Association, Committee on Business Law Libraries, 1966. 307 pp. This book is somewhat outdated, so the researcher is cautioned to look for newer offerings in volatile fields and to consult the latest editions/revisions of those books.

Howell, Margaret A. *Bibliography of Bibliographies of Legal Materials.* 2 vols. Newark, New Jersey: The Author, 1969. (1969-1971 supplement).

Other reference books, helpful to the legal researcher include:

Cheney, Frances N. *Fundamental Reference Sources.* Chicago: American Library Association, 1971.

White, Carl M. *Sources of Information in the Social Sciences—A Guide to the Literature.* 2nd ed. Chicago: American Library Association, 1973.

Body, Alexander C. *Annotated Bibliography of Bibliographies on Selected Government Publications and Supplementary Guides to the Superintendent of Documents Classification System.* Kalamazoo, Michigan: The Author, 1967. supplements in 1968, 1970, 1972, 1974.

Scores of books describing legal research, legal writing, legal citation and style are available and are listed in:

DeVergie, Adrienne C. comp. *English for Lawyers: A Bibliography of Style Manuals and Other Writing Guides.* Austin, Texas: University of Texas, Tarlton Law Library. Legal Bibliograph Series No. 9, November, 1975.

A few of these books are:

Cohen, Morris L. *Legal Research in a Nutshell.* 3rd ed. St. Paul: West Publishing Co., 1976.

Covington, Robert N. et al. *Cases and Materials for a Course on Legal Methods.* Mineola, N.Y.: Foundation Press, 1969.

Lloyd, David. *Finding the Law; A Guide to Legal Research.*

Dobbs Ferry, N.Y.: Oceana Publications, 1974.

Pollack, Ervin H. *Fundamentals of Legal Research.* 4th ed. Mineola, N.Y.: Foundation Press, 1973.

Price, Miles O. and Harry Bitner. *Effective Legal Research.* 3rd ed. Boston, Mass.: Little, Brown and Co., 1969.

Re, Edward D. *Brief Writing and Oral Argument.* 3rd ed. Dobbs Ferry, N.Y.: Oceana Publications, 1965.

Statsky, William P. *Legal Research Writing and Analysis: Some Starting Points.* St. Paul, Minn.: West Publishing Co., 1974.

Strunk, William. *The Elements of Style*, 2nd ed. New York: Macmillan, 1972.

Texas Law Review Manual on Style. 2nd ed. Austin, Texas: Texas Law Review, Inc., 1968.

Uniform System of Citation. 12th ed. Cambridge, Mass.: The Harvard Law Review Association, 1976. Variously known as the "Bluebook" or "Whitebook," this is the standard style manual for law review writing.

Wiener, F. Bernays. *Briefing and Arguing Federal Appeals.* Washington: Bureau of National Affairs, 1967.

Section 940   RESTATEMENTS

Since 1923, a body of judges, professors and practitioners called the American Law Institute has published statements of what it perceives as the common law in a particular area. Called Restatements, these cover most major areas of the law, *e.g.*, contracts, torts, property, agency, etc., and have come to enjoy the confidence of the bench and bar as statements of persuasive authority. Much of the credit for the Restatement's acceptance accrues to the Institute's practice of naming a respected scholar as Reporter of the law for each area, and Tennessee is honored that former Vanderbilt dean John Wade occupies this position presently. Although ideally the Restatements themselves, rather than the underlying cases should be cited, the Restatements do contain references to Tennessee cases. Separate Restatements indicating Tennessee authority have not been published except for the now outdated Schermerhorn, H. B. *Restatement of Conflict of Laws, Tennessee Annotations.* St. Paul: American Law Institute Publishers, 1935. 102 pp.

Section 950   PERIODICALS

An important but sometimes underutilized resource for legal research are the legal periodicals which attempt to keep the bar abreast of legal developments and to provide insightful commentary on the law. Chief among these are the law reviews. These are student edited journals that are published by the state's three accredited law schools. The state's legal periodicals are:

The Daily News. Published weekdays at 193 Jefferson Avenue, Memphis, Tennessee 38103. A legal newspaper, it contains notices of suits filed, land transactions, and similar legal notices.

The Docket. Published monthly by the Nashville Bar Association, V. 1, 1975-. Newsletter.

Hamilton County Herald. Published bi-weekly at 6131 Airways Boulevard, Chattanooga, Tennessee 37421. A legal newspaper, as described above.

Judicial Newsletter. Published four times annually by the Public Law Research and Service Program at the University of Tennessee, Knoxville, College of Law. V. 1, 1974-. This newsletter presents highlights of recent developments in legislation, *e.g.*, summary and analysis of Tennessee mental commitment procedures.

Memphis State University Law Review. Published four times annually by Memphis State University Law School. V. 1, 1970-. This law review is especially valuable to researchers of Tennessee law because its editorial policy aims to feature such law. The *Review* anticipates devoting an issue each year to a special topic of Tennessee law, such as the issues on the rules of civil procedure (1974) and administrative law (1976).

The Nashville Record. Published weekly at 107 Stahlman Building, Nashville, Tennessee 37201. A legal newspaper, as described above.

Race Relations Law Reporter. Published by Vanderbilt Law School from 1956 to 1968, now no longer published, this periodical played an important role in documenting the path of race-related litigation in the

United States. It was succeeded by the *Race Relations Law Survey*, published from 1969 to 1972, now no longer published. Both periodicals include cumulative indexes.

Ready for the Plaintiff. Published quarterly by the Tennessee Trial Lawyers Association, 1963-. Newsletter.

Tennessee Bar Association *Proceedings.* The proceedings of the annual meeting of the Tennessee Bar Association from 1882 through 1935 were published annually in pamphlet form by the Association. These near-forgotten *Proceedings* contain a rich storehouse of information about Tennessee law during that era, contained in bar addresses and reports. Numerous biographical sketches are included, too. An index to the *Proceedings* for the period 1882-1931 is contained in 10 TENN. L. REV. 193 (1932). The *Proceedings* were published as a part of the *Tennessee Law Review* from 1936 until 1970. Since that time the Association proceedings have been abstracted in the *Tennessee Bar Journal.*

Tennessee Bar Journal. Published quarterly by the Tennessee Bar Association. V. 1, 1965-. News items and short articles of an informal nature are published in this periodical. No cumulative index.

Tennessee Lawyer. Published eight times a year by the Tennessee Bar Association. V. 1, 1952-. This newsletter alerts the members of upcoming events affecting the bench and bar.

Tennessee Law Review. Published four times annually by the University of Tennessee, Knoxville, College of Law (Tennessee Law Review Association, Inc.) V. 1, 1922-. The state's oldest law review, it contains much overlooked commentary on Tennessee law including several articles on legal history and reform. A cumulative index for volumes 1-30 (1922-1963) was published in 1967. Each volume contains its own index, a practice followed by the state's other law reviews, too. An attempt to broaden the coverage of its material has resulted in an apparent de-emphasis of Tennessee law in recent years, yet the *Review* seeks a balanced coverage through inclusion of Tennessee-related articles such as Cook's annual survey of criminal law.

Vanderbilt Journal of Transnational Law. Published four times a year by Vanderbilt University School of Law. V. 5, 1971- (formerly *Vanderbilt International* V. 1-4, 1967-1971).

Vanderbilt Law Review. Published six times annually by Vanderbilt University School of Law. V. 1, 1947-. The policy of this law review is to publish articles, notes and comments on legal developments of national importance. Accordingly, Tennessee-related subjects are published only if they meet this criteria. This was not always true, however. For the years 1953 through 1964 it made an important contribution to Tennessee legal research through publication of its *Annual Survey of Tennessee Law.* This survey, written by professors and practitioners, included detailed analysis of case developments and their background and remains useful today. The *Survey* was indexed by case and subject matter in a pamphlet index volume attached to volume 18 (1964-65). The *Review* published a cumulative index for volumes 1-10 (1974 to 1957) in volume 10 (1957), and another such index for volumes 11-20 (1957-1964) in volume 20 (1967). Another cumulative index is scheduled for 1977.

Section 960   DIRECTORIES

Over thirty directories of lawyers (called law lists) have been approved by the American Bar Association giving names of "selected" counsel who practice in specialized fields. For a current list of such directories see: "A.B.A. Approved Law Lists," *Tennessee Bar Journal* 12 (May, 1976): 33-35. Among the more notable of these is the national directory of lawyers, Martindale-Hubbell Law Directory (Summit, N.J.: Martindale—Hubbell). Published annually, names are arranged by state and city. A specialized directory for the state is the Tennessee Legal Directory (Los Angeles: Legal Directories Publishing Co., Inc.).

which appears annually. The Tennessee Bar Association published a list of members in Tennessee Bar Journal 11 (November, 1975): 7-92. The Tennessee Trial Lawyers Association publishes an annual Directory.

Section 970   SPECIAL LIBRARIES

In 1973 there were at least one hundred and eighty special libraries in Tennessee. These were affiliated with an array of organizations and institutions such as colleges, churches, businesses, chambers of commerce, hospitals, and government agencies. Some of these libraries, such as those of the State Library and Archives, the State Planning Office, and the Municipal Technical Advisory Service have been described earlier. See sections 750, 752, 830. The following libraries are a few that may be useful to the legal researcher, although in many instances special permission must be received to use them since all are not open to the public. This list is drawn from: Gladish, Mary L. *Directory of Special Libraries of Tennessee.* Nashville: Tennessee Library Association, 1973. 91 pp.

Bureau of Business and Economic Research Library
Memphis State University, Memphis, TN 38111
(901) 454-2281

Bureau of Educational Research and Services
302 Ball Bldg. Memphis State University
Memphis, TN 38111
(901) 454-2362

Central Research Library
Oak Ridge National Laboratory
P. O. Box X, Oak Ridge, TN 37380
(615) 850-6836 or 483-8611

Chattanooga-Hamilton County Regional Planning Commission Library
123 East 7th, Chattanooga, TN 37402
(615) 266-7782

The Chattanooga Times Library
117 E. 10th St. P. O. Box 951
Chattanooga, TN 37401
(615) 756-1234

Graduate School of Management Resource Information Center
2505 West End Avenue, Nashville, TN 37203
(615) 322-2534

*Greater Chattanooga Area Chamber of Commerce Research
    Library*
819 Broad St., Chattanooga, TN 37402
(615) 267-2121

Hamilton County Governmental Library
102 E. 6th St., Chattanooga, TN 37402
(615) 267-3513

Joint University Libraries, Special Collections Dept.
21st Avenue South, Nashville, TN 37203
(615) 322-2807

Knox County Governmental Library
Knox County Courthouse, Knoxville, TN 37902
(615) 523-2257

Knoxville-Knox County Public Library Area Resource Ctr.
500 West Church Avenue, Knoxville, TN 37901
(615) 523-0781

Knoxville Metropolitan Planning Commission Library
City Hill Park, Knoxville, TN 37902
(615) 637-6310

Memphis and Shelby County Archives
161 Jefferson Street, Memphis, TN 38103
(901) 526-5736

Memphis Area Chamber of Commerce
42 South Second, Memphis, TN
(901) 523-2322

Memphis Commercial Appeal Library
495 Union Avenue, Memphis, TN 38101
(901) 526-8811

Memphis Public Library and Information Center
1850 Peabody, Memphis, TN 38104
(901) 528-2965

*Memphis Public Library and Information Center, Cossitt-
    Goodwyn Libraries*
33 S. Front Street, Memphis, TN 38103
(901) 528-2984

Memphis State University, School of Law Library
Central Avenue, Memphis, TN 38111
(901) 454-2426

*Metropolitan Government of Nashville and Davidson County
    Planning Commission*
Metropolitan Office Bldg., 2nd Ave. S. and Lindsley, P. O.
    Box 39, Nashville, TN 37202
(615) 259-6349

Nashville Banner Library
1100 Broadway, Nashville, TN 37203
(615) 255-5401

Nashville Tennessean Library
1100 Broadway, Nashville, TN 37203
(615) 255-1221

Public Library of Nashville and Davidson County,
    Area Research Center
8th Avenue N. and Union, Nashville, TN 37203
(615) 244-4700

Public Library of Nashville and Davidson County,
    Business Information Division
8th Avenue N. and Union, Nashville, TN 37203
(615) 244-4700

Tennessee Department of Employment Security,
    Research and Statistics Library
519 Cordell Hull Bldg., Nashville, TN 37211
(615) 741-2284

Supreme Court Law Library
Supreme Court Bldg.
Number 6, Highway 45 Bypass, Jackson, TN 38301
(901) 424-1247

Supreme Court Law Library
Supreme Court Bldg., 719 Locust Street
Knoxville, TN 37902
(615) 524-4537

Supreme Court Library
Supreme Court Bldg., 401 7th Avenue North
Nashville, TN 37219
(615) 741-2016

Tennessee Valley Authority Technical Library
E2B7—400 Commerce Avenue
Knoxville, TN 37902
(615) 632-3466

U. S. Department of Commerce
1st American Bank Bldg., Memphis, TN 38111
(901) 534-3213

University of Tennessee, Law Library
1505 West Cumberland Avenue
Knoxville, TN 37916
(615) 974-4381

Vanderbilt Law Library
Vanderbilt University, Nashville, TN 37203
(615) 322-2568

University of Tennessee, Special Collections Library
1401 West Cumberland, Knoxville, TN 37915
(615) 974-4480

Vanderbilt Television News Archive, Vanderbilt University
21st Avenue South, Nashville, TN 37203
(615) 322-2927

The following is a list of Tennessee law schools:

School of Law
Memphis State University
Memphis, TN 38152
(901) 454-2421
R. D. Cox, Dean

College of Law
The University of Tennessee
1505 West Cumberland Avenue
Knoxville, TN 37916
(615) 974-2521
Kenneth L. Penegar, Dean

School of Law
Vanderbilt University
Nashville, TN 37240
(615) 322-2615
Robert L. Knauss, Dean

Y.M.C.A. Night Law School, Inc.
1000 Church Street
Nashville, TN 37203
(615) 256-9153
Office: 1926 Castleman Drive
Nashville, TN 37215
J. G. Lackey, Dean

APPENDIX A

CHECK-LIST OF TENNESSEE SESSION LAWS*

General Assembly	Session	Remarks On Contents	Pages	Convened	Adjourned
Acts and Ordinances**		Territory South of the River Ohio, 1790-1796			
	1st		viiip	Aug. 25, 1794	Sept. 30, 1794
	2nd		101p	June 29, 1795	July 11, 1795
		State of Tennessee, 1796-	31p		
1st	1st		78p	Mar. 28, 1796	April 23, 1796
1st	2nd		13p	July 30, 1796	Aug. 9, 1796
2nd	1st		120p	Sept. 18, 1797	Oct. 28, 1797
2nd	2nd		70p	Dec. 3, 1798	Jan. 5, 1799
3rd	1st		136p	Sept. 16, 1799	Oct. 26, 1799
4th	1st		203+xxxvip	Sept. 21, 1801	Nov. 14, 1801
5th	1st		143+xiip	Sept. 19, 1803	Nov. 8, 1803
5th	2nd		71p	July 23, 1804	Aug. 4, 1804
6th	1st		91+3p	Sept. 16, 1805	Nov. 4, 1805
6th	2nd		113+ivp	July 28, 1806	Sept. 13, 1806
7th	1st		180+iip	Sept. 21, 1807	Dec. 4, 1807
7th	2nd		63+vip	April 3, 1809	April 22, 1809
8th	1st		155+vp	Sept. 18, 1809	Nov. 23, 1809
9th	1st		143+viiip	Sept. 16, 1811	Nov. 21, 1811
9th	2nd		88+8p	Sept. 7, 1812	Oct. 21, 1812

* This list adapted from CHECKLIST OF ACTS AND CODES OF THE STATE OF TENNESSEE, 1792-1939. Special Publications Series No. 5 Nashville: Tennessee Historical Records Survey Project, 1940: CHECKLIST OF TENNESSEE SESSION LAWS (Part I) in PRELIMINARY CHECKLIST OF TENNES- SEE LEGISLATIVE DOCUMENTS. Nashville: State Library and Archives, 1954; Pimsleur, CHECKLISTS OF BASIC AMERICAN LEGAL PUBLICATIONS. AALL Publications Series No. 4, Section 2. South Hackensack, N.J.: Fred B. Rothman, 1962.
** Issued by the Governor and Judges of the Territory between June 11, 1792 and March 21, 1793.

General Assembly	Session	Pages	Remarks on Contents	Convened	Adjourned
10th	1st	190+13p		Sept. 21, 1813	Nov. 20, 1813
11th	1st	284+22p		Sept. 18, 1815	Nov. 17, 1815
12th	1st	230+xiiip		Sept. 15, 1817	Nov. 25, 1817
13th	1st	140+xp	Pub.	Sept. 20, 1819	Nov. 30, 1819
13th	1st	208+xiip	Priv.	Sept. 20, 1819	Nov. 30, 1819
13th	2nd	46+vp	Pub.	June 26, 1820	July 31, 1820
13th	2nd	117+1+viiip	Priv.	June 26, 1820	July 31, 1820
14th	1st	226+xxix+1p	Pub. & Priv.	Sept. 17, 1821	Nov. 17, 1821
14th	2nd	176+xxvip	Pub. & Priv.	July 22, 1822	Aug. 24, 1822
15th	1st	286+xxvip	Pub. & Priv.	Sept. 15, 1823	Nov. 29, 1823
15th	2nd	175+xxiip	Pub. & Priv.	Sept. 20, 1824	Oct. 22, 1824
16th	Reg.	viii+1+396+xlviiip+Table	Pub. & Priv.	Sept. 19, 1825	Dec. 7, 1825
16th	Extra	xiv+59+xii+216+xlviiip	Pub. & Priv.	Oct. 16, 1826	Dec. 11, 1826
17th	Stated	vii+xii+xxvi+98+245+xxxp	Pub. & Priv.	Sept. 17, 1827	Dec. 15, 1827
18th	Stated	viii+147+xxxix+xv+308+L+1p	Pub. & Priv.	Sept. 21, 1829	Jan. 14, 1830
19th	Stated	vi+170p	Pub.	Sept. 19, 1831	Dec. 21, 1831
19th	Stated	ix+268p	Priv.	Sept. 19, 1831	Dec. 21, 1831
19th	Called	iv+72p	Pub.	Sept. 3, 1832	Oct. 22, 1832
19th	Called	vi+138p	Priv.	Sept. 3, 1832	Oct. 22, 1832
20th	1st	vi+147p	Pub.	Sept. 16, 1833	Dec. 2, 1833
20th	1st	ix+206p	Priv.	Sept. 16, 1833	Dec. 2, 1833
21st****	1st	viii+246+Tables	Pub.	Oct. 5, 1835	Feb. 22, 1836
21st	1st	ix+295p	Priv.	Oct. 5, 1835	Feb. 22, 1836
21st	Called	32p	Pub.	Oct. 3, 1836	Oct. 26, 1836
22nd	1st	xvi+507p	Acts	Oct. 2, 1837	Jan. 29, 1838
23rd	1st	x+291p	Acts	Oct. 7, 1839	Feb. 1, 1840

****Constitution of 1834, p1-17.

General Assembly	Session	Pages	Remarks on Contents	Convened	Adjourned
24th	1st	xiii+278+2p	Acts	Oct. 4, 1841	Feb. 7, 1842
24th	2nd	3+47p	Acts	Oct. 3, 1842	Nov. 16, 1842
25th	1st	xviii+356p	Acts	Oct. 2, 1843	Jan. 31, 1844
26th	1st	xvi+17—408p	Acts	Oct. 6, 1845	Feb. 2, 1846
27th	1st	xviii+17—486p	Acts	Oct. 4, 1847	Feb. 7, 1848
28th	1st	xx+625p	Acts	Oct. 1, 1849	Feb. 11, 1850
29th	1st	xxii+787p	Acts	Oct. 6, 1851	March 1, 1852
30th	1st	xx+17—833+	Acts	Oct. 3, 1853	March 6, 1854
		67p	School Laws***		
31st	1st	xx+627p	Acts	Oct. 1, 1855	March 3, 1856
32nd	1st	viii+124+viii+445p	Pub. & Priv.	Oct. 5, 1857	March 22, 1858
33rd	1st	xiii+143+xxiv+145—708p	Pub. & Priv.	Oct. 3, 1859	March 26, 1860
33rd	[1st] Extra	viii+127p+Chart† (Eastman)	Pub. & Priv.	Jan. 7, 1861	Feb. 4, 1861
33rd	[1st] Extra	viii+127p+Chart† (Griffith)	Pub. & Priv.		
33rd††††	[2nd] Extra	viii+103p	Pub. & Priv.	April 25, 1861	July 1, 1861
34th	1st [Reg]	vii+82+1p	Pub.	Oct. 7, 1861	March 20, 1862 [adj sine die]
34th	1st [Reg.]	vii+82+1p (Reprint Statute Law Book Co. 1897)	Pub.	Oct. 7, 1861	March 20, 1862 [adj sine die]
34th‡ [1865]	1st (1865) [1st Called]	12+xiii+178p	Pub. & Priv.	April 3, 1865	June 12, 1865 [adj with date]
34th [1865]	2nd (1865) [1st Adj]	476p	Pub. & Priv.	Oct. 2, 1865	May 28, 1866 [adj to meet Nov. 5]

***Compilation of Common School Laws.
††††Message of Gov. Isham G. Harris, pl-12 (sic 14).
‡‡‡Introductory Documents, xiiip; Message of Gov. W. G. Brownlow, pl-15.
†Compilation of Militia Law, p57-116.

General Assembly	Session	Pages	Remarks on Contents	Convened	Adjourned
34th [1866]	Extra [Special Called]	40p	Pub.	July 4, 1866	July 25, 1866 [adj sine die]
34th [1866]	2nd Adj [2nd Adj]	92+329p	Pub. & Priv.	Nov. 5, 1866	March 11, 1867 [adj sine die]
35th	1st	142+396p	Pub. & Priv.	Oct. 7, 1867	March 16, 1868
35th‡‡	Extra	55p	Pub.	July 27, 1868	Sept. 14, 1868
35th	2nd	80+viii+81—437p	Pub. & Priv.	Nov. 9, 1868	March 1, 1869
36th	1st	748p	Pub. & Priv.	Oct. 4, 1869	March 7, 1870
36th†	2nd	xxxii+238p	Acts	May 9, 1870	July 11, 1870
36th	3rd	200+1p	Acts	Dec. 5, 1870	Feb. 6, 1871
37th	1st	257p	Acts	Oct. 2, 1871	Dec. 16, 1871
37th	Called	75+1p	Acts	March 12, 1872	April 1, 1872
38th	1st	243+1+xp	Acts	Jan. 6, 1873	March 25, 1873
39th	1st	361+xviip	Acts	Jan. 4, 1875	March 24, 1875
40th	1st	303+1p	Acts	Jan. 1, 1877	March 27, 1877
40th	1st Extra	32p	Acts	Dec. 5, 1877	Dec. 11, 1877
	2nd Extra			Dec. 11, 1877	Dec. 28, 1877
40th	1st Extra	32p	Acts	Dec. 5, 1877	Dec. 11, 1877
	2nd Extra		Acts	Dec. 11, 1877	Dec. 28, 1877
		(Reprint Statute Law Book Co. 1938)			
41st	1st	388+1+xiiip	Acts	Jan. 6, 1879	April 1, 1879
41st	Called	39+3p	Acts	Dec. 16, 1879	Dec. 24, 1879
42nd	1st	376p	Acts	Jan. 3, 1881	April 7, 1881
42nd	1st Extra	38+1p	Acts	Dec. 7, 1881	Dec. 26, 1881
42nd	2nd Extra	80+	Acts	April 6, 1882	April 27, 1882
42nd	3rd Extra	40p		April 27, 1882	May 22, 1882
43rd	1st	471+1p	Acts	Jan. 1, 1883	March 30, 1883

‡‡Message of Gov. W. G. Brownlow, p5-13.
†New constitution of 1870, xxiip.

174

General Assembly	Session	Pages	Remarks On Contents	Convened	Adjourned
44th	1st	371p	Acts	Jan. 5, 1885	April 9, 1885
44th	Extraordinary	134p	Acts	May 25, 1885	June 13, 1885
45th	1st	525p	Acts	Jan. 3, 1887	March 29, 1887
46th	1st	603p	Acts	Jan. 7, 1889	May 7, 1889
46th	2nd	125p	Acts	Feb. 24, 1890	March 15, 1890
46th	3rd			March 15, 1890	March 18, 1890
47th	1st	611p	Acts	Jan 5, 1891	March 30, 1891
47th	Extraordinary	132p	Acts	Aug. 31, 1891	Sept. 21, 1891
48th	1st	576p	Acts	Jan. 2, 1893	April 10, 1893
49th	[1st]	664p	Acts	Jan. 7, 1895	May 14, 1895
49th	2nd			May 27, 1895	June 17, 1895
49th	2nd Extra	55+3p	Acts	Sept. 7, 1896	Sept. 26, 1896
50th	1st	xxx+878p	Acts	Jan. 4, 1897	May 1, 1897
50th	2nd	112p	Acts	Jan. 17, 1898	Feb. 5, 1898
51st	1st	1345+2p	Acts	Jan. 2, 1899	April 24, 1899
52nd	1st	1327p	Acts	Jan. 7, 1901	April 25, 1901
53rd	1st	1707p	Acts	Jan. 5, 1903	April 16, 1903
54th	1st	1406+1p	Acts	Jan. 2, 1905	April 17, 1905
55th	1st	2332p	Acts	Jan. 7, 1907	April 16, 1907
56th	1st	6+2355p	Acts	Jan. 4, 1909	May 1, 1909
57th	1st	10+17—390p	Pub.	Jan. 2, 1911	July 9, 1911
57th	1st	10+17—2127p	Priv.	Jan. 2, 1911	July 9, 1911
58th	1st	9+349+	Pub.	Jan. 6, 1913	Aug. 23, 1913
	1st Extra	1+351—657+	Pub.	Sept. 8, 1913	Sept. 27, 1913
	2nd Extra	1+659—743p	Pub.	Oct. 3, 1913	Oct. 17, 1913
58th	1st	9+1191+	Priv.	Jan. 6, 1913	Aug. 23, 1913
	1st Extra	1+1193—1635p	Priv.	Sept. 8, 1913	Sept. 27, 1913
59th	1st	8+738p	Pub.	Jan. 4, 1915	May 17, 1915

General Assembly	Session	Pages	Remarks on Contents	Convened	Adjourned
59th	1st	19+	Pub. & Priv. suppl.	Jan. 4, 1915	May 17, 1915
59th	Extra	20—63p	Pub.	March 21, 1916	March 31, 1916
60th	1st	8+2279p	Priv.	Jan. 4, 1915	May 17, 1915
60th	1st	8+668p	Pub.	Jan. 1, 1917	April 10, 1917
61st	1st	8+2636p	Priv.	Jan. 1, 1917	April 10, 1917
61st	1st	8+971p	Pub.	Jan. 6, 1919	April 17, 1919
61st	1st	8+2620p	Priv.	Jan. 6, 1919	April 17, 1919
61st	Extraordinary	481p	Pub. & Priv.	Aug. 9, 1920	Sept. 4, 1920
62nd	1st	9+738p	Pub.	Jan. 3, 1921	April 11, 1921
62nd	1st	9+1627p	Priv. v. 1	Jan. 3, 1921	April 11, 1921
62nd	1st	1628—3076p	Priv. v. 2	Jan. 3, 1921	April 11, 1921
63rd	1st	11+620p	Pub.	Jan. 1, 1923	April 1, 1923
63rd	1st	11+1400p	Priv. v. 1	Jan. 1, 1923	April 1, 1923
63rd	1st	1401—2568p	Priv. v. 2	Jan. 1, 1923	April 1, 1923
64th	1st	11+729p	Pub.	Jan. 5, 1925	April 16, 1925
64th	1st	14p	Pub. suppl.	Jan. 5, 1925	April 16, 1925
64th	1st	11+1472p	Priv. v. 1	Jan. 5, 1925	April 16, 1925
64th	1st	1473—2926p	Priv. v. 2	Jan. 5, 1925	April 16, 1925
65th	1st	11+531p	Pub.	Jan. 3, 1927	May 6, 1927
65th	1st	11+1498p	Priv. v. 1	Jan. 3, 1927	May 6, 1927
65th	1st	1499—2805p	Priv. v. 2	Jan. 3, 1927	May 6, 1927
66th	1st	11+644p	Pub.	Jan. 7, 1929	April 14, 1929
66th	1st	xv+1306p	Priv. v. 1	Jan. 7, 1929	April 14, 1929
66th	1st	1307—2757p	Priv. v. 2	Jan. 7, 1929	April 14, 1929
66th	Extraordinary	xxxviii+1+151+222p	Pub. & Priv.	Dec. 2, 1929	Dec. 14, 1929
67th	1st	11+1+619p	Pub.	Jan. 5, 1931	July 2, 1931
67th	1st	11+1064p	Priv. v. 1	Jan. 5, 1931	July 2, 1931
67th	1st	2+1067—2218p	Priv. v. 2	Jan. 5, 1931	July 2, 1931
67th	1st Extra	16+564p	Pub. & Priv.	Nov. 16, 1931	Nov. 21, 1931
67th	2nd Extra		Pub. & Priv.	Nov. 30, 1931	Dec. 19, 1931

General Assembly	Session	Pages	Remarks on Contents	Convened	Adjourned
68th	1st	11+669p	Pub.	Jan. 2, 1933	April 22, 1933
68th	1st	11+1064p+Index	Priv. v. 1	Jan. 2, 1933	April 22, 1933
68th	1st	1065—2023p	Priv. v. 2	Jan. 2, 1933	April 22, 1933
69th	1st	12+626+2+xxvip	Pub.	Jan. 7, 1935	April 22, 1935
69th	1st	12+1116+1+xvip	Priv. v. 1	Jan. 7, 1935	April 22, 1935
69th	1st	2+1125—2187+3+xvip	Priv. v. 2	Jan. 7, 1935	April 22, 1935
69th	Extra	896p	Pub. & Priv.	July 15, 1935	Aug. 3, 1935
70th	[1st] Extra	1440p	Pub.	Dec. 16, 1936	Dec. 19, 1936
	Regular			Jan. 4, 1937	May 21, 1937
70th	Regular	1439p	Priv. v. 1	Jan. 4, 1937	May 21, 1937
70th	Regular	1445—2720p	Priv. v. 2	Jan. 4, 1937	May 21, 1937
70th	2nd Extra	597p	Pub. & Priv.	Oct. 11, 1937	Oct. 30, 1937
	3rd Extra			Nov. 8, 1937	Nov. 19, 1937
71st	1st	1133p	Pub.	Jan. 2, 1939	March 10, 1939
71st	1st	1976p	Priv.	Jan. 2, 1939	March 10, 1939
72nd	1st	705p	Pub.	Jan. 6, 1941	Feb. 15, 1941
72nd	1st	1928p	Priv.	Jan. 6, 1941	Feb. 15, 1941
73rd	1st	599p	Pub.	Jan. 4, 1943	Feb. 11, 1943
73rd	1st	1686p	Priv.	Jan. 4, 1943	Feb. 11, 1943
	1st Extra	14+82p	Pub.	April 10, 1944	April 13, 1944
74th	1st	827p	Pub.	Jan. 1, 1945	March 2, 1945
74th	1st	1903p	Priv.	Jan. 1, 1945	March 2, 1945
75th	1st	1120p	Pub.	Jan. 6, 1947	March 14, 1947
75th	1st	1760+51p	Priv. v. 1	Jan. 6, 1947	March 14, 1947
75th	1st	1+1761—3487+51p	Priv. v. 2	Jan. 6, 1947	March 14, 1947
76th	1st	1386p	Pub.	Jan. 3, 1949	April 15, 1949
76th	1st	1504+31p	Priv. v. 1	Jan. 3, 1949	April 15, 1949
76th	1st	1+1505—3018p	Priv. v. 2	Jan. 3, 1949	April 15, 1949
77th	1st	1497p	Pub.	Jan. 1, 1951	March 16, 1951

General Assembly	Session	Pages	Remarks on Contents	Convened	Adjourned
77th	1st	2176p+30p	Priv.	Jan. 1, 1951	March 16, 1951
78th	1st	1258p	Pub.	Jan. 5, 1953	April 10, 1953
78th	1st	1992p	Priv.	Jan. 5, 1953	April 10, 1953
79th	1st	1600p	Pub.	Jan. 3, 1955	March 18, 1955
79th	1st	1481p	Priv.	Jan. 3, 1955	March 18, 1955
80th	1st	1894p	Pub.	Jan. 7, 1957	March 22, 1957
80th	1st	1317p	Priv.	Jan. 7, 1957	March 22, 1957
80th	1st Extra	37p	Pub.	May 6, 1958	May 17, 1958
81st	1st	1400p	Pub.	Jan. 5, 1959	March 20, 1959
81st	1st	1268p	Priv.	Jan. 5, 1959	March 20, 1959
82nd	1st	1417p	Pub.	Jan. 2, 1961	March 17, 1961
82nd	1st	1543p	Priv.	Jan. 2, 1961	March 17, 1961
82nd	1st Extra	25p	Pub.	May 29, 1962	June 7, 1962
83rd	1st	1772p	Pub.	Jan. 7, 1963	March 22, 1963
83rd	1st	932p	Priv.	Jan. 7, 1963	March 22, 1963
84th	1st	1494p	Pub.	Jan. 4, 1965	March 19, 1965
84th	1st Extra	75p	Pub.	May 10, 1965	May 27, 1965
84th	1st	1051p	Priv.	Jan. 4, 1965	March 19, 1965
84th	2nd Extra	151p	Pub.	March 14, 1966	March 31, 1966
85th	1st	1538p	Pub.	Jan. 3, 1967	May 26, 1967
85th	Adj.	923p	Pub.	Feb. 13, 1968	April 3, 1968
85th	1st & Adj.	1909p	Priv.	Jan. 3, 1967	April 3, 1968
86th	1st	1456p	Pub.	Jan. 7, 1969	May 9, 1969
86th	1st	796p	Priv.	Jan. 7, 1969	May 9, 1969
86th	2nd	1137p	Pub.	Jan. 13, 1970	Feb. 20, 1970
86th	2nd	797—1317p	Priv.	Jan. 13, 1970	Feb. 20, 1970
87th	1st	1784p	Pub.	Jan. 5, 1971	May 31, 1971
87th	1st	800p	Priv.	Jan. 5, 1971	May 31, 1971
87th	2nd	1261p	Pub.	Feb. 7, 1972	April 14, 1972
87th	2nd	1262—2449p	Pub.	Feb. 7, 1972	April 14, 1972

General Assembly	Session	Pages	Remarks on Contents	Convened	Adjourned
87th	2nd	801—1716p	Priv.	Feb. 7, 1972	April 14, 1972
88th	1st	14+1452+34	Pub.	Jan. 2, 1973	May 4, 1973
88th	1st	16+1455—2144+22	Pub.	Jan. 2, 1973	May 4, 1973
88th	1st	556+16	Priv.	Jan. 2, 1973	May 4, 1973
88th	2nd	1008+16	Pub.	Jan. 8, 1974	April 25, 1974
88th	2nd	1008—2020+30	Pub.	Jan. 8, 1974	April 25, 1974
88th	2nd	834+15	Priv.	Jan. 8, 1974	April 25, 1974
89th	1st	1762+79	Pub.	Jan. 7, 1975	June 12, 1975
89th	1st	758+15	Priv.	Jan. 7, 1975	June 12, 1975
89th	2nd	1002+20	Pub.	Jan. 14, 1976	March 19, 1976
89th	2nd	1003—2003+77	Pub.	Jan. 14, 1976	March 19, 1976
89th	2nd	269+10	Priv.	Jan. 14, 1976	March 19, 1976

APPENDIX B

CHECK-LIST OF LEGISLATIVE JOURNALS*

no printed records of "House of Representatives"

General Assembly	Session	Pages	Remarks On Contents	Convened	Adjourned
1st	1st	(35p.)** [40p.]†	Legislative Council	Feb. 24, 1794	Mar. 1, 1794
			House	Aug. 25, 1794	Sept. 30, 1794
	1st	(43p.) [48p.]	Legislative Council	Aug. 25, 1794	Sept. 30, 1794
	2nd	(14p.) [18p.]	House	June 29, 1795	July 11, 1795
	2nd	(20p.) [22p.] (32p.) [38p.]	Jr. Const. Convention	June 29, 1795	July 11, 1795
	1st	(49p.) 72p.††	Senate	Jan. 11, 1796	Feb. 6, 1796
	1st	(54p.) 80p.	House	Mar. 28, 1796	April 23, 1796
	2nd	(24p.) 34p.	Senate	Mar. 28, 1796	April 23, 1796
	2nd	(28p.) 40p.	House	July 30, 1796	Aug. 9, 1796
		[103p.]	Senate	July 30, 1796	Aug. 9, 1796
2nd	1st	((121+iiip.))†††	House & Senate	Sept. 18, 1797	Oct. 28, 1797
	1st	[112p.]		Sept. 18, 1797	Oct. 28, 1797

* This list adapted from CHECKLIST OF TENNESSEE LEGISLATIVE JOURNALS (Part II) in PRELIMINARY CHECKLIST OF TENNESSEE LEGISLATIVE DOCUMENTS. Nashville: State Library and Archives, 1954.

** Page numbers in parentheses refer to a collection of these journals reprinted in 1852, the journals usually cited because the original printed journals for these years were not "discovered" until 1971. The former is: Journal of the Territorial Councils of the Senate and House of Tennessee. Knoxville: Roulstone, 1794-1796. Reprint. Nashville: McKenzie and Brown, 1852. The latter are in possession of the University of Tennessee-Knoxville Library, but are described in: John Dobson, The Lost Roulstone Imprints. Knoxville: The University of Tennessee Library, Occasional Pub. No. 2, Winter 1975.

† The page numbers in brackets refer to the original printed journals as described in The Lost Roulstone Imprints, see note ** supra.

†† Page numbers shown below refer to original printed journals which are generally available, as is the case with most late 19th and 20th century journals.

††† Page numbers shown in double parentheses refer to a collection of printed journals of the Second General Assembly which was published in 1933. It is: Mrs. John T. Moore (comp.), Journals of the Senate and House of the Second General Assembly, September 18, 1797-December 3, 1798. Kingsport: Southern Publishers, Inc. and State Library and Archives, Publication No. 1, 1933.

General Assembly	Session	Pages	Remarks On Contents	Convened	Adjourned
2nd	2nd	((2+125—258+vp.))	Supp.		
2nd	2nd	((2+261—266+ip.))	Supp.		
2nd	2nd	((2+269—369+iiip.))	Senate	Dec. 3, 1798	Jan. 5, 1798
2nd	2nd	((2+373—481+ivp.))	House	Dec. 3, 1798	Jan. 5, 1798
3rd	1st	not found in printed form	Senate	Sept. 16, 1799	Nov. 26, 1799
3rd	1st	not found in printed form	House	Sept. 16, 1799	Nov. 26, 1799
4th	1st	184p.	Senate	Sept. 21, 1801	Nov. 14, 1801
4th	1st	141p.	House	Sept. 21, 1801	Nov. 14, 1801
5th	1st	172p.	Senate, contains impeachment trials of David Campbell	Sept. 19, 1803	Nov. 8, 1803
5th	1st	166p.	House	Sept. 19, 1803	Nov. 8, 1803
5th	2nd	98p.	Senate	July 27, 1804	Aug. 4, 1804
5th	2nd	82p.	House	July 23, 1804	Aug. 4, 1804
6th	1st	152p.	Senate	Sept. 16, 1805	Nov. 4, 1805
6th	1st	116p.	House	Sept. 16, 1805	Nov. 4, 1805
6th	2nd	110p.	Senate	July 28, 1806	Sept. 13, 1806
6th	2nd	103+1p.	House	July 28, 1806	Sept. 13, 1806
7th*	1st	197p.	Senate	Sept. 21, 1807	Dec. 4, 1807
7th	1st	166p.	House	Sept. 21, 1807	Dec. 4, 1807
7th	2nd	82p.	Senate	April 3, 1809	April 22, 1809
7th	2nd	98p.	House	April 3, 1809	April 22, 1809
8th	1st	200p.	Senate	Sept. 18, 1809	Nov. 23, 1809
8th	1st	196p.	House	Sept. 18, 1809	Nov. 23, 1809
9th	1st	224p.	Senate	Sept. 16, 1811	Nov. 21, 1811
9th	1st	292p.	House	Sept. 16, 1811	Nov. 21, 1811
9th†	2nd	133+2p.	Senate	Sept. 7, 1812	Oct. 21, 1812

* Includes impeachment trial of Isaac and John Phillips, see p.80.
† Includes impeachment trial of William Cocke, see p.31.

General Assembly	Session	Pages	Remarks On Contents	Convened	Adjourned
9th	2nd	152p.	House	Sept. 7, 1812	Oct. 21, 1812
10th	1st	[MS and printed copies burned]	Senate		Nov. 20, 1813
10th	1st	[MS and printed copies burned]	House	Sept. 21, 1813	Nov. 20, 1813
11th	1st	236p.	Senate	Sept. 18, 1815	Nov. 17, 1815
11th	1st	304p.	House	Sept. 18, 1815	Nov. 17, 1815
12th	1st	220p.	Senate	Sept. 15, 1817	Nov. 25, 1817
12th	1st	312, 325-328, 229p.	House	Sept. 15, 1817	Nov. 25, 1817
13th	1st	333p.	Senate	Sept. 20, 1819	Nov. 30, 1819
13th	1st	301p.	House	Sept. 20, 1819	Nov. 30, 1819
13th	2nd	175p.	Senate	June 26, 1820	July 31, 1820
13th	2nd	204p.	House	June 26, 1820	July 31, 1820
14th	1st	345p.	Senate	Sept. 17, 1821	Nov. 17, 1821
14th	1st	390+	House	Sept. 17, 1821	Nov. 17, 1821
		391—400p.	Jr of the Committee†††		
14th	2nd	218p.	Senate	July 22, 1822	Aug. 24, 1822
14th	2nd	166+	House	July 22, 1822	Aug. 24, 1822
		2p	Jr of the Committee†††		
15th	1st	309p.	Senate	Sept. 15, 1823	Nov. 29, 1823
15th	1st	352p.	House	Sept. 15, 1823	Nov. 29, 1823
15th	2nd	200+	Senate	Sept. 20, 1824	Oct. 22, 1824
		ivp	Jr of the Committee†††		
15th	2nd	201p.	House	Sept. 20, 1824	Oct. 22, 1824
16th	1st	228, 225—452 +	Senate	Sept. 19, 1825	Dec. 7, 1825
		452—456p.	Jr of the Committee†††		
16th	1st	492p.	House	Sept. 19, 1825	Dec. 7, 1825

††† Of the Whole of Both Houses on the Resolution for the call of a Convention.

General Assembly	Session	Pages	Remarks On Contents	Convened	Adjourned
16th	Called	303+1+	Senate	Oct. 16, 1826	Dec. 11, 1826
16th	Called	305—307p. 356+	Jr of the Committee† House	Oct. 16, 1826	Dec. 11, 1826
17th	Stated	357—359p. 520p.	Jr of the Committee† Senate	Sept. 17, 1827	Dec. 15, 1827
17th	Stated	674+	House	Sept. 17, 1827	Dec. 15, 1827
18th	Stated	675, 676p. 144, 142—692+1+ Fold Sheet+ 156p.	Jr of the Committee† Senate	Sept. 21, 1829	Jan. 14, 1830
18th	Stated	836p.+Fold Sheet	Court of Impeach.†† House	Sept. 21, 1829	Jan. 14, 1830
19th	Stated	355+1+	Senate	Sept. 19, 1831	Dec. 21, 1831
19th	Stated	357—442p.	Court of Impeach.††† House	Sept. 19, 1831	Dec. 21, 1831
19th	Called	414p. 150+ 153p.	Senate House	Sept. 3, 1832	Oct. 22, 1832
20th	1st	315p.+Table	Senate	Sept. 16, 1833	Dec. 2, 1833
20th	1st	422p.+Table	House	Sept. 16, 1833	Dec. 2, 1833
21st	1st	534p.+Table	Senate	Oct. 5, 1835	Feb. 22, 1836
21st	1st	707p.+Table	House	Oct. 5, 1835	Feb. 22, 1836
21st	Called	64+2+ 88p.	Senate & Reports House & Appendix	Oct. 3, 1836	Oct. 26, 1836
22nd	1st	498+ 499—628+2 Charts	Senate Appendix	Oct. 2, 1837	Jan. 29, 1838
22nd	1st	620+ 621—893p.	House Appendix	Oct. 2, 1837	Jan. 29, 1838
23rd	1st	548+ 549—567p.	Senate Appendix	Oct. 7, 1839	Feb. 1, 1840

† Of the Whole of Both Houses on the Resolution for the call of a Convention.
†† Of Nathaniel W. Williams. These pages also found bound without senate journal.
††† Of Joshua Haskell.

General Assembly	Session	Remarks On Contents	Convened	Adjourned	Pages
23rd	1st	House / Appendix	Oct. 7, 1839	Feb. 1, 1840	664+ / 665—958p.
24th	1st	Senate / Appendix	Oct. 4, 1841	Feb. 7, 1842	712+ / 64, 81—85, 70, 71,88 / 73—81, 98, 83—198p.
24th	1st	House / Appendix	Oct. 4, 1841	Feb. 7, 1842	958+ / 214p.
24th	Called	Senate / Appendix	Oct. 3, 1842	Nov. 16, 1842	204+ / 28+
24th	Called	House / Appendix	Oct. 3, 1842	Nov. 16, 1842	221+ / 28p.
25th	1st	Senate / Appendix	Oct. 2, 1843	Jan. 31, 1844	739+ / 264p.
25th	1st	House / Appendix	Oct. 2, 1843	Jan. 31, 1844	812+ / 264p.
26th	1st	Senate / Appendix	Oct. 6, 1845	Feb. 2, 1846	566+ / 350p.
26th	1st	House / Appendix	Oct. 6, 1845	Feb. 2, 1846	629+2 Plates+ / 350p.
27th	1st	Senate / Appendix	Oct. 4, 1847	Feb. 7, 1848	732+ / 464p.+ 2 Plates
27th	1st	House / Appendix	Oct. 4, 1847	Feb. 7, 1848	1048+ / 333p.+2 Plates
28th	1st	Senate / Appendix	Oct. 1, 1849	Feb. 11, 1850	848+ / [no. p.605, 2 p.606] 381+1p.
28th	1st	House / Appendix	Oct. 1, 1849	Feb. 11, 1850	918+ / 2+443p.
29th	1st	Senate / Appendix	Oct. 6, 1851	March 1, 1852	882+Chart+ / 338p.

General Assembly	Session	Pages	Remarks On Contents	Convened	Adjourned
29th	1st	1008+ / 326p.	House / Appendix	Oct. 6, 1851	March 1, 1852
30th	1st	792+ / 296+1p.	Senate / Appendix	Oct. 3, 1853	March 6, 1854
30th	1st	1192+ / 296+1p.	House / Appendix	Oct. 3, 1853	March 6, 1854
31st	1st	773+344, 1, 146—176, 377—580 +1+189+5p. [p.4 (580) blank]	Senate / Appendix	Oct. 1, 1855	March 3, 1856
31st	1st	965+1+344, 1, 146—176, 377—580 +1+189+5p.	House / Appendix	Oct. 1, 1855	March 3, 1856
32nd	1st	906p.	Senate	Oct. 5, 1857	March 22, 1858
32nd	1st	932p.	House	Oct. 5, 1857	March 22, 1858
33rd	1st	847p.	Senate	Oct. 3, 1859	March 26, 1860
33rd	1st	1240p.	House	Oct. 3, 1859	March 26, 1860
33rd	[1st] Extra.	189+	Senate	Jan. 7, 1861	Feb. 4, 1861
33rd	2nd Extra.	256p.	House		
33rd		204+	Senate	April 25, 1861	July 1, 1861
		224p.	House		
34th**	1st [Reg.]		Senate	Oct. 7, 1861 / Jan. 20, 1862 / Feb. 20, 1862†††	Dec. 21, 1861 / Feb. 15, 1862‡ / March 20, 1862
34th**	1st [Reg]		House	Oct. 7, 1861 / Jan. 20, 1862 / Feb. 20, 1862†††	Dec. 21, 1861 / Feb. 15, 1862‡ / March 20, 1862
34th [1865]	1st (1865) [1st Called]	255+	Senate	April 3, 1865	June 12, 1865 [adj sine die]

** The House Journal was printed in 1957. **House Journal. Thirty-fourth General Assembly.** (Robert H. White ed.) Nashville: Tennessee Historical Commission, 1957. No Senate records have been discovered.

††† Met at Memphis.

‡ Met informally on Sunday, Feb. 16, 1862.

General Assembly	Session	Pages	Remarks On Contents	Convened	Adjourned
34th [1865]	1st (1865) [1st Called]	155p. 316+	Appendix House	April 3, 1865	June 12, 1865 [adj sine die]
34th [1865]	2nd (1865) [1st Adj.]	155p. 700p. [p.635 blank, 698 called 798]	Appendix Senate	Oct. 2, 1865	May 28, 1866 [adj to meet Nov. 5]
34th [1865]	2nd (1865) [1st Adj.]	676p.	House	Oct. 2, 1865	May 28, 1866 [adj to meet Nov. 5]
34th [1866]	Extra. [Special Called]	65p.	Senate	July 4, 1866	July 25, 1866 [adj sine die]
34th [1866]	Extra. [Special Called]	73p.	House	July 4, 1866	July 25, 1866 [adj sine die]
34th [1866]	2nd. Adj. [2nd Adj.]	520+	Senate	Nov. 5, 1866	March 11, 1867 [adj sine die]
34th [1866]	2nd Adj. [2nd Adj.]	168p. 447+	Appendix House	Nov. 5, 1866	March 11, 1867 [adj sine die]
Senate as Court of Impeachment		168p. 207p.	Appendix People of Tenn. vs. Thomas N. Frazier	May 11, 1867	June 4, 1867
35th	1st	586p.	Senate	Oct. 7, 1867	March 16, 1868
35th	1st	808p.	House	Oct. 7, 1867	March 16, 1868
35th	Extra.	223p.	Senate	July 27, 1868	Sept. 14, 1868
35th	Extra.	279p.	House	July 27, 1868	Sept. 14, 1868

General Assembly	Session	Pages	Remarks On Contents	Convened	Adjourned
35th	Adj.	363p.	Senate	Nov. 9, 1868	March 1, 1869
35th	Adj.	520p.	House	Nov. 9, 1868	March 1, 1869
36th	1st	555p.	Senate	Oct. 4, 1869	March 7, 1870
36th	1st	1010p.	House	Oct. 4, 1869	March 7, 1870
36th	[2nd] Adj.	521p.	Senate	May 9, 1870	July 11, 1870
				Dec. 5, 1870	Feb. 6, 1871
36th	Adj. [2nd] Adj.	944+1p.	House	May 9, 1870	July 11, 1870
				Dec. 5, 1870	Feb. 6, 1871
37th	1st	476+	Senate	Oct. 2, 1871	Dec. 16, 1871
		526+1p.	Appendix		
		534+	House		
		526+1p.	Appendix		
37th	Extra.	111+	Senate	March 12, 1872	April 1, 1872
		85+1p.	Appendix		
37th	Extra.	164+1+	House	March 12, 1872	April 1, 1872
		85+1p.	Appendix		
38th	1st	509+	Senate	Jan. 6, 1873	March 25, 1873
		[p.501 blank]	Gov's. Message (John C. Brown)		
		30+xxxi+1+	Appendix		
		33—139p.+2 Tables			
38th	1st	571+	House	Jan. 6, 1873	March 25, 1873
		30+xxxi+1+	Gov's. Message (John C. Brown)		
		33—139p.+2 Tables	Appendix		
39th	1st	799p.	Senate	Jan. 4, 1875	March 24, 1875
39th	1st	805+1p.	House	Jan. 4, 1875	March 24, 1875
40th	1st	727p.	Senate	Jan. 1, 1877	March 27, 1877
40th	1st	961p.	House	Jan. 1, 1877	March 27, 1877
40th†	1st Extra.	286+1p.	Senate & House	Dec. 5, 1877	Dec. 11, 1877
	2nd Extra.			Dec. 11, 1877	Dec. 28, 1877

† Includes Appendix to House Journal, p.225-239, "Report of the Special Committee on the State Debt."

General Assembly	Session	Pages	Remarks On Contents	Convened	Adjourned
41st	1st	770p.	Senate	Jan. 6, 1879	April 1, 1879
41st	1st	1097p.	House	Jan. 6, 1879	April 1, 1879
41st	Called	51+	Senate	Dec. 16, 1879	Dec. 24, 1879
		60p.	House		
42nd	1st	759p.	Senate	Jan. 3, 1881	April 7, 1881
42nd	1st	1095p.	House	Jan. 3, 1881	April 7, 1881
42nd	Extra.	85p.	Senate	Dec. 7, 1881	Dec. 26, 1881
42nd	1st Extra.	108p.	House	Dec. 7, 1881	Dec. 26, 1881
42nd	2nd Extra.	165+1+	Senate	April 6, 1882	April 27, 1882
42nd	3rd Extra.	116p.	Senate	April 27, 1882	May 22, 1882
42nd	2nd Extra.	246+	House	April 6, 1882	April 27, 1882
42nd	3rd Extra.	162p.	House	April 27, 1882	May 22, 1882
43rd	1st	842p.	Senate	Jan. 1, 1883	March 30, 1883
43rd	1st	979p.	House	Jan. 1, 1883	March 30, 1883
44th	1st	698+1p. [p.679 blank]	Senate	Jan. 5, 1885	April 9, 1885
44th	1st	950p.	House	Jan. 5, 1885	April 9, 1885
44th	1st Extra.	140+	Senate	May 25, 1885	June 13, 1885
		1+10p.	Appendix†		
44th	1st Extra.	204+	House	May 25, 1885	June 13, 1885
		1+10p.	Appendix†		
45th	1st	830p.	Senate	Jan. 3, 1887	March 29, 1887
45th	1st	1092p.	House	Jan. 3, 1887	March 29, 1887
46th	1st	877p.	Senate	Jan. 7, 1889	May 7, 1889
46th	1st	907+1p.	House	Jan. 7, 1889	May 7, 1889
46th	1st Extra.	155+	Senate	Feb. 24, 1890	March 15, 1890
46th	2nd Extra.	10+	Senate	March 15, 1890	March 18, 1890
		1+xivp.	Senate		

† Message of Gov. William B. Bate.

General Assembly	Session	Pages	Remarks On Contents	Convened	Adjourned
46th	1st Extra.	174p.	House	Feb. 24, 1890	March 15, 1890
	2nd Extra.			March 15, 1890	March 18, 1890
47th	1st	535p.	Senate	Jan. 5, 1891	March 30, 1891
47th	1st	542+1p.	House	Jan. 5, 1891	March 30, 1891
47th	Extraordinary	167p.	Senate	Aug. 31, 1891	Sept. 21, 1891
47th	Extraordinary	199p.	House	Aug. 31, 1891	Sept. 21, 1891
48th	1st	851p.	Senate	Jan. 2, 1893	April 10, 1893
48th	1st	953p.	House	Jan. 2, 1893	April 10, 1893
	Senate as Court of Impeachment††		People of Tenn. vs. J. J. DuBose	April 11, 1893	June 2, 1893
49th†††	1st	732p.	Senate	Jan. 7, 1895	May 14, 1895
49th	1st	641+2p.	House	Jan. 7, 1895	May 14, 1895
49th	Extraordinary	112p.	Senate	May 27, 1895	June 17, 1895
49th	Extraordinary	160p.	House	May 27, 1895	June 17, 1895
49th	2nd Extra.	102+	Senate	Sept. 7, 1896	Sept. 26, 1896
		115p.	House		
50th	1st	1139p.	Senate	Jan. 4, 1897	May 1, 1897
50th	1st	1344p.	House	Jan. 4, 1897	May 1, 1897
50th	Extraordinary	132+	Senate	Jan. 17, 1898	Feb. 5, 1898
		167p.	House		
51st	1st	1069+1+ 1071—1133+1+ 1135—1227p.	Senate Addenda	Jan. 2, 1899	April 24, 1899
		1463p.	House	Jan. 2, 1899	April 24, 1899
51st	1st	925p.	Senate	Jan. 2, 1899	April 24, 1899
52nd	1st	1118p.	House	Jan. 7, 1901	April 25, 1901
52nd	1st	861+1+	Senate	Jan. 7, 1901	April 25, 1901
53rd	1st	863—898+ 899—967+1p.	Senate Appendix	Jan. 5, 1903	April 16, 1903

†† Not found in printed form.
†††T p erroneously marked May 27, 1895. Contains joint convention in Contest for Governor, Peter Turney vs. H. Clay Evans, see p.144.

General Assembly	Session	Pages	Remarks On Contents	Convened	Adjourned
53rd	1st	969+1+	House	Jan. 5, 1903	April 16, 1903
		970—1025+1+	Appendix†		
		1027—1106+1p.			
54th	1st	735+1+	Senate	Jan. 2, 1905	April 17, 1905
		737—980+	Appendix		
		981—1045p.			
54th	1st	949p.	House	Jan. 2, 1905	April 17, 1905
55th	1st	963+1+	Senate	Jan. 7, 1907	April 16, 1907
		965—1017+	Appendix		
		1019—1093p.			
55th	1st	1115p.	House	Jan. 7, 1907	April 16, 1907
56th	1st	834+	Senate	Jan. 4, 1909	May 1, 1909
		835—956+	Appendix		
		957—1028p.			
56th	1st	1104p.	House	Jan. 4, 1909	May 1, 1909
57th	1st	1129p.	Senate	Jan. 2, 1911	July 7, 1911
57th	1st	1375p.	House	Jan. 2, 1911	July 7, 1911
58th	1st	1512p.	Senate	Jan. 6, 1913	Aug. 23, 1913
	1st. Extra.			Sept. 8, 1913	Sept. 27, 1913
	2nd Extra.			Oct. 13, 1913	Oct. 17, 1913
58th	1st	1660p.	House	Jan. 6, 1913	Aug. 23, 1913
	1st Extra.			Sept. 8, 1913	Sept. 27, 1913
	2nd Extra.			Oct. 13, 1913	Oct. 17, 1913
59th	1st	1167+1+	Senate	Jan. 4, 1915	May 17, 1915
		1169—1172+	Appendix††		
		1173—1306p.			

† Report of Penitentiary Committee.
†† Inaugural address of Governor Tom C. Rye.
††† Not found in printed form.

General Assembly	Session	Remarks On Contents	Pages	Convened	Adjourned
59th	1st	House	1443+1p.	Jan. 4, 1915	May 17, 1915
59th	Extraordinary	Senate & House	235p.	March 21, 1916	March 31, 1916
Senate as Court of Impeachment†††		People of Tenn. vs. Jesse Edgington		April 24, 1916	June 16, 1916
	Senate as Court of Impeachment	People of Tenn. vs. Z. N. Estes	324p.	June 16, 1916	July 29, 1916
60th	1st	Senate	1611p.	Jan. 1, 1917	April 10, 1917
60th	1st	House	1470p.	Jan. 1, 1917	April 10, 1917
61st	1st	Senate	1536p.	Jan. 6, 1919	April 17, 1919
61st	1st	House	1482p.	Jan. 6, 1919	April 17, 1919
61st	Extraordinary	Senate & House	496p.	Aug. 9, 1920	Sept. 4, 1920
62nd	1st	Senate	1582p.	Jan. 3, 1921	April 11, 1921
62nd	1st	House	1706p.	Jan. 3, 1921	April 11, 1921
63rd	1st	Senate	1160+1p.	Jan. 1, 1923	April 1, 1923
63rd	1st	House	1307+1p.	Jan. 1, 1923	April 1, 1923
64th	1st	Senate	1385+1p.	Jan. 5, 1925	April 16, 1925
64th	1st	House	1541p.+ Errata Slip	Jan. 5, 1925	April 16, 1925
65th	1st	Senate	1202p.	Jan. 3, 1927	May 6, 1927
65th	1st	House	1797+1p.	Jan. 3, 1927	May 6, 1927
66th	1st	Senate	2+1294p.	Jan. 7, 1929	April 14, 1929
66th	1st	House	2+1767p.	Jan. 7, 1929	April 14, 1929
66th	Extraordinary	Senate & House	3+484p.	Dec. 2, 1929	Dec. 14, 1929
67th	1st	Senate	1583p.	Jan. 5, 1931	July 2, 1931
67th	1st	House	2011p.	Jan. 5, 1931	July 2, 1931
67th	1st Extra.	Senate & House	3+908p.	Nov. 16, 1931	Nov. 21, 1931

General Assembly	Session	Pages	Remarks On Contents	Convened	Adjourned
68th	1st	2+1394+1p.	Senate	Jan. 2, 1933	April 22, 1933
68th	1st	2+2033+1p.	House	Jan. 2, 1933	April 22, 1933
69th	1st	2+1440p.	Senate	Jan. 7, 1935	April 22, 1935
69th	1st	2+1963+1p.	House	Jan. 7, 1935	April 22, 1935
69th	Extraordinary	2+416+	Senate	July 15, 1935	Aug. 3, 1935
		2+647+1p.	House		
70th	[1st] Extra.	1447p.	Senate	Dec. 16, 1936	Dec. 19, 1936
	1st			Jan. 4, 1937	May 21, 1937
70th	1st Extra.	2096p.	House	Dec. 16, 1936	Dec. 19, 1936
	1st			Jan. 4, 1937	May 21, 1937
70th	2nd Extra.	800p.	Senate & House	Oct. 11, 1937	Oct. 30, 1937
	3rd Extra.			Nov. 8, 1937	Nov. 19, 1937
71st	1st	1413p.	Senate	Jan. 2, 1939†	March 10, 1939
71st	1st	1797+2p.	House	Jan. 2, 1939	March 10, 1939
72nd	1st	1018p.	Senate	Jan. 6, 1941	Feb. 15, 1941
72nd	1st	1419p.	House	Jan. 6, 1941	Feb. 15, 1941
73rd	1st	1014p.	Senate	Jan. 4, 1943	Feb. 11, 1943
73rd	1st Extra.	1382+2p.	House	April 10, 1944	April 13, 1944
	1st Extra.			Jan. 4, 1943	Feb. 11, 1943
				April 10, 1944	April 13, 1944
74th	1st	1279p.	Senate	Jan. 1, 1945	March 2, 1945
74th	1st	1479p.	House	Jan. 1, 1945	March 2, 1945
75th	1st	1694+1p.	Senate	Jan. 6, 1947	March 14, 1947
75th	1st	1959p.	House	Jan. 6, 1947	March 14, 1947
76th	1st	1954+1p.	Senate	Jan. 3, 1949	April 15, 1949
76th	1st	2509p.	House	Jan. 3, 1949	April 15, 1949
77th	1st	1666p.	Senate	Jan. 1, 1951	March 16, 1951
77th	1st	2189p.	House	Jan. 1, 1951	March 16, 1951
78th	1st	1779+1p.	Senate	Jan. 5, 1953	April 10, 1953

†T p erroneously marked Jan. 8, 1939.

General Assembly	Session	Pages	Remarks On Contents	Convened	Adjourned
78th	1st	2143p.	House	Jan. 5, 1953	April 10, 1953
79th	1st	1693+1p.	Senate	Jan. 1, 1955	March 18, 1955
79th	1st	2083p.	House	Jan. 1, 1955	March 18, 1955
80th	1st	1596+2p.	Senate	Jan. 1, 1957	March 22, 1957
80th	1st	1876p.	House	Jan. 1, 1957	March 22, 1957
80th	1st	1092, vii,1093-1179p.	Senate & House	May 6, 1958	May 17, 1958
	Extraordinary Senate as Court of Impeachment	+347p.	People of Tenn. vs. Raulston Schoolfield	May 21, 1958	July 12, 1958
81st	1st	1483p.	Senate	Jan. 5, 1959	March 20, 1959
81st	1st	1751p.	House	Jan. 5, 1959	March 20, 1959
82nd	1st	953p.	Senate	Jan. 2, 1961	March 17, 1961
82nd	1st	1153p.	House	Jan. 2, 1961	March 17, 1961
82nd	1st	55+81p.	Senate & House	May 29, 1962	June 7, 1962
83rd	Extraordinary				
83rd	1st	1002p.	Senate	Jan. 7, 1963	March 22, 1963
83rd	1st	1148p.	House	Jan. 7, 1963	March 22, 1963
84th	1st	1069+90p.	Senate	Jan. 4, 1965	March 19, 1965
84th	1st Extra.	1245+140p.	House	May 10, 1965	May 27, 1965
84th	1st Extra.			May 10, 1965	May 27, 1965
84th				Jan. 4, 1965	March 19, 1965
85th	1st	1391p.	Senate	Jan. 3, 1967	May 26, 1967
85th	1st	1718p.	House	Jan. 3, 1967	May 26, 1967
85th	2nd	11+1393—2300p.	Senate	Feb. 13, 1968	April 3, 1968
85th	2nd	28+1719—2805p.	House	Feb. 13, 1968	April 3, 1968
86th	1st	1117p.	Senate	Jan. 7, 1969	May 9, 1969
86th	1st	1367p.	House	Jan. 7, 1969	May 9, 1969
86th	2nd	1+1118—1988p.	Senate	Jan. 13, 1970	Feb. 20, 1970
86th	2nd	28+1369—2331p.	House	Jan. 13, 1970	Feb. 20, 1970

General Assembly	Session	Pages	Remarks On Contents	Convened	Adjourned
87th	1st	1621+19p.	Senate	Jan. 5, 1971	May 31, 1971
87th	1st Extra.		House	March 23, 1971	March 23, 1971
87th	1st	1829+15p.		Jan. 5, 1971	May 31, 1971
87th	1st Extra.			March 23, 1971	March 23, 1971
87th	2nd	1623—3377p.	Senate	Feb. 7, 1972	April 13, 1972
87th	2nd	1831—3925p.	House	Feb. 7, 1972	April 13, 1972
88th	1st	1670p.	Senate	Jan. 2, 1973	May 4, 1973
88th	1st	2026p.	House	Jan. 2, 1973	May 4, 1973
88th	2nd	13+2027—3088	House	Jan. 8, 1974	April 25, 1974
88th	2nd	3089—4218	House	Jan. 8, 1974	April 25, 1974
88th	2nd	1697—2694	Senate	Jan. 8, 1974	April 25, 1974
88th	2nd	2695—3641	Senate	Jan. 8, 1974	April 25, 1974
89th	1st	24+934p.	House	Jan. 7, 1975	June 12, 1975
89th	1st	935—1759	House	Jan. 7, 1975	June 12, 1975
89th	1st	28+1414p.	Senate	Jan. 7, 1975	June 12, 1975

LIST OF TENNESSEE REPORTS
AND TENNESSEE DECISIONS (Southwestern Reporter)

Tennessee Reports Volume	Reporter	Reporter Series Number	Approximate Years of Cases
1	Overton	1	1791–1813
2	Overton	2	1802–1817
3	Cooke	1	1811–1813
3A	Cooke	2	1814
4	Haywood	3	1816–1817
5	Haywood	4	1817–1818
6	Haywood	5	1818
7	Peck	1	1821–1824
8	Martin & Yerger	1	1825–1827
9	Yerger	1	1820–1831
10	Yerger	2	1820–1830
11	Yerger	3	1832
12	Yerger	4	1833
13	Yerger	5	1825–1833
14	Yerger	6	1834
15	Yerger	7	1834–1835
16	Yerger	8	1835
17	Yerger	9	1836
18	Yerger	10	1836–1837
19	Meigs	1	1838
20	Humphreys	1	1839–1840
21	Humphreys	2	1840–1841
22	Humphreys	3	1842
23	Humphreys	4	1843–1844
24	Humphreys	5	1844–1845
25	Humphreys	6	1845–1846
26	Humphreys	7	1846–1847
27	Humphreys	8	1847–1848
28	Humphreys	9	1848–1849
29	Humphreys	10	1848–1850
30	Humphreys	11	1850–1851
31	Swan	1	1851–1852
32	Swan	2	1852–1853
33	Sneed	1	1853–1854
34	Sneed	2	1854–1855
35	Sneed	3	1855–1856
36	Sneed	4	1856–1857
37	Sneed	5	1857–1858
38	Head	1	1858
39	Head	2	1858–1859
40	Head	3	1859
41	Coldwell	1	1860
42	Coldwell	2	1865–1866
43	Coldwell	3	1866
44	Coldwell	4	1867
45	Coldwell	5	1867–1868
46	Coldwell	6	1868–1869
47	Coldwell	7	1869–1870
48	Heiskell	1	1870
49	Heiskell	2	1870
50	Heiskell	3	1870–1871
51	Heiskell	4	1871
52	Heiskell	5	1871
53	Heiskell	6	1871
54	Heiskell	7	1871–1872

Tennessee Reports Volume	Reporter	Reporter Series Number	Approximate Years of Cases
55	Heiskell	8	1871–1876
56	Heiskell	9	1871–1872
57	Heiskell	10	1872–1873
58	Heiskell	11	1872
59	Heiskell	12	1873–1874
60	Baxter	1	1871–1873
61	Baxter	2	1872–1873
62	Baxter	3	1873–1874
63	Baxter	4	1874–1875
64	Baxter	5	1875
65	Baxter	6	1872–1873
66	Baxter	7	1872–1874
67	Baxter	8	1874–1876
68	Baxter	9	1876–1878
69	Lea	1	1878
70	Lea	2	1878–1879
71	Lea	3	1879
72	Lea	4	1879–1880
73	Lea	5	1880
74	Lea	6	1880–1881
75	Lea	7	1881
76	Lea	8	1881–1882
77	Lea	9	1882
78	Lea	10	1882
79	Lea	11	1883
80	Lea	12	1883–1884
81	Lea	13	1884
82	Lea	14	1884–1885
83	Lea	15	1885
84	Lea	16	1885–1886
85	Pickle	1	1886–1887
86	Pickle	2	1887–1888
87	Pickle	3	1888–1889
88	Pickle	4	1889–1890
89	Pickle	5	1890
90	Pickle	6	1890–1891
91	Pickle	7	1891–1892
92	Pickle	8	1892–1893
93	Pickle	9	1893–1894
94	Pickle	10	1894–1895
95	Pickle	11	1895
96	Pickle	12	1895–1896
97	Pickle	13	1896
98	Pickle	14	1896–1897
99	Pickle	15	1897
100	Pickle	16	1897–1898
101	Pickle	17	1898–1899
102	Pickle	18	1898–1899
103	Pickle	19	1899
104	Pickle	20	1899–1900
105	Pickle	21	1900
106	Pickle	22	1900–1901
107	Pickle	23	1901
108	Pickle	24	1901–1902
109	Cates	1	1902
110	Cates	2	1902–1903
111	Cates	3	1902–1903
112	Cates	4	1903–1904
113	Cates	5	1904

Tennessee Reports Volume	Reporter	Reporter Series Number	Approximate Years of Cases
114	Cates	6	1904–1905
115	Cates	7	1905
116	Cates	8	1905–1906
117	Cates	9	1906
118	Cates	10	1906–1907
119	Cates	11	1907
120	Cates	12	1907–1908
121	Cates	13	1908
122	Cates	14	1908–1909
123	Cates	15	1909–1910
124	Cates	16	1910–1911
125	Cates	17	1911
126	Cates	18	1911–1912
127	Cates	19	1912–1913
128	Thompson	1	1913
129	Thompson	2	1913–1914
130	Thompson	3	1913–1914
131	Thompson	4	1914–1915
132	Thompson	5	1914–1915
133	Thompson	6	1915
134	Thompson	7	1915–1916
135	Thompson	8	1915–1916
136	Thompson	9	1916
137	Thompson	10	1916
138	Thompson	11	1917
139	Thompson	12	1917–1918
140	Thompson	13	1917–1918
141	Thompson	14	1918–1919
142	Thompson	15	1919–1920
143	Thompson	16	1920–1921
144	Thompson	17	1920–1921
145	Thompson	18	1920–1921
146	Thompson	19	1921–1922
147	Thompson	20	1922
148	Thompson	21	1923
149	Thompson	22	1923
150	Thompson	23	1924
151	Thompson	24	1924
152	Thompson	25	1923–1925
153	Thompson	26	1925–1926
154	Smith	1	1925–1926
155	Smith	2	1926–1927
156	Smith	3	1926–1927
157	Smith	4	1927–1928
158	Smith	5	1928
159	Smith	6	1929
160	Smith	7	1929–1930
161	Smith	8	1929–1930
162	Smith	9	1930–1931
163	Smith	10	1930–1931
164	Smith	11	1931–1932
165	Beeler	1	1931–1932
166	Beeler	2	1932–1933
167	Beeler	3	1933–1934
168	Beeler	4	1934
169	Beeler	5	1934–1935
170	Beeler	6	1933–1936
171	Beeler	7	1936–1937

Tennessee Reports Volume	Reporter	Reporter Series Number	Approximate Years of Cases
172	Beeler	8	1936–1937
173	Beeler	9	1937–1938
174	Beeler	10	1937–1939
175	Beeler	11	1938–1939
176	Beeler	12	1939–1940
177	Beeler	13	1940–1941
178	Beeler	14	1941–1942
179	Beeler	15	1942
180	Beeler	16	1943–1944
181	Beeler	17	1944
182	Beeler	18	1944–1945
183	Beeler	19	1945–1946
184	Beeler	20	1946–1947
185	Beeler	21	1947–1948
186	Beeler	22	1947–1948
187	Beeler	23	1947–1949
188	Beeler	24	1948–1949
189	Beeler	25	1949–1950
190	Beeler	26	1949–1950
191	Beeler	27	1950–1951
192	Beeler	28	1950–1951
193	Beeler	29	1950–1951
194	Beeler	30	1951–1952
195	Beeler	31	1952–1953
196	Beeler	32	1953–1954
197	McCanless	1	1953–1954
198	McCanless	2	1954–1955
199	McCanless	3	1954–1955
200	McCanless	4	1956
201	McCanless	5	1956–1957
202	McCanless	6	1957–1958
203	McCanless	7	1958
204	McCanless	8	1958–1959
205	McCanless	9	1959
206	McCanless	10	1960
207	McCanless	11	1960
208	McCanless	12	1960–1961
209	McCanless	13	1960–1961
210	McCanless	14	1961–1962
211	McCanless	15	1961–1963
212	McCanless	16	1962–1963
213	McCanless	17	1963–1964
214	McCanless	18	1963–1964
215	McCanless	19	1964
216	McCanless	20	1964–1965
217	McCanless	21	1964–1965
218	McCanless	22	1965–1966
219	McCanless	23	1966
220	McCanless	24	1966–1967
221	McCanless	25	1967–1968
222	McCanless	26	1967–1968
223	Pack	1	1968–1969
224	Pack	2	1969–1970
225	Pack	3	1970–1971

End of **Tennessee Reports;** Tennessee cases now officially reported in **South-western Reporter (Tennessee Decisions)**

226	Pack	4	475-479 S.W.2d	1971–1972
227	Pack	5	480-485 S.W.2d	1971–1972
228	Pack	6	486-490 S.W.2d	1972–1973
229	Pack	7	491-495 S.W.2d	1972–1973
230	Pack	8	496-499 S.W.2d	1972–1973
231	Rice	1	500-505 S.W.2d	1973–1974
232	Ashley	1	506-511 S.W.2d	1973–1974
233	Ashley	2	512-516 S.W.2d	1973–1974
234	Ashley	3	517-521 S.W.2d	1974–1975
235	Ashley	4	522-526 S.W.2d	1974–1975
236	Ashley	5	527-529 S.W.2d	1975
237	Ashley	6	530-533 S.W.2d	1975–1976
238	McLemore	1	534-539 S.W.2d	1975–1976
239	McLemore	2	540-543 S.W.2d	1976

Index

Abbreviations, 162
Abstract, 84
Accounting, 150
Acts.
    See Session laws; Public acts;
      Private acts
Acts from 1715 to present, 35
Administration of justice.
    See Executive Secretary of the
      Supreme Court
Administrative agencies, 127–129
    boards, 127–128
    commissions, 127–128
    committees, 127–128
    councils, 127–128
    departments, 127
    Reports, 136–137
Administrative law
    rules and regulations, 130–132
      Official Compilation, 131
    treatises, 152
Administrative Procedures Act, 130
Administrative Register, 130
Admission to the Union, 11
    cession acceptance, 9
    in 1866, 14
Adoption, 109
Advisory Commission on Rules, 115
Agency law, 152
Agency reports.
    See headings by name of issuing
      agency, *e.g.*, Law Revision Commis-
      sion. See also Public documents;
      List of Tennessee State Publications;
      Libraries; State Library and Archives
Agriculture—Department, 127
American Annotated Cases (Ann. Cas.),
    93
American Digest System, 118
American Jurisprudence (Am. Jur.), 160
American Law Institute, 162
American Law Reports (A.L.R.), 84–85
American State Reports (Am. St. R.),
    93
Annotations, 116
    early, 117
Annual Survey of Tennessee Law, 165
    index, 165
Appellate Court Nominating Commission.
    97
Appellate courts.
    See by name of court, *e.g.*, Supreme
      Court of Tennessee; Court of
      Criminal Appeals; Court of Chancery
      Appeals
    intermediate, 1873–1925, 71
    opinions, 93–94
    practice before, 162
    Reports, 93–95
Arbitration Commission, 71
Attorney General, 132
    Opinions, 134
      index, 84
Attorneys, 165
Automobiles, 152, 159

Banking—Department, 127
Bankruptcy Court, 133
Bar admission requirements, 34, 103–104
Bibliographies, 47, 161
    See also *Tennessee History: A
      Bibliography*
Bill drafting, 46
Bills, 137
Biographies, 90
Blue Book, 128
Board of Law Examiners, 34, 103–104
Briefs and records, 96
Business law.
    See Uniform Commercial Code. See

also specific headings, *e.g.*, Sales;
    Secured transactions.

Calendars, court, 96–97
Canons of Judicial Ethics, 34
Cession acts, 6, 9
Chancery Appeals Decisions, 94
Chancery Appeals Reports, 94
Chancery courts, 76
    Reports, 78
    rules, 35, 99, 102, 104–105, 108
Chapter laws.
    See Session laws; Public acts;
      Private acts
Charters.
    See Municipal ordinances. *See also*
      specific topics, *e.g.*, Corporations
Charters, colonial, 2
Charters, incorporation.
    See Corporations
Circuit courts, 75
    rules, 99–103
      civil, 35, 100–105
      local, 107–108
Citation form, 162
Citators, 121.
    *See also Shepard's Tennessee Cita-
      tions; Shepard's Ordinance Law
      Annotations; Shepard's Acts and
      Cases by Popular Name*
Cities, 141.
    See Municipal ordinances; Municipal
      Technical Advisory Service
    and county consolidation, 142
    and private acts, 141
    indexed, 121
    early law, 153
    treatises, 155
    types of government, 141, 142
City Attorney opinions, 145
Civil procedure, rules.
    See Rules of procedure—Tennessee;
    See *also* headings under specific
      courts; *e.g.*, Circuit; General
      Sessions; Supreme Court
Code of Professional Responsibility, 35
Codes.
    See Statutes, Tennessee
Commerce Clearing House loose-leaf
    services, 149
Commercial law.
    See Uniform Commercial Code. See
      also specific headings, *e.g.*, Sales;
      Secured transactions
Common law acceptance, 6
Comptroller, 139
    publications, 139–140
Conservation—Department, 127
Constituents "Hot Line".
Constitutional Amendments.
    See Limited Constitutional Conven-
      tions, 16
    Amendment of 1853, 13
Constitutions, 30, 152
    See also Limited Constitutional
      Conventions, 16
    annotations, early, 15
    federal, 30, 152
    in T.C.A., 15
    of 1796, 9, 10
    of 1834, 11
    of 1870, 15
Consumer law, 149
Contracts, 152
Copyright, 155
Corporations, 149–150, 152–153
    Business Corporation Act, 38
Corpus Juris Secundum (C.J.S.) 160
Corrections—Department, 127
County government, 146–148
    See also County officials; County

records; County Technical Assistance
Service
and private acts, 146
collected, 146
indexed, 121
Quarterly Court, 147
resolutions, 147
County judges, 80
rules, 109–110, 158–159
County officials, 139–140
directory, 147
County records, 137–138
County Technical Assistance Service, 147
publications, 147
Court of Appeals, 72–73
Reports, 95
rules, 104
Court of Chancery Appeals, 71–72
Reports, 94
Court of Civil Appeals, 72
Reports, 94–95
Court of Criminal Appeals, 73–74
Reports, 95
rules, 104
Court reports.
*See Tennessee Reports; Tennessee
Decisions; Southwestern Reporter.
See also* headings under specific
courts, *e.g.,* Court of Appeals
Court rules, 99.
See Rules of procedure—Tennessee;
Rules of procedure—federal; Bar
admission requirements. *See also*
headings for specific courts, *e.g.,*
Circuit-local rules; *see also Shepard's
Tennessee Citations*
Courts of Tennessee, 65.
See listings under name of court:
Chancery; Circuit; County Judge;
Court of Appeals; Criminal; General
Sessions; Juvenile, Law and Equity;
Municipal; Probate; Supreme Court;
see also trial courts
Criminal courts, 75
law, 107, 153, 165
rules, 106–108
Criminal procedure, 106–107, 153–154
Cumberland Compact, 4

Declaratory judgments, 38
Definitions.
See dictionaires, words and phrases
Dictionaries, 160
Digests, 117.
*See West's Tennessee Digest; Michie's
Digest of Tennessee Reports
American Digest,* 118
early, 119
Directories.
See Law lists
Discovery, 105
District Attorney General's Conference,
114
District courts, 111
Divorce, 109, 154
Domestic relations courts, 80, 109
See also family law
Drug control, 38, 107

Economic and Community Development—
Department, 127
Education—Department, 127
Education law, 42, 154
Elections, 154
Eminent domain, 156
Employment Security—Department, 127
Encyclopedias, 160
Environmental law, 149
Equity, 76–78, 102, 154
Estate planning.
See wills and estate administration
Evidence, 154
Executive orders, 132
Executive Secretary, Supreme Court, 97

Family law, 61, 80, 109, 154
Federal courts, 111
Federal Reporter, 111
Federal rules, 111–113
appellate rules—Sixth Circuit, 112
local rules, 112
Federal Supplement, 111
Finance and Administration—
Department, 127
Fiscal Review Committee, 53, 62–63
Form books, 150–151, 158
Franchise, 14
Franklin, State of, 5
Future interests, 156

General Assembly, 43
See journals
action on bills, 50
See legislation introduced
committee membership, 50
current members, 50
special committees, 62–63
General Services—Department, 127
General Sessions Courts, 79–80
rules, 108, 111
Gibson's Suits in Chancery, 102
Governmental Guide: Tennessee, 128
Government in Tennessee, 2
Government publications.
*See List of Tennessee State
Publications*
Governor
executive orders, 132
messages, 2
proclamations, 132
vetoes, 44, 50
Guides (Tennessee), 128

Haywood and Cobbs' Revisal, 21
Haywood's Revisal, 20
Hearings, 50
Higgins Reports, 95
History of a Lawsuit, 100–101
History of Tennessee, 1
Human Services—Department, 127

Income tax, federal, 157
Insurance, 155
Insurance—Department, 127
International law, 165
Interstate compacts, 45

Jacksonian Democracy, 1, 12, 69
Journals, 49, App. B
House and Senate, 1794–1796, 9
unbound, 51
Judges
list of, 90
memorials, index to, 90
Judicial conferences, 113
Judicial Council, 114–115
Judicial districts, 75–76
Judicial Standards Commission, 98
Judicial system
diagram, 65
Jurisdiction of state courts.
See headings under specific court,
e.g., Circuit Court
Jury instructions, 155
Justice of the Peace, 79–80, 159–160
Juvenile courts and law, 80, 110

Labor—Department, 127
Labor law, 149–150, 155
Land law.
See property law
Landlord and tenant, 40, 156
Law and equity courts, 78–79
Law libraries, 168
Law lists, 165–166
Law reviews, 163–165
Law Revision Commission, 59
general reports, 59–60
topical reports, 60–62

Law schools, 168
Lawyers' Reports Annotated (L.R.A.), 93
Leases, 40, 156
Legal ethics, 155
Legal forms, 150–151
Legal newspapers, 163
Legal periodicals, 163–165
Legal research manuals, 161
Legal writing, 161–162
Legislation.
    See statutes; public acts; private acts; Tennessee Code Annotated
    special-prohibited, 12
Legislative committees
    Fiscal Review, 53, 62–63
    Legislative Council, 53–59
    Services Committee
    special committees, 62–63
Legislative Council Committee, 53–59
    final reports, 1954–1966, 54-55
    topical reports, 1966–, 55–59
Legislative debates, 50
Legislative history, 34, 46, 49
Legislative intent, 46, 49
    See also legislative history
Legislative publications.
    See topics by committee, e.g., Legislative Council—Topical Reports, 1966–; see also, List of State Publications; see also, General Assembly—Special Committees
Legislation introduced
    bill history report, 52
    Chief Clerk's index, 51
    sponsor index, 51
    status of, 50
    Unofficial Index, 51
Legislative Record, 50
Legislative reporting services, 52
    CCLC Legislative Newsletter, 52
    Tennessee Journal, 52
Legislature.
    See General Assembly
Legislators' Manual, 53
Libraries
    See law libraries, research and special libraries
Limited Constitutional Conventions, 16
List of Tennessee State Publications, 136
Loose-leaf services, 149

Manuscripts, 138
Martindale-Hubbell Law Directory, 165
Medical jurisprudence, 157
Memphis State University Law Review, 105, 130, 163
Memphis State University School of Law, 168
Mental health, 42
Mental Health and Mental Retardation—Department, 127
Messages of the Governors, 1796–1907, 2
Method of citing, 162
Michie's Digest of Tennessee Reports, 118
Military—Department, 127
Military government, 1862, 14
Milliken and Vertrees' Code, 23
Model acts, 37
Moore's Federal Practice, 112
Municipal courts, 81, 107
Municipal ordinances, 141–145, 155
    city attorney opinions, 145
    home rule, 142
    larger cities, 142
        codes, 143
    Shepard's Ordinance Law Annotations, 145
    smaller cities, 143
    treatises, 155

National Reporter System, 85
Newspapers

legal, 163
    microfilmed, 137
Non-profit corporations, 38

Opinions, Attorney General, 132
Opinions, court
    See headings for specific court, e.g., Supreme Court of Tennessee
    unpublished, 82
Ordinances.
    See municipal ordinances, municipal courts
Organic law, 1

Parallel citations, 83, 85, 95
Partnership Act, 40
Patents, 155
Periodicals (Tennessee), 163–165
Personnel—Department, 127
Popular Name, Acts and Cases by, 122, 124
Prentice-Hall loose-leaf services, 149
Private acts, 44
    and public acts, 43
    by county, 121, 146
    index to, 121
Probate code, 40
Probate courts, 80, 109–110
    See wills and estate administration
    rules, 109–110
Proclamations, 132
Products liability, 149, 156
Property law, 156
Public acts, 43
    and resolutions, 44
    codification, 43
    compilation since 1796, App. A
    early compilations, 48
    territorial, 48, App. A
Public documents, 135–137, 52–64
    collections of, 136–137
    custody, 138
    index, 135–137
    Monthly Checklist, 136
Public Health—Department, 127
Public Service Commission, 140

Race Relations Law Reporter, 163
Railroad Commission, 140
Records.
    See public documents
Real property, 156
Referees Commission, 71
Reference books, 161
Research and special libraries, 137, 139, 144, 166–168
Research books.
    See legal research books
Residential landlord and tenant, 40
Resolutions, 44–45
Restatements of the Law, 162
Revenue—Department, 127
Rules of procedure—federal.
    See federal rules
Rules of procedure—Tennessee
    appellate 35, 103–104, 115
    civil, 35, 104–105
    criminal, 106–107
    early rules (pre-1970), 100–101
    local, 108-111. See headings under specific courts, e.g., Circuit; General Sessions; Probate

Safety—Department, 127
Sales, 158
Scott's Revisal, 20
Secession, 13
Secured transactions, 150, 158
Securities law, 150, 157
Session laws, 43, App. A.
    See public acts, private acts
    early compilations, 48
    indexes, 120
    territorial, 48, App. A

Shepard's Acts and Cases by Popular Name, 122, 124
Shepard's Tennessee Citations, 121
  Statute Edition, 122
    court rules, 123
Sheriff, 140
Simultaneous Death Act, 41
Sixth Circuit Court of Appeals, 111
  reports, 111
  rules, 112
Slavery, 12, 13
Southwestern Reporter, 82–83, 85, App. C
Southwest Territory, 9
State Constitution-Making, with Especial Reference to Tennessee, 1, 10
State documents, 135–137
  See public documents; State Library and Archives; *List of Tennessee State Publications*. See also specific headings under issuing agency, *e.g.*, Law Revision Commission
Statehood, 11
State Library and Archives, 137
State officials, 126–128
State Planning Office, 138
  library, 139
  publications, 139
State Publications, Monthly Checklist, 136
State reports, 82–96.
  See headings under specific court, *e.g.*, Supreme Court
  discontinued, 82, 95
  parallel citations, 82, 85, 95
Statistics, 128
Statutes, federal, 111–113
Statutes, Tennessee, 19
  See Tennessee Code Annotated. See also, Shepard's Tennessee Citations—Statute Edition
  early, 9, 19–28
  repealed, 7
  Code of 1858, 21
  Haywood and Cobbs' Revisal, 21
  Haywood's Revisal, 20
  Michie's Tennessee Code, 27
  Milliken and Vertrees' Code, 23
  1932 Code, 26
  1950 Supplement, 28
  Scott's Revisal, 20
  Shannon's Code (1917), 25
  Shannon's Supplements, 23, 24, 26
  Thompson and Steger's Compilation, 22
  Williams' Code, 27
Statutory interpretation, 46
Studies in the Constitutional History of Tennessee, 1, 10
Style manuals, 161–162
Superior Courts of Law and Equity, 68
Supreme Court of Errors and Appeals, 68
Supreme Court of Tennessee, 67–70
  briefs and records, 96
  clerks, 96
  history, 67–70
  jurisdiction, 69–70, 102–103
  libraries, 168
  opinions, 81
    slip, 83
    standards for publication, 81
    unofficial reporting services, 84
    unpublished, 82
  Reports, 82–96
    See Tennessee Reports.
    miscellaneous reports, 91–93
    Shannon's Unreported Cases, 91
    Thompson's Unreported Cases, 91
  rules, 34, 103–104, 115
Suggested State Legislation, 46

Table of cases, 118
Taxation, federal, 157
  business, 157
  personal and estate, 157
Taxation, state, 150

Tennessee Administrative Register, 130
Tennessee Appeals Reports, 95
Tennessee Bar Association
  Proceedings, 1882–1935, 164
Tennessee Bar Journal, 164
Tennessee Blue and White Book, 85
Tennessee Code Annotated, 28–36
  See specific topics by name, *e.g.*, Uniform Commercial Code; acts from 1715 to present; tables; bar admission requirements
  code section origins, 34, 35
  constitutions, 30
  index, use of, 34–46, 120
  non-statutory material, 34–35
    See specific topics, *e.g.*, tables; Code of Professional Responsibility
  repealed uncodified acts, 36
  section numbering system, 33
  supplements, 28–29, 36
  tables, earlier codes, 35
  titles, list of, 29–33
Tennessee Code Commission, 28, 30, 128
Tennessee Criminal Appeals Reports, 95
Tennessee Decisions, 82, 95, App. C
Tennessee Digest, West, 118
  See also, Michie's Tennessee Digest
Tennessee History: A Bibliography, 2
Tennessee Journal, 52
Tennessee Law Review, 164–165
Tennessee Law Revision Commission, 59
Tennessee Practice (West), 105, 158
Tennessee Reports, 82–83, 85–90, App. C
  alphabetized (table of cases), 118
  citation of, 83, 88
  last report, 82
  index (1875), 121
  parallel citation, 83
  revisions, 85–90
    Cooper's edition, 87–89
    Shannon's edition, 89–90
    special features of, 90–91
Tennessee Rules of Court, 1976, 99, 104
  See Rules of procedure—Tennessee
Texts, 151–160
Thompson and Steger's Compilation, 22
Torts, 149, 156–157
Tourist Development—Department, 127
Trade regulation, 150
Transportation—Department, 127
Treatises, 151–160
Trial courts, 74
  See listings under name of court, *e.g.*, Circuit; General Sessions
Trials, 151, 157–158
Trusts, 158
T.T.L.A. Opinions Service, 84

Uncodified law.
  See private acts
Uniform Commercial Code, 34, 38, 158
Uniform laws, 37
  Uniform Laws Annotated, 41
United States Code Annotated, 111–112
Uniform System of Citation, 162
University of Tennessee, College of Law, 168
U. S. Constitution, 30, 152
U. S. Court of Appeals, 111
  rules, 112
  Sixth Circuit, 111
U. S. District Courts, 111
  reports, 111
  rules, 112
U. S. Law Week, 150

Vanderbilt Journal of Transnational Law, 165
Vanderbilt Law Review, 165
Vanderbilt Law School, 168
Veterans Affairs—Department, 127
Vetoes, 44, 50
Vital Statistics Act, 41

Watauga Association, 3
West's Tennessee Digest, 118
West's Tennessee Practice, 105, 158
West's Tennessee Rules of Court, 1976,
  99
Wills and estate administration, 109–110,
  158–159

Women, 159
Words and phrases, 118
Workmen's compensation, 42, 159

Y.M.C.A. Night Law School, 168

Zoning, 156